Teachers Reflecting on Boredom in the Language Classroom

Reflective Practice in Language Education
Series Editor: Thomas S. C. Farrell, Brock University

This series covers different issues related to reflective practice in language education and includes an introductory book which introduces these areas. The other books in the series clarify the different approaches that have been taken within reflective practice and outline current themes that have emerged in the research on various topics and methods of reflection that have occurred.

Published:

Reflective Practice in ELT
Thomas S. C. Farrell

Cooperative Learning through a Reflective Lens
George M. Jacobs, Anita Lie and Siti Mina Tamah

Exploring the Principles of Reflective Practice in ELT: Research and Perspectives from Turkey
Edited by Bahar Gün and Evrim Üstünlüoğlu

Micro-Reflection on Classroom Communication: A FAB Framework
Hansun Zhang Waring and Sarah Chepkirui Creider

Reflecting on Leadership in Language Education
Edited by Andy Curtis

Reflective Practice in TESOL Service-Learning
Cynthia J. Macknish

Surviving the Induction Years of Language Teaching:
The Importance of Reflective Practice
Thomas S.C. Farrell

The Reflective Cycle of the Teaching Practicum
Fiona Farr and Angela Farrell

Using Video to Support Teacher Reflection and Development in ELT
Laura Baecher, Steve Mann and Cecilia Nobre

Forthcoming:

English Language Teacher Beliefs
Farahnaz Faez and Michael Karas

Language Teacher Identity and Reflective Practice
Zia Tajeddin

Teachers Reflecting on Boredom in the Language Classroom

Mirosław Pawlak

Mariusz Kruk

Joanna Zawodniak

SHEFFIELD UK   BRISTOL CT

Published by Equinox Publishing Ltd.
UK: Office 415, The Workstation, 15 Paternoster Row, Sheffield, South Yorkshire S1 2BX
USA: ISD, 70 Enterprise Drive, Bristol, CT 06010

www.equinoxpub.com

First published 2024

British Library Cataloguing-in-Publication Data
A catalogue record for this book is available from the British Library.

ISBN-13   978 1 80050 421 9   (hardback)
           978 1 80050 422 6   (paperback)
           978 1 80050 423 3   (ePDF)
           978 1 80050 467 7   (ePub)

Library of Congress Cataloging-in-Publication Data

Names: Pawlak, Mirosław, author. | Kruk, Mariusz, 1971- author. | Zawodniak, Joanna, author.
Title: Teachers reflecting on boredom in the language classroom / Mirosław Pawlak, Mariusz Kruk, Joanna Zawodniak.
Description: Sheffield, South Yorkshire ; Bristol, CT : Equinox Publishing Ltd, 2024. | Series: Reflective practice in language education | Includes bibliographical references and index. | Summary: "This book investigates teacher and student boredom from the perspective of the teacher and illustrates how thinking about different aspects of this negative emotion might enhance reflective practices"-- Provided by publisher.
Identifiers: LCCN 2023030839 (print) | LCCN 2023030840 (ebook) | ISBN 9781800504219 (hardback) | ISBN 9781800504226 (paperback) | ISBN 9781800504233 (pdf) | ISBN 9781800504677 (epub)
Subjects: LCSH: Language and languages--Study and teaching--Psychological aspects. | Languages, Modern--Study and teaching--Psychological aspects. | Classroom environment--Psychological aspects. | Motivation in education. | Boredom.
Classification: LCC P53.7 .P39 2024 (print) | LCC P53.7 (ebook) | DDC 418.0071--dc23/eng/20231016
LC record available at https://lccn.loc.gov/2023030839
LC ebook record available at https://lccn.loc.gov/2023030840

Typeset by Sparks Publishing Services Ltd – www.sparkspublishing.com

Contents

Series Editor's Preface

When I first saw the title of this new book, *Teachers Reflecting on Boredom in the Language Classroom*, by Mirosław Pawlak, Mariusz Kruk, and Joanna Zawodniak, I must say I was a bit surprised as I had not even considered before that teachers can in fact become bored with their work. Yes, I am aware that students can become bored, but I had figured that teachers may be too busy to become bored. After reading this excellent book, I wonder now how I missed the fact, as pointed out by these wonderful authors, that just like their students in second language education, teachers are also bound to exhibit a range of emotions and boredom, as they point out, is surely no exception. Although the authors say that they found writing this book an extremely enriching and rewarding experience that has helped *them* to reflect on and better understand the complexity of teachers' perspectives on L2 boredom, they also said the book was not easy to write in view of the scarcity of helpful points of reference and the need to come up with ideas, suggestions and recommendations basically from scratch. However, now that they have written this excellent book, they said that they would be happy if they encourage at least some teachers to reflect on the boredom that they themselves and their learners experience, so that they will feel that they have accomplished their goal in undertaking to write this book in the first place. I believe they have more than accomplished their goal of contributing their expert knowledge to the betterment of language teachers' lives.

Teachers Reflecting on Boredom in the Language Classroom reports on a study in which Polish teachers at different educational levels were requested to reflect on the boredom that their learners and they themselves experience in second language lessons as well as the strategies that can be employed to prevent or reduce the detrimental effects of this negative emotion. The results of the research project, together with theoretical accounts of boredom and prior empirical evidence, the authors point out, serve as a backdrop for some concrete recommendations for dealing with teacher boredom but also provide a point of departure for hands-on activities which can encourage reflective practice with respect to this aversive emotion in second language education.

The 7 chapters (as well as an introduction and conclusion and two appendices) provide background on learner boredom that readers will be interested in but mostly the book focuses on teacher boredom and how we can reflect on its presence and decide on what strategies we can employ to try to reduce this 'negative' emotion. Chapter 1, *Emotions in the Language Classroom*, sets the scene for the discussion of boredom by explaining the role of emotions in second language learning and teaching as well as offering a succinct synthesis of existing empirical investigations in this area. Chapter 2, *Conceptualizing Boredom*, offers a definition of boredom and its typologies, its relationship to related concepts such as disengagement or demotivation, as well as its potential links to teacher well-being and teacher burnout. Chapter 3, *Perspectives on Boredom, its Causes and Solutions,* outlines the main theoretical accounts of boredom and provides insights into the reasons for the occurrence of this negative emotion, both in learners and teachers, and the ways in which it can be improved. Chapter 4, *Researching Boredom in L2 Learning and Teaching*, provides the rationale for conducting empirical research into boredom experienced by learners and teachers, and offers an overview of the main foci of such research as well as the crucial methodological choices that can be made in this respect, Chapter 5, *Boredom in the L2 Classroom: Listening to Teachers' Voices*, provides a description of the methodology of the research project, the findings and an overall discussion of these. Chapter 6, *Integrating Theory and Practice: Reflective Practice with Respect to Boredom*, attempts to situate reflection on second language boredom within a broader framework for reflective practice, and offers concrete principles and guidelines for preventing and coping with learner and teacher boredom. Chapter 7, *Awareness-raising Activities Stimulating Reflection on L2 Boredom*, presents a number of hands-on activities intended to encourage teachers to reflect on boredom in a variety of ways. Finally, the conclusion succinctly synthesizes the contents and considers future research directions in relation to teacher boredom. Also included in each chapter are regular reflection breaks in order to help practitioners digest what they have read, better understand the ideas discussed, and relate the different issues touched upon to everyday teaching.

Throughout *Teachers Reflecting on Boredom in the Language Classroom* the authors attempted to shed light on the ways in which second language teachers at different educational levels view the causes and symptoms of boredom afflicting their learners as well as themselves, the link between this emotion experienced by the two groups, and strategies that can be employed to prevent and combat this negative phenomenon in both cases. I believe they were very successful with this main aim as this emotion is seldom if ever discussed in language teacher education courses or professional development programs. Readers will especially benefit from knowing the concrete guidelines offered in Chapter 6 and the awareness-raising activities included in Chapter 7 and in the spirit of this entire book series, *Reflective Practice in Language Education*, teachers at all levels (and other interested stakeholders) can be encouraged to engage in their own reflections on boredom within their practice. Pre-service and in-service language teachers, language teacher educators, and teachers and teacher educators beyond language education will find the details about reflecting on boredom outlined and discussed in this book very useful, engaging, and enlightening. *Teachers Reflecting on Boredom in the Language Classroom* will certainly benefit all teachers and other education stakeholders to become (more) reflective practitioners throughout their lives.

Thomas S. C. Farrell
Series Editor, *Reflective Practice in Language Education*

Introduction

It has long been recognized that the process of second and foreign language (L2) learning as well as its outcomes is mediated by a range of individual difference (ID) factors, with the effect that thousands of studies have been conducted to shed light on the contribution of such factors (see Dörnyei, 2005; Dörnyei & Ryan, 2015; Gregersen & MacIntyre, 2014; Griffiths & Soruç, 2020; Pawlak, 2020a; Pawlak & Kruk, 2022). One area in which such individual variation manifests itself concerns different emotions that can emerge in the language classroom, impacting both learners and their teachers (Gkonou, Dewaele, & King, 2020; Kruk & Pawlak, 2022; Oxford, 2021). For example, a commonly used group-work task involving decision-making is bound to trigger quite extreme emotions in learners, such as enjoyment, pride or shame, which could be related to their communicative ability or self-efficacy. At the same time, the way in which the task proceeds or its outcomes could evoke diverse emotions in teachers, who might also enjoy the activity if they choose to contribute to the discussion in various groups, become proud when they see progress made by their students, or feel shame when they realize that the activity is unsuccessful since it may not have been properly premeditated and introduced.

While for several decades the main focus of second language acquisition (SLA) research has been on the negative emotion of anxiety (MacIntyre, 2017), recent years have seen a major extension of the spectrum of emotions that have become the focus of empirical investigation, a shift that can be mainly attributed to the impact of positive psychology (MacIntyre, Gregersen, & Mercer, 2019). One such emotion is *boredom*, a potentially highly detrimental phenomenon that has been demonstrated to pervade educational settings, the learning and teaching of additional languages being by no means an exception. This said, even though this aversive emotion has been quite thoroughly examined in the field of educational psychology, with some scholars even looking at its causes and effects outside the classroom (e.g., Dettmers et al., 2011; Mann & Robinson, 2009; Pekrun, Goetz, Daniels, Stupnisky, & Perry, 2010), the same cannot be said about the domain of SLA research, where boredom still remains a relative newcomer. It is surely true that the number of relevant studies has grown exponentially in the last two or three years and that the accumulated empirical evidence has allowed a better understanding of the causes of boredom in L2 learning in different contexts (e.g., Li, 2021; Nakamura, Darasawang, & Reinders, 2021; Pawlak, Kruk, & Zawodniak, 2020a), has resulted in successful attempts to establish the factor structure underlying this negative emotion (e.g., Li, Dewaele, & Hu, 2021; Pawlak, Kruk, Zawodniak, & Pasikowski, 2020b), and has managed to shed light on its links to some other ID factors as well as attainment (e.g., Dewaele, Botes, & Greiff, 2022; Li & Wei, 2022; Pawlak, Zarrinabadi, & Kruk, 2022a). This said, such research is still in its infancy and it has a long way to go before it can determine the effects of boredom on the process and product of L2 learning inside and outside the classroom, illuminate intricate interactions with other ID factors or establish the feasibility and effectiveness of pedagogical interventions in this respect.

One of the reasons why the research undertaken thus far has been blatantly lacking is the fact that it has for the most part focused on boredom manifested by learners, giving only scant attention to how this negative emotion is perceived, experienced and handled by L2 teachers (e.g., Dumančić, 2018). Such a situation is clearly unfortunate for several reasons. First, as elucidated above, similarly to learners, teachers are also bound to exhibit a range of emotions, and boredom is surely no exception. The problem is that, when teachers become bored themselves, they might release their grip over what is happening in the classroom, be slow to react when things start to go wrong and in general fail to take optimal instructional decisions, with negative consequences for the learning opportunities that students are afforded. Second, when boredom is beginning to negatively impact the learning process, whether in the classroom or outside, teachers are, realistically speaking, the only actors who can take steps to ameliorate the problem. For this to happen, however, they need to be able to reflect on the causes of their learners' boredom as well as their own, the manifestations of this negative emotion as well as the potential strategies that can be employed to prevent it or diminish its deleterious effects. Third, according to crossover theory (cf. Bakker, Westman, & Van Emmerick, 2009; Hatfield, Cacioppo, & Rapson, 1994), people interacting with each other in different situations have a tendency to adjust their emotions in order to synchronize them, a phenomenon that has been referred to as *emotional contagion* (see section 2.2. in Chapter 1). This certainly also applies to teachers and learners in the L2 classroom, with the effect that teacher boredom can influence learner boredom and the other way around. Thus, if teachers wish to effectively deal with L2 boredom, they not only need to address this negative emotion in their learners but also be able to identify its triggers and symptoms in themselves, and devise ways of combating it.

The present book represents an effort to address the existing gap in the literature and can be seen as a natural extension upon the present authors' previous endeavors to examine the negative emotion of boredom in L2 learners, mostly university students majoring in English and representing relatively high levels of proficiency (e.g., Kruk, 2016, 2021b; Pawlak et al., 2020b; Pawlak, Zawodniak, & Kruk, 2020c, 2020d; Zawodniak, Kruk, Pawlak, 2021; see Chapter 4 for an overview of selected, relevant studies). To be more specific, in addition to offering a necessary overview of key theoretical issues and the existing empirical evidence, the volume reports on a study in which Polish teachers at different educational levels were requested to reflect on the boredom that their learners and themselves experience in L2 lessons as well as the strategies that can be employed to prevent or reduce the detrimental effects of this negative emotion. The results of the research project, together with theoretical accounts of boredom and prior empirical evidence, then serve as a basis for concrete recommendations for dealing with learner and teacher boredom but also provide a point of departure for hands-on activities which can encourage reflective practice with respect to this aversive emotion in L2 education. We are deeply convinced that reflection of this kind constitutes the requisite first step if L2 teachers are ever expected to take boredom seriously and embark on concrete actions intended to diminish its negative effects on the L2 learning process.

The book has been divided into seven chapters. Chapter 1, *Emotions in the Language Classroom*, aims to set the scene for the discussion of boredom by explaining the role of emotions in L2 learning and teaching as well as offering a succinct synthesis of existing empirical investigations in this area. Chapter 2, titled *Conceptualizing Boredom*, offers a definition of the emotion in question alongside its typologies, its relationship to related concepts such as disengagement or demotivation, as well as its potential links to teacher well-being and teacher burnout. In Chapter 3, *Perspectives on Boredom, its Causes and Solutions*, the main theoretical accounts of boredom are outlined, which allows insights into the reasons for the occurrence of this negative emotion, both in learners and teachers, and the ways in which it can be ameliorated. Chapter 4, entitled *Researching Boredom in L2 Learning and Teaching*, provides the rationale for conducting empirical investigations into boredom experienced by learners and teachers, offers an overview of the main foci of such research as well as the crucial methodological choices that can be made in this respect, and includes examples of relevant, selected studies. The last three chapters constitute the core of the monograph and testify to its innovative contribution to the field. Chapter 5, titled *Boredom in the L2 Classroom: Listening to Teachers' Voices*, provides a description of the methodology of the research project, presents its findings and offers a discussion of these findings against the backdrop of previous theory and empirical evidence, also highlighting the limitations of the study. In Chapter 6, *Integrating Theory and Practice: Reflective Practice with Respect to Boredom*, an effort is made to situate reflection on L2 boredom within a broader framework for reflective practice, and concrete principles and guidelines for preventing and coping with learner and teacher boredom are offered. Chapter 7, titled *Awareness-raising Activities Stimulating Reflection on L2 Boredom*, presents a number of hands-on activities intended to encourage teachers to reflect on boredom in a variety of ways. Finally, the conclusion succinctly synthesizes the contents of the volume and considers future research directions in relation to teacher boredom.

Although the book is intended for broad audiences, including SLA theorists and researchers, teacher trainers, materials developers and coursebook writers, it is our sincere hope that it will also prove to be appealing to language teachers in different contexts and at different educational levels. With this in mind, we have tried to make the narrative as accessible as possible and also included in each chapter regular reflection breaks in order to help practitioners digest what they have read, better understand the ideas discussed and relate the different issues touched upon to everyday teaching. We believe that such an approach is important because, if L2 boredom is to be successfully addressed, this needs to happen on the ground rather than as a result of theoretical discussions at conferences and publications in top-tier journals. More broadly, such an approach holds the promise of bridging the gap between theory, research and classroom practice (cf. Sato & Loewen, 2022). On a personal note, this book was not easy to write in view of the scarcity of helpful points of reference and the need to come up with ideas, suggestions and recommendations basically from scratch. Because of challenges of this kind, however, it was also an extremely enriching and rewarding experience that has helped the authors themselves to reflect on and better understand the complexity of teachers' perspectives on L2 boredom. If we encourage at least some teachers to reflect on the boredom that they themselves and their learners experience, we will feel that we have accomplished our goal in undertaking to write this book in the first place.

Chapter 1

Emotions in the Language Classroom

INTRODUCTION

This chapter focuses on emotions as part and parcel of learning and teaching a second or foreign language (L2) in the classroom. Such emotions are therefore approached from the perspective of not only learners but also teachers since it is the way they (emotions) interact in different situations that are bound to affect what transpires during a given lesson and impact to a considerable extent learning outcomes. More specifically, the chapter pays equal attention to positive emotions (i.e., curiosity, enjoyment, love, hope, pride) and negative emotions (i.e., anxiety, shame, guilt and anger with the exception of boredom which is discussed in Chapter 2) as jointly shaping the L2 learning environment. The role of emotions in L2 education is depicted in connection with the most influential models and theories shedding light on the affective dimension of human life in general and the endeavor of L2 learning and teaching in particular. The description of emotions in the language classroom is accompanied by a handful of comments on related studies which, albeit recently growing in number, are still few and far between, especially when it comes to teacher emotions. One important caveat is that the negative emotion of boredom will not be presented here as, being the main thrust of this book, it will be discussed in more detail in the following chapters.

1.1 POSITIVE PSYCHOLOGY

The term *positive psychology* (PP) was proposed by Seligman (2002), who defined it as the scientific study of human virtues that may enable individuals to flourish and improve the quality of life. Although PP focuses on the idea of well-being, it does not neglect less optimistic aspects of human existence, such as, for instance, difficulties, setbacks or disappointments, approaching them from a more promising perspective of one's strengths and resources that can optimize attempts to successfully deal with these problematic situations (MacIntyre & Mercer, 2014; Seligman & Csikszentmihalyi, 2000).

Positive psychology draws on the *well-being theory*, which uses the acronym PERMA to spell out and elaborate on the characteristics of a flourishing individual. The model is composed of five both eudaimonic (i.e., referring to the experience of self-actualization and meaningful purpose in life) and hedonic (i.e., concerning the experience of pleasure and enjoyment) intrinsically motivating indicators of well-being: *positive emotion* (P), *engagement* (E), *relationships* (R), *meaning* (M) and *achievement* (A) (Seligman, 2011). *Positive emotion* has been shown to directly lead to a state of happiness and to involve the acceptance of unfortunate or unsuccessful moments in the past alongside the anticipation of positive future. Positive emotions (e.g., hope, interest, joy, love, compassion, pride, amusement or gratitude) can be cultivated by spending time and cooperating with people of one's own choosing, doing enjoyable activities or reflecting on things that one is good at. Positive emotions may also enable individuals to minimize the adverse effects of negative emotions and, at the same time, enhance their resilience (cf. Georgoulas-Sherry & Kelly, 2019; Tugade & Fredrickson, 2004). The next indicator of well-being is *engagement*, which refers to the state of being actively and intensely involved or engrossed in doing something. Engagement can be increased by carefully observing the learning environment, seeking ways of getting old things done in novel ways as well as identifying and taking advantage of one's character strengths (Lam, Wong, Yang, & Liu, 2012; Shernoff, 2013). Engagement is followed in the PERMA model by *relationships* (R), which refer to an individual's eternal need for belongingness and feeling supported or valued by other people. Creating good interpersonal relationships depends on the ability/readiness to join a class or group that one perceives as interesting, ask questions so as to learn more about group members and look at other people through the lens of their strengths rather than weaknesses. The fourth element of the PERMA model is *meaning* (M) that is searched for out of the need for a sense of worth and purpose in life, which helps face up to the challenges and difficulties encountered. Meaning can be built by using one's potential and passion as well as finding new, creative activities that would best capitalize upon persons' resources. The fifth indicator of well-being within the model in question is *accomplishment* (A), also referred to as *mastery* or *competence*, which results from persisting and succeeding in pursuing and attaining one's goals. The achievement of these goals depends on an individual's self-motivation and it can lead him or her to look at what has been attained with a sense of pride (Seligman, 2011). L2 learners' accomplishment can be viewed from several perspectives, comprising the development/improvement of general L2 proficiency, effective L2 use in various situations, completion of a language course, or manifestation of self-regulated behavior (Oxford,

2015, 2016a). Obviously, the PERMA model is also applicable to teachers with all the five elements being relevant to the jobs they perform. For example, positive emotions can enhance the effectiveness of the instructional practices employed (P), experimenting with new techniques is likely to lead to greater engagement (E), good rapport with learners may facilitate classroom interactions using the L2 (R), frequent reliance on communicative tasks related to learners' and teachers' everyday lives can make classroom instruction more meaningful (M), whereas tangible learners' progress is bound to result in the conviction that instruction has been effective and has led to the accomplishment of envisaged goals (A).

The interplay of the five components of well-being comprising the PERMA model (Seligman, 2011) has been stressed and elaborated on in Oxford's (2016b) EMPATHICS model, which is directly related to English language teaching (ELT). The model is more complex and elaborate, thus representing an improvement on PERMA for two reasons. First, it is more comprehensive because it includes a greater number of what could be referred to as "ingredients" of well-being: emotion and empathy; meaning and motivation; perseverance together with resilience, hope and optimism; agency and autonomy; time; hardiness and habits of mind; intelligences; character strengths; as well as self-factors including self-efficacy, self-concept, self-esteem and self-verification. Second, in line with the tenets of complex dynamic systems theory (CDST; Larsen-Freeman, 2016), the model stresses constant interactions between these elements, together with their dynamism, nonlinearity and unpredictability. As such, the EMPATHICS model may help better understand why some students' sense of well-being is higher than that of others who do not fully enjoy L2 learning. It can also do the same for L2 teachers, accounting at least to some extent for the nature of their instructional practices as well as the effectiveness of these practices.

It is not surprising that PP needs tools that can be employed to determine the extent to which the different components of well-being are present in individuals, including learners and teachers in academic settings. One such instrument is the *Values in Action Inventory of Strengths* (VIA), which draws on a 5-point Likert scale to measure and assess 24 positive character traits that have been categorized into six groups: transcendence, wisdom, humanity, courage, temperance and justice (Peterson & Park, 2009). The VIA inventory can be employed to raise individuals' awareness of their strengths, which may help them capitalize on those that benefit them in a more active and conscious way. This in turn may enhance self-directed learning, thus contributing to greater well-being and lower psychological inhibition or distress (Peterson & Seligman, 2004), as well as better equipping students to effectively cope with the challenges of the L2 learning process. One could also argue that such awareness can enhance teachers' well-being, making them more autonomous, confident, creative, engaged, motivated, resilient and simply more effective in achieving their instructional goals. As a result, teachers are likely to pay more attention to and to more profoundly profit from the positive aspects of the L2 classroom realities (MacIntyre & Mercer, 2014; cf. Pawlak, 2009, 2019).

> **Reflective Break**
> - What is your understanding of the term *positive psychology*?
> - What is your understanding of the term *emotion*?
> - Do you think that teachers' awareness of their students' emotions can contribute to more effective L2 instruction? Why or why not?
> - Would you agree with the assumption that learners' awareness of their teachers' emotions can also influence what happens in the classroom and learning outcomes? Please justify.

1.2 OVERVIEW OF EMOTION-FOCUSED THEORIES

Specialists have attempted to provide different theoretical explanations concerning the role of emotions. In the following subsections two such theories are briefly presented: the broaden-and-build theory (Fredrickson, 1998) and the crossover theory (Hatfield et al., 1994).

1.2.1 The Broaden-and-Build Theory

Formulated by Fredrickson (1998) and aimed at capturing the essence of certain positive emotions, comprising joy, interest, contentment, pride and love, the *broaden-and-build theory* posits that such emotions have the potential to extend individuals' awareness and enhance novel, insightful thoughts and actions. These changes in turn are likely to contribute to building up long-term personal resources that are conducive to effective intellectual, social, artistic and physical functioning (Fredrickson, 2001). More specifically, this theory holds that positive emotions can add to the state of flourishing and well-being through enriching thought-action repertoires which can in due course become a deterrent to the protracted effects of negative emotions (Fredrickson, Mancuso, Branigan, & Tugade, 2000).

The broaden-and-build theory rests on five core, empirically supported propositions. The first of them is based on the assumption that *positive emotions widen the spectrum of thought-action repertoires*. In other words, when individuals experience any of these emotions, they are eager and willing to create, explore or play with things that fascinate them and attract their attention. At such moments, they display unusual, flexible, innovative, integrative and efficient thought patterns which equip them with enduring resources likely to help them succeed in the future (e.g.,

Estrada, Isen, & Young, 1997). As for the second core proposition, it posits that *positive emotions can undo lingering negative emotions*, which implies that cultivating the former can become a way of correcting or warding off the aversive effects of the latter, thus contributing to one's psychological well-being (e.g., Fredrickson & Branigan, 2005). The third proposition states that *positive emotions fuel psychological resilience* understood as the ability to effectively address and adapt to problematic or stressful situations. Positive affect and positive beliefs are therefore treated as a means of dealing with different kinds of adversity (e.g., Fredrickson & Joiner, 2002; Tugade & Fredrickson, 2004), also including difficulties encountered in L2 learning contexts (cf. MacIntyre & Gregersen, 2012). According to the fourth tenet, *positive emotions help build and sustain personal resources* that can be physical, intellectual, and social in nature (e.g., Aspinwall, 2001). Finally, the fifth core proposition assumes that, by broadening the scopes of attention and cognition, *positive emotions should augment and improve individuals' psychological and physical well-being*. It is these extended scopes of attention and cognition that can make coping with adverse situations easier and more effective. It is noteworthy that this coping ability can serve as a predictor of potential experiences of positive emotions (e.g., Fredrickson, 2004; Fredrickson & Joiner, 2002).

The broaden-and-build theory can be capitalized on in the L2 classroom, which is a unique learning environment where students are expected to communicate in a language they have not fully mastered yet and where they are constantly evaluated by the teacher, all of which contributes to high levels of stress and uncertainty. This theory shows that once a positive meaning is found in adversity, it is possible to experience positive emotions and approach the learning process with the acceptance of occasional problems or failures rather than with frustration and annoyance. The tenets of the broaden-and-build theory without doubt also apply to L2 teachers since positive affect can help them effectively deal with the exigencies of the classroom, which can have a beneficial effect on their well-being (see section 6 in Chapter 2).

Reflective Break
- What is your own understanding of the broaden-and-build theory?
- Do you agree with the beneficial effects of positive emotions that this theory assumes?

1.2.2 The Crossover Theory

The *crossover theory* focuses on the idea of *emotional contagion* as a tendency to synchronize moods, verbal/non-verbal signals and postures with those experienced and transferred by another person (Hatfield et al., 1994), which is likely to enhance mutual understanding and social cohesion between interaction partners (Anderson, Keltner, & John, 2003). Consequently, this theory highlights the role of transcending the boundaries of one's own emotions as well as more conscious psychological states in increasing group dynamics (Barsade, 2002). Originally focused on work-related stress and strain, it has evolved to encompass such states and emotions, both positive and negative, as well-being, flow, burnout, depression, anger and joy (e.g., Bakker et al., 2009; Westman, 2001).

The crossover phenomenon draws on three basic mechanisms. The first, referred to as *primitive emotional contagion*, is connected with unconscious imitation of one's interlocutor's behavior that is responded to with similar emotions. The second mechanism draws on the receiver's empathy as an explanation for emotional convergence, while the third one underlines the dependence of such convergence upon mediating variables, such as, for example, instructional behavior (Hatfield et al., 1994; Hennig-Thurau, Groth, Paul, & Gremler, 2006; Westman, 2001). Most importantly, in light of the issues raised in this book, the crossover theory was incorporated into the teaching and learning contexts by Frenzel, Goetz, Stephens and Jacob (2009) in their *model of reciprocal causation between teacher emotions, instructional behavior and student outcomes*. Specifically, this model underlines that there is a mutual influence between teachers' emotions and their instructional behaviors, which affects students' motivation, competence level and social-emotional skills.

While extensively investigated in professional contexts, mainly with regard to the states of well-being, burnout and stress, the crossover theory has only recently garnered the attention of researchers interested in its influence on academic settings, though not in particular in relation to the L2 classroom. It is worth mentioning at this juncture three studies examining the crossover effects in educational contexts. In one empirical investigation, Bakker (2005) set out to investigate the extent to which 178 music teachers' flow experience could be transferred to their 605 students. Quantitative analysis of questionnaire-derived data demonstrated that teachers' peak levels of flow were significantly and positively correlated to the frequency of comparable experiences reported by their students. Flow crossover was shown to be both a conscious and unconscious process. This is because, for one thing, it included students' deliberate recognition of their teachers' commitment to work, which evidently enhanced their intrinsic motivation to perform well, and, for another, it drew on the direct imitation of their happy and cheerful teachers. Frenzel et al.'s (2009) quantitative study, in turn, aimed to obtain insights into the emotional transmission between 71 math teachers' and their 1542 students' self-reported enjoyment. The findings revealed a significant positive association between teacher and student enjoyment, the latter being impacted by the former. While Bakker's (2005) and Frenzel et al.'s (2009) studies drew on trait-based self-reports allowing for the retrospective examination of the participants' emotional crossover processes, in their research project, Becker, Goetz, Morger and Ranellucci (2014) were more concerned with actual emotions experienced and observed by students over a period of two weeks. More specifically, the study was carried out among 149 students in four different kinds of classes (i.e., German, English, French, mathematics) for the purpose of investigating the relationship between their momentary emotions (i.e., joy, anger and anxiety) and perceived teachers' emotions as well as those teachers' instructional behaviors. Using the experience sampling technique, the researchers demonstrated that teachers' emotions were an important determinant of students' emotions with regard to all four school domains. At the same time, students' enjoyment and anger were significantly related to teachers' instructional practices, which was not the case with anxiety, a possible reason being that self-reported levels of this negative emotion were low. It is also noteworthy that emotional convergence between teachers and students was both a conscious, empathy-based process and an unconscious, emotional contagion-dependent phenomenon. Since the intensity of the association between teachers' and students' emotions did not differ across the four subject domains, the researchers concluded that the crossover effects involved universal rather than context-specific processes (cf. Hatfield et al., 1994).

> **Reflective Break**
> - What is your own understanding of the crossover theory?
> - Have you experienced emotional contagion in your own L2 learning and teaching? Please provide one or more examples.
> - In your opinion, is emotional contagion more of a conscious or unconscious process? Please justify.

1.3 POSITIVE AND NEGATIVE EMOTIONS IN THE L2 CLASSROOM

While the previous section has provided theoretical accounts of the role of emotions in different contexts, there is a need at this point to focus more squarely on the various positive and negative emotions that affect L2 learning and teaching processes. On the whole, emotions can be referred to as desirable or undesirable domain non-specific, socially mediated responses which can be experienced in a pleasant (positive) or an unpleasant (negative) way (Dewaele & Pavelescu, 2019; Feldman Barrett, 2017; MacIntyre & Gregersen, 2012). These responses emerge from an aroused state of an organism and, as such, they bring about physiological changes that are accompanied by specific feelings, thoughts and memories translating into a number of tendencies to act (Goleman, 2006). Although, on the face of it, negative emotions may seem unnecessary for effective and/or successful functioning of an individual, the issue is much more complex and ambivalent, which is why it deserves to be explained in more detail. First of all, it has to be realized that positive and negative emotions are not dichotomous entities situated on the opposite sides of the same continuum; rather, they are two qualitatively different aspects of experience (Plutchik, 1980). Another important thing is that in certain circumstances positive emotions can lead to negative outcomes, while negative emotions can result in positive consequences. For example, this is the case with happiness, the intense pursuit of which is reported to contribute to depression, misery and loneliness (Gruber, Mauss, & Tamir, 2011), or with anger which might in some situations culminate in better performance on a competitive task (Tamir & Bigman, 2014).

With respect to positive emotions, they are viewed as one's own internal dialog that, albeit primarily drawing on positive affect, comprises not only pleasant emotions (e.g., joy, love, interest) but also cognition needed for the interpretation of particular situations or events and certain behaviors, such as, for example, expressing gratitude, surprise or admiration. Positive emotions reflect an individual's openness to new experience and attempts to find meaning in life. As postulated by the broaden-and-build theory (Fredrickson, 1998, 2003; Fredrickson & Branigan, 2001) that was described above, positive emotions have the potential to extend the range of thoughts and actions by creating the urge to seek novelty, push the boundaries of possibility, investigate the surrounding environment or play with the unknown (cf. Csikszentmihalyi, 1990; Ryan & Deci, 2000). Following this line of reasoning and at the same time looking from the perspective of L2 learning, positive emotions can be viewed as opening individuals to absorbing the target language (Tugade & Fredrickson, 2007). They can also encourage teachers to approach their instructional process in novel, creative and challenging ways.

Negative emotions are defined as unpleasurable, usually disruptive, negative affect-flavored responses to aversively perceived aspects of the environment. Although negative emotions may inhibit the achievement of one's goals, they can prove helpful in at least a few situations. First, they can serve as a point of reference for comprehending and appreciating the real value of positive emotions. Second, they can act on an evolutionary basis motivating individuals not to give up when confronted with obstacles or setbacks (Ching & Chan, 2020). Third, negative emotions can enhance cognitive conflict processing, thus enabling individuals to better understand confusing signals (Kanske & Kotz, 2011). Fourth, such emotions can facilitate emotional conflict processing, meaning that they can help individuals tackle serious emotional problems (Zinchenko, Obermeier, Kanske, Schröger, & Kotz, 2017). Viewed in this way, the awareness of negative emotions can help both teachers and learners better appreciate the overall climate of the L2 classroom and take concrete actions to eliminate phenomena that can get in the way of effective L2 education.

In light of the above considerations, it is warranted to dedicate the subsequent sections of this chapter to the description of selected positive and negative emotions that have been reported to shape what transpires in the L2 classroom. Two important caveats are in order at this juncture. For one thing, it is noteworthy that emotion research conducted to date has mainly been concerned with language learning processes rather than L2 teaching practices whose emotional dimension still remains the empirical terra incognita and this tendency is clearly visible in the following overview. Moreover, this overview deliberately omits the description of the negative emotion of boredom, which is discussed in considerable detail in the remainder of the book.

Reflective Break
- In your opinion, is it possible for positive emotions to influence negative ones and/or the other way round? Is it the case with your students? What emotions does it refer to? Provide one or two examples in this respect.

1.3.1 Positive Emotions

The following subsections are concerned with such positive emotions that can emerge in the process of L2 learning and teaching as curiosity, enjoyment, love, hope and pride. In each case, first, the relevant theoretical background is briefly touched upon and, second, some empirical evidence is presented as well.

Curiosity

Curiosity is regarded as a positive motivational-emotional construct that has so far been underexplored in L2 learning contexts. It refers to an eager and strong desire to acquire, experience and benefit from new knowledge which assumes the form of inquisitive thinking and as a result encourages exploratory behavior (Csikszentmihalyi, 1990; Litman, 2005; Oudeyer, Gottlieb, & Lopes, 2016). Curiosity is an intrinsically rewarding and definitely pleasant experience which can be divided into *perceptual curiosity* and *epistemic curiosity* (Loewenstein, 1994). The former is a sensory experience resulting from exposure to visual, auditory or tactile stimuli, whereas the latter is a kind of cognitive phenomenon motivating individuals to reach higher levels of understanding that is of particular importance in learning and teaching processes (Loewenstein, 1994). Epistemic curiosity can further be conceptualized as both *interpersonal*, driven by a desire to gain information about other persons' experiences, and *intrapersonal*, including inquisitive introspection for the purpose of gaining greater insight into one's own thoughts and feelings (Litman, Robinson, & Demetre, 2017). Intrapersonal curiosity is particularly relevant here since it may have a role to play in L2 teachers' self-reflection and self-evaluation as well as in the understanding and improving of the quality of their relationships with students.

It is warranted at this juncture to mention the *interest-deprivation (I/D) theory of curiosity* proposed by Litman and Jimerson (2004), who indicate that inquisitive thinking and exploratory behavior can be triggered by both the induction and reduction of this emotion. To put it more precisely, gathering information is a rewarding experience as it either induces a positive feeling of interest, which is the case for *I-type curiosity*, or reduces the negative feeling of uncertainty caused by cognitive dissonance between new knowledge and prior knowledge, which is typical of *D-type curiosity*. Litman and Jimerson's (2004) model was used by Mahmoodzadeh and Khajavy (2019) as a framework for conceptualizing *language learning curiosity* (LLC), which was described as a distinct variable likely to foster and sustain enjoyment, interest and desire to learn a new language in connection with the first language (L1) which has already been mastered. As a result, the researchers theorized LLC both as a feeling of interest, triggered while seeking ways of using the L2 for communicative purposes, and as a feeling of deprivation, evoked in the process of searching for possibilities of filling gaps in L2 knowledge.

Accordingly, Mahmoodzadeh and Khajavy (2019) developed and validated the *Language Learning Curiosity Scale* (LLCS) which was used in their mixed-methods triangulation study conducted among 334 Iranian EFL learners. They demonstrated that LLC was positively associated with enjoyment and willingness to communicate (WTC), whereas it was negatively correlated to anxiety. Additionally, curiosity about foreign language learning was reported to be a socially situated phenomenon in the sense that this positive emotion could be best shaped through joint student, teacher and peer efforts and cooperation. At the same time, it was shown that implementing activities which will contribute to students' curiosity about language learning is more important than creating a low-anxiety classroom environment. Mahmoodzadeh and Khajavy (2019) also emphasize that more research is needed to determine the extent to which teachers can help cultivate LLC. An interesting study was also carried out by Takkac Tulgar (2018) among 10 learners of Turkish as a second language with the aim of examining the impact of curiosity on the L2 learning process. The analysis of the data obtained from reflective reports showed that curiosity had a positive influence on the participants' linguistic, sociocultural and pragmatic knowledge of the target language, which overall contributed to holistic L2 development.

Reflective Break
- How does curiosity as a feeling of interest and deprivation manifest itself among learners and teachers in the L2 classroom? Can you think of examples from your own teaching practice?
- Do you agree with Mahmoodzadeh and Khajavy's (2019) claim that establishing a language classroom and activities which contribute to learners' curiosity about learning a foreign language is more crucial than forming a low-anxiety classroom environment? Justify your point of view.

Enjoyment

In contrast to curiosity, *enjoyment* is the most frequently examined positive emotion in L2 learning. It is defined as a positive affective state that draws on the combination of challenge, interest, fun, happiness, sense of meaning and sense of pride, thus facilitating the learning process (Dewaele & Li, 2021). Its activation depends on the degree of students' autonomy as well as on whether they are given opportunities to seek novelty and pursue challenging goals (Dewaele & MacIntyre, 2014). Enjoyment is reported to positively correlate to increased motivation, engagement and WTC as well as to more satisfying actual and self-perceived L2 performance (Botes, Dewaele, & Greiff, 2021). This positive emotion is also known to mediate the relationship between such variables as, for instance, grit and foreign language performance (FLP) (Wei, Gao, & Wang, 2019) or teacher enthusiasm and student social-behavioral engagement (Dewaele & Li, 2021). It is notable that enjoyment cannot be equated with pleasure which is merely connected with the completion of an action or a task. This is because enjoyment assumes additional dimensions of intellectual focus, sustained or heightened attention as well as increased challenge (Boudreau, MacIntyre, & Dewaele, 2018).

Dewaele and MacIntyre (2016) identified two dimensions of foreign language enjoyment (FLE): the *social dimension*, connected with a positive classroom atmosphere as well as supportive teachers and peers, and the *private dimension*, concerning the cognition that accompanies FLE and a sense of achievement. It is also possible to distinguish various sources of FLE, including teacher-related factors (e.g., friendliness, patience, behavior types), peer-related factors (e.g., student collaboration), self-factors (e.g., age, gender, L2 attitude, attitude towards the teacher), content (e.g., the degree of difficulty and novelty) as well as factors tied to L2 classroom environment (e.g., Dewaele & MacIntyre, 2019; Dewaele, Franco Magdalena & Saito, 2019; Jiang, 2020). Of these five sources, teachers have been found to be particularly influential in impacting student enjoyment. Different studies have yielded examples of emotional transmission from teachers to students. In one of them, carried out among 564 Chinese EFL undergraduate students with the help of a mixed-methods approach, Jiang and Dewaele (2019) showed that teacher-specific variables (e.g., the teacher's sense of humor and friendliness) were more predictive of FLE than learner-internal factors. Another study worth mentioning is the quantitative research project conducted by Li, Huang and Li (2021) among 1718 EFL high school students and 1295 university EFL students in China. It was revealed that the participants' enjoyment was significantly, positively associated with their teachers' interest in and passion for teaching, academic and emotional support as well as attempts to create a positive climate in the classroom (cf. Farrell, 2014a; Frenzel et al., 2009).

Another interesting line of inquiry approaches FLE and foreign language classroom anxiety (FLCA) as complementary emotions that dynamically interact in the L2 classroom environment, where the former may considerably reduce the debilitating effect of the latter (e.g., Dewaele & Dewaele, 2017; Dewaele & MacIntyre, 2016). It has also been demonstrated that FLE is related to gender. For instance, in Dewaele and MacIntyre's (2014) mixed-methods study carried out among 1746 multilingual participants, females turned out to experience more enjoyment than males. It should be added that greater FLE was reported by the participants whose L2 proficiency level was higher, who studied more foreign languages and who were older. It was in this study that Dewaele and MacIntyre introduced the *Foreign Language Enjoyment Scale* (FLES), which was later on adapted for speakers of different languages (e.g., Li, Jiang, & Dewaele, 2018).

Reflective Break

- In your opinion, which dimension of FLE is more important in the L2 classroom: the private or the social dimension? Why do you think that is?
- Looking back on your own learning and teaching experiences, have you ever noticed a link between learner and teacher enjoyment? Please provide examples.
- Do you regard enjoyment and anxiety as two sides of the same coin in the L2 learning process? Do you think the same may refer to the L2 teaching experience? Provide one or two examples in this respect.

Love

Although *love* is among the most essential and universal human emotions in the sense that it immediately follows physical survival and safety needs (Newton, 2011), it has only recently caught the attention of applied linguists. This is because they realized that investigating this emotion may contribute to the rehumanizing of education, that is, establishing closer interpersonal relationships in learning environments, which has the potential to bring about social change (Barcelos, 2021).

Consequently, love can be defined as a social disposition that arises from and develops through interpersonal relationships. The experience of love therefore entails a sense of responsibility and respectfulness while cooperating with others (Chabot, 2008). This primary focus on the social and relational quality of love is what makes this emotion different from enjoyment, which is a two-dimensional, both socially and privately oriented construct (Dewaele & MacIntyre, 2016).

As has been so adeptly expressed by Barcelos and Coelho (2016), "love unfolds and reveals itself in the space between teachers and learners in the language classroom" (p. 137). This implies that a peaceful, friendly and/or supportive classroom environment needs to be firmly grounded in mutual trust, respect and agreement as well as a strong belief in one's own abilities. Just a handful of studies have focused on examining the role of love in L2 educational settings and they are mostly qualitative in nature. In a multiple case study conducted with four EFL Romanian high school students, Pavelescu and Petrić (2018) aimed to identify positive emotions experienced by the participants over a period of one semester and determine which of them were the most salient. The analysis of the data gleaned from a written language learning history task, interviews and lesson observations demonstrated that, unlike enjoyment, love appeared to be the driving force of L2 learning and as such it motivated the participants to seek ways of overcoming the difficulties they encountered and dedicate more effort to the learning process. As a result, love was found to broaden the students' cognition and encourage greater engagement. Another study was conducted by Barcelos (2021) in order to examine one Brazilian university EFL student-teacher's L2 learning process and teaching trajectories from the very beginning of her L2 learning experience. The analysis of the narrative written by the participant revealed that love occupied an important place in her identity as a prospective EFL teacher, feeding into inner and interpersonal peace that she needed for herself and her students. Pedagogical implications emerging from this study highlighted love as the emotion likely to help teachers make better decisions with regard to their self-improvement and develop their individual identities (cf. Farrell, 2019). Barcelos (2021) also appealed for including love as content in L2 teaching courses so as to raise student-teachers' awareness of the role that this emotion can play in their future teaching practice, in particular in shaping relationships with students.

Reflective Break
- Do you agree that love is an important positive emotion in the language classroom? Why or why not?

Hope

The emotion of *hope* plays an important role in the L2 learning process, especially in relation to its motivational dimension, which can be seen in Dörnyei's (2009) model of L2 motivational self system drawing on a self-internalized image of future self that L2 learners strive for (cf. Papi, 2010). Hope is a desire for particular things to happen, which provides individuals with large amounts of energy they are ready to invest in the accomplishment of their goals (Ahmed, 2010). It is a threefold concept, including goals, pathways to problem solution and agency, which jointly pave the way for individuals to interact with their environment (Snyder, 2002). This clearly shows that for hopeful people goals have to be accompanied by plans for accomplishment and self-referential, agentic thinking that underlies personal growth and change. It should be added that students who are high-hopers are also able to flexibly design alternative pathways when goal attainment is impeded by unpredictable obstacles or pitfalls (Lopez et al., 2004). A similar mechanism can be hypothesized in the case of teachers characterized by high levels of hope as they more readily embark on alternative courses of action when the instructional practices applied fail to live up to their expectations. Importantly, hope, with its proactive, goal-directed orientation, should not be confused with optimism which has attributional quality and is thus associated to a greater extent with merely formulating expectations towards future life (Shorey, Snyder, Rand, Hockemeyer, & Feldman, et al., 2002).

At this point, it is worth presenting two studies approaching the emotion of hope from L2 teacher and L2 learner perspectives. The first was Hiver's (2016) 12-month mixed-methods attempt to investigate 19 novice South Korean EFL teachers' perceptions of hope and its role in the first year of their teaching practice. Using a hope rating scale, introspective journals and stimulated-recall interviews, the researcher revealed that for those teachers hope was a context-specific, emergent outcome rather than an inactive state. In other words, hope emerged in response to the environmental demands that they needed to face up to. The study also demonstrated the relationship between teachers' hope and hardiness mechanisms, such as commitment and challenge, that can protect their self-concept from self-doubt and anxiety. The second study, which relied on qualitative data, was carried out by Ross and Rivers (2018) among eight university-level Australian ESL learners with the aim of exploring their emotional experiences, including hope, in their English-speaking out-of-class environment. The analysis of the data collected through semi-structured interviews showed that hope was not in the least related to the participants' formal learning context but to their future ability and readiness to confidently and fluently use ESL in a variety of naturalistic contexts favorable to achieving a communicative purpose.

Pride

Pride is a self-conscious emotion evoked by individuals' perceptions of an accomplishment to which they ascribe personal value or by the impression that what they have achieved is appreciated by others, which may result in boosting their self-esteem or in improving other people's appraisals of attained outcomes (Muris & Meesters, 2014). In the case of L2 learners, this positive emotion can be evoked by superior performance on an exam, the results of which determine admission to university or success in a national competition that is likely to bring about admiration from others. When it comes to L2 teachers, they can take personal pride in the top performance of one of their students on a final examination but also in the fact that they get a reward from educational authorities that may be coveted by their colleagues. Regarding self-related pride, it can be divided into *authentic pride*, which is connected with particular individual attainments, and *hubristic pride*, which pertains to this emotion in global terms. While authentic pride conveys definitely positive connotations, hubristic pride may be viewed in terms of self-aggrandizing properties usually attributed to egotistic or haughty individuals, which is why this emotion, albeit generally perceived as a character strength, should not be treated as unambiguously positive (Tracy & Robins, 2004). It is also crucial to differentiate between pride as a temporary, situation-dependent state and a trait-like nature of self-esteem, with the former being a significant predictor of the latter.

Pride can be meaningfully linked to L2 learning experience, which was shown in the study conducted by Ross and Stracke (2016). They investigated how this emotion was experienced by 12 tertiary-level learners of English as a second language (ESL) in Australian universities with respect to two different contexts: situated learning environment and out-of-class social interaction. Interviews demonstrated that the participants felt pride in the learning context mainly as a result of good grades or praise from classmates, whereas they did not experience this emotion in response to successful task performance without concrete rewards. When it comes to the communicative contexts outside the classroom, the participants felt pride more frequently and, unlike the context of formal learning, they did not expect external rewards (cf. Dörnyei, 2005, 2009). Interestingly, in certain situations they felt "non-pride" as they did not always have the impression that the ability to use English is something to be particularly proud of. Since some of the participants' perceptions of pride were negative, it can be assumed that this emotion involves a certain degree of dimensionality. The study offers pedagogical implications which pertain to the importance of creating conditions conducive to experiencing pride in formal learning settings (e.g., shorter, more achievable tasks ensuring their successful completion, more explicit presentation of L2 issues). In addition, L2 classes need to revolve around positive psychology aspects so that the experience of positive emotions could be extended and enhanced.

> **Reflective Break**
> - Are you inclined to see pride as a positive or negative experience in L2 learning and teaching? Why?
> - Can you think of situations in your L2 learning and teaching that made you particularly proud?
> - What were they and what effect did this emotion have on your future actions?

1.3.2 Negative Emotions

In the present section, we will outline and discuss the following negative emotions that affect L2 learning and teaching: anxiety, which was for a long time the only emotion considered by SLA researchers, as well as shame, guilt and anger. As was the case with positive emotions, some theoretical issues will be briefly presented and then examples of relevant studies will be provided.

Anxiety

Foreign language anxiety (FLA) is without doubt the most studied individual difference (ID) variable in SLA research. This emotion can be defined as "a distinct complex of self-perceptions, beliefs, feelings, and behaviors related to classroom language learning arising from the uniqueness of the language learning process" (Horwitz, Horwitz, & Cope, 1986, p. 128). This uniqueness results from the fact that although L2 students are expected to learn and use a language that they have not yet fully mastered, they are constantly evaluated not only by the most competent speaker in the classroom, that is, the teacher, but also by their peers, which is why they repeatedly experience feelings of tension, uneasiness, uncertainty and frustration (Horwitz et al., 1986; Piechurska-Kuciel, 2011). FLA is accompanied by a number of psycho-physiological symptoms, including, for instance, trembling, tenseness, accelerated pulse rate, perspiring, forgetfulness or avoidance behaviors (Horwitz et al., 1986).

Anxiety is usually classified into *state anxiety,* referring to its transitory nature, and *trait anxiety*, concerning a more stable tendency to experience apprehension (Ellis, 2008; Woodrow, 2006). Additionally, the concept of *situation-specific anxiety* was introduced to address L2 learning contexts and to underline the multifaceted character of this emotion (MacIntyre & Gardner, 1991). Anxiety can also be *facilitating*, when individuals increase their efforts to improve L2 use in order to compare more favorably to others, and *debilitating*, when L2 use is abandoned as a result of avoiding the source of perceived failure (Scovel, 1991). As for the internal structure of FLA, Horwitz et al. (1986) differentiated three subcomponents, that is, *communication apprehension, test anxiety* and *fear of negative evaluation*. The first deserves special attention as it plays a crucial role in the L2 classroom where students frequently experience speaking difficulties resulting from limited control of communicative situations, accompanied by awareness of undergoing constant evaluation. *Communication apprehension* encompasses oral communication anxiety, when speaking in pairs or groups, "stage fright", when speaking in public, and receiver anxiety, when encountering problems with understanding spoken messages (Horwitz et al., 1986).

There are several distinctive sources of FLA. One of them refers to learner beliefs about L2 learning, including, for example, attaching special importance to particular TL subsystems or to the conviction that some students are more capable of learning the target language than others. Another source of FLA is connected with teacher beliefs about language teaching which refer, for example, to the presumed necessity to correct all errors made by students, to constantly act as a controller or to stick to one language teaching method that is considered to be more effective than others. Anxiety can also derive from personal and interpersonal anxieties which are caused by, for example, low self-esteem, competitiveness or communication apprehension. Yet another source of FLA is associated with beliefs about teacher-learner interactions, which can be exemplified by learner uncertainty and fear as to how their errors will be perceived by others, not only the teacher but also peers. Anxiety is often also related to classroom procedures which primarily comprise situations when learners are required to speak in the L2 in front of their classmates or when they are called on to speak by the teacher. The final FLA source, not surprisingly, is language testing, which of course can take on many different forms (Young, 1991).

There are three major approaches to investigating FLA, namely, *confounded, specialized* and *dynamic*, which correspond to distinct stages in the study of this construct (MacIntyre, 2017). The *confounded approach* refers to studies which draw upon anxiety-focused ideas that were derived from a wide array of sources without paying special attention to the phenomenon of anxiety as experienced by language learners. It was then that FLA researchers mainly relied on psychological measures of anxiety. The *specialized approach* focuses on situation-specific anxiety with its definitions, underlying ideas and studies dedicated to investigating the place of this construct in the L2 learning process. It is in this stage that foreign language anxiety was conceptualized and that the *Foreign Language Classroom Anxiety Scale*

(FLCAS) was developed by Horwitz et al. (1986). Studies that represent the specialized approach typically set out to examine the relationship between anxiety and different learner variables, such as, for example, personality (e.g., Dewaele, 2002), perceived competence (e.g., MacIntyre, Noels, & Clément, 1997) or WTC (MacIntyre et al., 1997). Lastly, the *dynamic approach* encompasses studies dedicated to examining how anxiety fluctuates while interacting with different ID factors, such as boredom, WTC or motivation (e.g., Gregersen, MacIntyre, & Meza, 2014; Kruk, 2021a, 2022).

While L2 learner anxiety has been an extensively researched topic, the same cannot be said about teacher anxiety, which still remains an underexplored issue, be it in educational psychology, in English instruction or in teaching any other foreign language. In an attempt to fill this gap, Frenzel et al. (2016) conducted a study aimed at validating *Teacher Emotions Scales* (TES) which they had developed to enable the measurement of such teacher emotions as enjoyment, anger and anxiety. The study was carried out among teachers and students from Germany and Canada with the help of TES and student reports on teacher behavior. Quantitative analysis demonstrated that while neither enjoyment nor anger were significantly correlated to teacher self-efficacy and job satisfaction, there was a strong negative relationship between these variables and teacher anxiety. A negative association was also revealed between teacher anger and students' perception of variety in the instruction they received as well as between perceived teacher support and fast-paced instruction. Surprisingly, teacher anger was shown to be positively linked to student-perceived withitness. Not less importantly, anxiety was found to pose a greater threat to teacher well-being than to the quality of instruction.

Reflective Break
- Do you agree that anxiety can be not only a negative but also a positive experience in L2 learning?
- What can be done to reduce communication apprehension among L2 learners?
- Can you think of situations in which you feel anxiety as an L2 teacher? How do you cope with such situations?

Shame, Guilt and Anger

Shame, guilt and *anger* are negatively valanced emotions that, although differing in their characteristics, are interconnected and occur in similar situations, which is why they are described in the same section. To begin with, both shame and guilt can be classified as self-conscious, moral and other-oriented emotions since they are influenced by a shamed person's appraisal of other people's feelings, thoughts and judgments (Ekman, 2003). At the same time, anger belongs to the family of basic (core) emotions out of which all other emotions are composed and which evolved to serve adaptive purposes (Lazarus, 1991). Irrespective of their nature, the three emotions can be experienced by learners and their teachers alike. For example, while L2 learners may feel ashamed, guilty or even angry when they perform below their expectations on an oral interview, teachers can manifest similar emotions when a meticulously prepared demonstration lesson for their colleagues turns out to be a dismal failure.

Shame is not easy to define, mainly because it is a complex and elusive emotion intertwined not only with other emotions, but also with personality traits and cultural standards. It is strongly connected with feelings of guilt, regret and/or sadness experienced by an individual because of having done something wrong (*Merriam-Webster*, 2015). Individuals feel shame because of criticism directed at their global self, encompassing self-evaluation, self-regulation and acceptance or rejection by others, which components are of considerable significance for the language classroom. Consequently, shame emerges from one's fear that this global self will be threatened and, in effect, damaged (Kam & Bond, 2008). This negative emotion is manifested by withdrawal or defensive behaviors which are accompanied by helplessness, powerlessness and weakness (Wilson, 2016). Galmiche (2017) proposed the tentative notion of *foreign language classroom shame* (FLCS) which she characterized as a complex, self-evaluative emotion that emerges and dynamically fluctuates in the L2 classroom at all levels of proficiency and has a debilitating effect on L2 learners. This emotional state was shown to be comprised of a number of interconnected factors, including learner beliefs, feelings, personality traits and contextual factors. Galmiche (2017) used this definition in her qualitative study spanning two years and conducted with 30 French participants learning different L2s. The aim of the study was to investigate perceptions of shame in L2 learning. The analysis of the data obtained from in-depth, semi-structured interviews demonstrated that shame was the most frequently reported negative emotion when compared to frustration and anxiety. It was also shown that shame reduced students' linguistic confidence as well as their sense of identity and self-esteem. Based on such findings, the researcher highlighted the importance of the teacher's ability to recognize symptoms indicative of their students' shame so as to prevent its occurrence.

When it comes to *guilt*, while experiencing it, L2 learners are primarily focused on particular behaviors of theirs rather than on their global self, which implies critical thoughts about what they have done and may result in remorse, tension or regret (Tangney & Dearing, 2003). Guilt encourages compensatory actions alongside a desire to apologize but, since it does not cause damage to learners' self, it is less painful than shame. This is also the reason why guilty students are ready to take responsibility for their behavior rather than pinning the blame on others (Teimouri,

2018). Shame and guilt were investigated in Teimouri's (2018) research project carried out for the purpose of validating a scenario-based questionnaire, the *Second Language Test of Shame and Guilt Affect* (L2-TOSGA), which was used to measure the L2 students' IDs in relation to proneness to shame and guilt in L2 learning. The findings revealed that shame was strongly and negatively associated with the participants' motivation and language achievement, while guilt was found to be positively related to these two variables.

As far as *anger* is concerned, it can be defined as an intense and destructive emotional state involving such feelings as annoyance, displeasure, irritation and belligerence (Spielberger & Reheiser, 2009). These feelings can be experienced in the L2 classroom when, for example, students who encounter some difficulties realize that they would not have to deal with them if they could use their mother tongue (Wilson, 2016). In such cases, anger can be balanced with the teacher's attempt to improve their relationship with students by, for example, providing positive feedback or discussing rules constituting a code of conduct. An interesting picture of anger emerges from Cook's (2006) mixed-methods study aimed at investigating the impact of shame and anxiety on learning English by 30 ESL college students in the United States. The data gathered from in-depth interviews and self-report questionnaires demonstrated that multiple shame episodes were mainly caused by the participants' perceived deficiency in L2 ability. Special attention should be paid to the observed shame-anger sequence revealing that students' shame responses culminated in the use of anger as a defense strategy.

Reflective Break

- In your opinion, is it possible to differentiate the symptoms of shame, guilt and anger in the L2 classroom? Can you provide examples of such symptoms for each of these emotions?
- Can you think of a situation when you experienced shame, guilt or anger in your teaching? What were the catalysts of these negative emotions?

The following activities are more general in nature and they are aimed to encourage reflection on all of the positive and negative emotions discussed in this chapter, stressing their interaction in the language classroom:

- Which of the positive and negative emotions discussed above do you find to be the most and the least relevant to your teaching practice?
- Can you think of situations in your teaching practice where such emotions affected the course of a class? What exactly happened?
- Can you think of a situation in which a positive emotion resulted in a negative outcome? Describe the situation. Why did it happen?

- Can you think of a situation in which a negative emotion resulted in a positive outcome? Describe the situation. Why did it happen?
- Research shows that emotions can be contagious. Have you observed this phenomenon in your teaching experience? Can you provide examples of emotions transmitted from teachers to students (or vice versa)? When did it happen? What effect did it have on your students?
- What are the most common emotions displayed by your students during language lessons? Please, provide some examples.
- Make a list of things which make your learners manifest positive emotions in language lessons. Which positive emotions are related to these issues? Why?
- Make a list of things which contribute to your learners' manifestation of negative emotions in language lessons. Which negative emotions are related to these issues? Why?
- Do you think that language teachers should interfere with emotions experienced by their students? If yes, how? If not, why?
- Do you judge the success of your lessons based on your observations of emotions (negative and/or positive) your students manifest during language lessons?

CONCLUSION

This chapter has presented the role of positive and negative emotions in L2 education in relation to the theories which highlight the advantages of fostering the long neglected affective dimension of language learning and teaching. Emotions, whether positive or negative, have therefore been discussed as the driving force of students' and teachers' behavior, motivating them to undertake goal-directed actions. Consequently, a traditional stance on education as a primarily cognitive process thoroughly controlled by the teacher has been called into question. In a similar vein, teacher and student emotions have been shown to be interrelated, the former being an important predictor of the latter, but that relationship also potentially being reciprocal. Interestingly and importantly, all nine emotions that have been covered in this chapter do not exist in isolation, which is why they escape uniform specifications and which shows that adroitly addressing them in the L2 classroom may pose a formidable challenge. It is essential to realize that emotions have the potential to become powerful enhancers not only of L2 learning but also of L2 teaching, as well as that reflecting on their nature and mechanisms may help better understand and optimize these processes. The remainder of this book is dedicated to one specific emotion, that is, boredom, as experienced, perceived and combated by foreign language learners and teachers.

Chapter 2

Conceptualizing Boredom

INTRODUCTION

This chapter provides an in-depth description of boredom, with the main focus on its place in the processes of L2 learning and teaching. It was not until recently that the concept of boredom attracted the attention of applied linguists, which is the reason why it still remains an underexplored and therefore underappreciated emotion in the L2 classroom (cf. Chapman, 2013; Daschmann, Goetz, & Stupnisky, 2011; Goetz et al., 2014). This is also true for teachers whose perception of specific activities as boring depends more on their own beliefs, convictions, sentiments and assumptions than on their students' opinions, expectations and preferences, not to mention insights from carefully designed research projects that are still evidently few and far between (see Chapter 4 for a discussion of such research). At the same time, empirical evidence in the field of educational psychology (e.g., Goetz, Frenzel, Pekrun, Hall, & Lüdtke, 2007; Pekrun et al., 2010; Tulis & Fulmer, 2013) strongly suggests that boredom is the most intense and the most commonly experienced academic emotion and that it has been on the increase among adolescent student populations in relation to different subjects (e.g., social studies, math, foreign languages). Consequently, it is warranted to examine the phenomenon of boredom more closely with respect to its various types, causes and manifestations that may impact the learning and teaching of additional languages. This is because a thorough understanding of the convoluted and equivocal nature of this intriguing emotion may facilitate the search for effective ways of successfully dealing with it in L2 learning environments. The chapter begins with the presentation of the definitions of boredom that are followed by a discussion of its typologies and description of its after-class dimension. Lastly, the role of disengagement, demotivation and lack of interest in the experience of boredom is addressed. It should be stressed that although most of the theorizing concerning boredom has been focused on learners, many of its mechanisms may also apply to the experience of this negative emotion in the case of teachers, including L2 teachers.

2.1 DEFINITIONS OF BOREDOM

Boredom is not an easy concept to define, given its complex structure, numerous antecedents, different degrees of intensity, and tendency to dynamically interact with a wide range of other individual difference factors (cf. Ally, 2008; Caldwell, Darling, Payne, & Dowdy, 1999). The concept used to be presented in self-referential terms as, for instance, anguish, listlessness, tedium, doldrums, lethargy, languor or the blahs, which clearly shows its distressing, vague and debilitating nature (Bridgeland, Bruce, & Hariharan, 2013; Goldberg, Eastwood, LaGuardia, & Danckert, 2011; Vodanovich, 2003). Over the centuries, boredom has been the object of interest of various philosophers, poets and essayists who depicted it as the psychological Sahara (Brodsky, 1995) or the vacuity of soul (Schopenhauer, [1819] (2008)), which obviously reveals how devastating this experience can be. As one of the most common academic emotions (Goetz & Frenzel, 2006; Goetz et al., 2014; Nett, Goetz, & Hall, 2011; Pekrun et al., 2010), boredom certainly calls for a more detailed description referring to its internal structure, types and antecedents.

Boredom has thus far been defined in a variety of ways addressing its multifarious qualities. The most general and at the same time the most popular definition was provided by Fahlman (2009), who characterized boredom as an emotion, an affect, a feeling, a drive or a state encompassing disengagement, dissatisfaction, inattention, impaired vitality and disturbed time perception. She refers to this phenomenon as a "silent" emotion since it does not contribute to students' disruptive behaviors as much as anger and anxiety. Boredom is also categorized as an achievement emotion which is an inseparable part of academic contexts, that is, those related to in-class and out-of-school learning alike (Pekrun, 2006; Pekrun, Goetz, Frenzel, Barchfeld, & Perry, 2011). This aversive emotion results from a lack of activity from which students (or teachers) could derive pleasure and enjoyment and, therefore, they perceive the learning (or teaching) environment as meaningless (Eastwood, Frischen, Fenske, & Smilek, 2012). This is why they are demotivated and hence reluctant to participate in classroom activities, as a result of which their engagement in self-regulated learning wanes and they are less likely to invest cognitive effort in what they are expected to do (Preckel, Götz, & Frenzel, 2010). As soon as learners realize they cannot do what would be of interest to them, they switch to avoidance behaviors (Mann & Robinson, 2009; Pekrun et al., 2010). It is also worth alluding to the definition put forward by the present authors which refers to boredom as a state of disengagement arising from a lack of interest and involvement (Kruk, Pawlak, & Zawodniak, 2021). Finally, it is notable that despite its discrete nature, boredom may be associated with such conditions as anhedonia, apathy and depression (Goldberg et al., 2011).

Boredom can be viewed from psychological and social/sociological perspectives, which is warranted, given its equivocal and complex nature (Weinerman & Kenner, 2016). In psychology, it is defined as an enduring (trait) or transitory (state) affective phenomenon which may severely hamper the learning process (Acee et al., 2010; Daniels, Tze, & Goetz, 2015; Nett, Goetz, & Daniels, 2010). When looking at boredom through a sociological lens, it is possible to explain its mechanisms in relation to adolescents and young adults who find it difficult to accept the adult system of values to which they react with different manifestations of this negative emotion. More precisely, boredom is understood here as a vital part of the individual's persona adopted for the sake of resisting the rules and restrictions created and enforced by the educational system (Larson & Richards, 1991).

Proponents of some of the definitions disagree with regard to the arousal aspect of boredom, which means that there is no consensus among them concerning whether it emerges from higher or lower activation of peripheral physiological processes. For instance, Fisher (1993) as well as Harris (2000) assert that boredom is a painful, low-arousal condition attributed to an uninteresting and/or uninvolving environment. Contrary to this stance, Barbalet (1999) refers to boredom as a state of high arousal giving rise to restlessness and irritability rather than acceptance or resignation (see also Berlyne, 1960). Concurrently, Vogel-Walcutt, Fiorella, Carper and Schatz (2012) consider boredom to be a condition of both increased and suppressed arousal stemming from individual learner differences and/or situation-specific variables. Leary, Rogers, Canfield and Coe (1986) postulate the existence of an optimal level of arousal that is not likely to be triggered by boredom which is experienced above or below this optimum point. Boredom is also approached from the perspective of gifted individuals but it remains controversial whether it is more likely to be ascribed to low- or high-ability learners (Preckel et al., 2010). On the one hand, this negative emotion characterizes low-ability and low-achieving students who resort to avoidance behaviors triggered by the anticipation of failure, but, on the other hand, it might as well afflict gifted students who lack sufficient challenge or stimulation. This is what is likely to happen when more gifted students attend classes geared to average-ability learners, which may lead to procrastination and unwillingness to invest effort in completing the tasks at hand (Larson & Richards, 1991; Pekrun et al., 2010).

As has been repeatedly indicated above, systematic boredom-related research conducted by educational psychologists and sociologists has portrayed it as a complex, non-obvious phenomenon that cannot be unanimously classified as an exclusively emotional condition. Consistent with this standpoint, Nett et al. (2010) and Pekrun (2006) approach boredom as a multidimensional state concurrently impacted by affective, cognitive, expressive, motivational and physiological factors. This implies that boredom is usually an unpleasant experience giving individuals the impression of being stuck at a particular point in time. It decreases arousal levels and brings with it a variety of verbal and non-verbal manifestations, which entails a desire to seek solutions to cope with this aversive situation. The multifarious nature of boredom, reflected in the controversy over its place in the learning process (Martin, Sadlo & Stew, 2006), contributes to its uniqueness (Daniels et al., 2015), which is a good reason to explore it in an in-depth manner.

> **Reflective Break**
> - What is your understanding of the construct of *boredom*?
> - Which definition(s) of boredom presented in this section do you find the most appealing? Please, explain your choice.
> - How would you define boredom for you as a teacher?
> - Do you think that we can differentiate between learner and teacher boredom in the L2 classroom? Why or why not?

2.2 BOREDOM FROM A TYPOLOGICAL PERSPECTIVE

Given that boredom is a complex and multidimensional phenomenon, different authors have set out to shed more light on its essence categorizing it into distinct subtypes which would facilitate and enhance the understanding of its internal mechanisms as well as principles underlying changes in its intensity. As a result, several typologies have been proposed. One of them divides this negative emotion into *endogenous* boredom, which comes from within the individual, and *reactive* boredom, which arises in response to environmental stimuli (Neu, 1998). Another typology differentiates between *task-focused* boredom, which refers to situations where students have to deal with tasks which they perceive as meaningless, and *self-focused* boredom, which is connected with frustration-inducing learning contexts (Acee et al., 2010). According to other researchers (e.g., Malkovsky, Merrifield, Goldberg, & Danckert, 2012; Weir, 2013), boredom is a condition that can lead either to *lethargy*, when students are overwhelmed by the experience of apathy, or to *agitation*, when large amounts of their inner energy remain unused. Yet another group of authors, those mainly representing the philosophical and psychoanalytic orientation (e.g., Maddi, 1970; O'Connor, 1967), propose the concept of *chronic* or *existential* boredom, which shares some features with depression. Interesting as all these classifications of boredom may be, there are two more that deserve special attention when it comes to the unique context of L2 learning because they emphasize the complexity of this negative emotion in its entirety. They also show its dynamic, unpredictable and detrimental nature, elaborate on its multiple interactions with a variety of ID factors and specify the role of its various intensities in the adoption of coping strategies. These two typologies will be discussed in greater detail in the following two sections.

> **Reflective Break**
> - How do your learners express the feeling of boredom during lessons?
> - Make a list of the most common manifestations of boredom in your language lessons.
> - In your experience, is boredom more likely to lead to inactivity (i.e., lethargy) or agitation that may lead to disruptive behaviors in the L2 classroom? Can you provide examples from your teaching practice?

2.2.1 State Boredom vs. Trait Boredom

Just like other ID factors that have long been the focus of second language acquisition (SLA) research (e.g., learning strategies, self-esteem, anxiety, motivation; see e.g., Gregersen & MacIntyre, 2014; Griffiths & Soruç, 2020; Pawlak, 2020a; Pawlak & Kruk, 2022, for overviews), boredom can be understood as a situation-specific experience (i.e., state boredom) or as a more enduring tendency attributed to individuals (i.e., trait boredom).

With regard to *state boredom,* it is the most studied category that can be characterized as a temporary, context-dependent, short-lasting condition stemming from one's perception that the learning environment is uninteresting and insufficiently stimulating (Bench & Lench, 2013; Fahlman, 2009). Students, including L2 learners, can experience state boredom in many different situations, when, for example, they are not given the opportunity to make their own choices and, as a result, take control over their own learning. Alternatively, this can happen when teachers do not adjust topics and activities to their students' expectations, abilities or proficiency levels, which may culminate in a lack of interest and unwillingness to participate in what transpires in the classroom. Other contributors to boredom may include unclear or unfocused goals which are therefore difficult to pursue and various institutional constraints (e.g., the need to follow a set coursebook) which may inhibit the learning process and make it less involving (Vogel-Walcutt et al., 2012; Weinerman & Kenner, 2016). State boredom is the product of low arousal that is induced by disinterest, dissatisfaction or frustration, and it is known to constantly fluctuate over time and pose difficulties in concentrating on tasks to be completed. This said, some researchers (e.g., Vogel-Walcutt et al., 2012) opt for conceptualizing state boredom as arising not only from decreased energy but also from heightened, situation-specific arousal. While state boredom is a negative psychological condition, it can be reversed and as such it can become a motivating experience of seeking new goals and effective ways of confronting this problematic situation (Sharp, Hemmings, Kay, Murphy, & Elliott, 2017; Vogel-Walcutt et al., 2012). Importantly, many of the characteristics of state boredom discussed here may apply as well to teachers, who, for example, may become uninvolved and go through the motions when having to adhere to an externally imposed curriculum or assigning repetitive coursebook tasks and activities in the L2 classroom.

When it comes to *trait boredom*, it is usually referred to as *boredom proneness* that is an integral part of human personality. As such, it is symptomatic of individuals who exhibit a higher disposition to experience this aversive and debilitating emotion, which results in a permanent lack of interest and disengagement. Boredom proneness can be either external or internal in nature. *External boredom proneness* pertains to a tendency to perceive the surrounding environment as uninvolving and the resultant intention to search for novelty and excitement. *Internal boredom proneness* concerns the inability to find and attend to interesting things to do (Macklem, 2015). Students who are more susceptible to experience boredom also display a general tendency to give in to negative rather than positive emotions. This is why they can find it difficult to control anger in everyday life, which can make them experience higher levels of impulsivity and aggression than their peers (Barnett & Klitzing, 2006; Dahlen, Martin, Ragan, & Kuhlman, 2004). Students characterized by boredom proneness usually exhibit high levels of extraversion, although, at the same time, their behaviors are indicative of shyness and inclination to be easily hurt (Gordon, Wilkinson, McGown, & Jovanoska, 1997). Obviously, teachers are also bound to vary with respect to boredom proneness, which inevitably translates into their response to the instructional practices they implement.

As revealed by research findings, trait boredom interacts with a wide range of factors such as, for example, negative affect (e.g., hostility and aggression), loneliness, depression, health symptoms, and various dysfunctional behaviors (e.g., sleep disorder, eating disorders, drug abuse) (Gana, Deletang, & Metais, 2000; Gordon et al., 1997; Kass, Wallace, & Vodanovich, 2003; Mercer-Lynn, Hunter, & Eastwood, 2013; Vodanovich & Rupp, 1999). Likewise, boredom-prone individuals have been reported to drop out of school, get lower grades and be low academic achievers experiencing anxiety, decreased motivation and unwillingness to speak as well as considerable amounts of anxiety and stress (Berryhill, Linney, & Fromewick, 2009; Bridgeland et al., 2013; Daschmann et al., 2011; Kass et al., 2003; LePera, 2011; Toohey, 2011). One could assume that high levels of trait boredom could also be responsible for teacher stress which is known to be triggered by student aggression and problematic teacher-student interactions, and which may finally lead to symptoms of professional burnout (Wettstein, Kühne, Tschacher, & La Marca, 2020).

Regardless of evident differences between state and trait boredom, these two emotional conditions are viewed as overlapping, which implies that an individual can have a stable tendency to be bored while simultaneously experiencing this negative emotion at a particular point in time as a result of exposure to unchallenging and/or unrewarding stimuli (Fahlman, 2009; Todman, 2003). For example, a learner may be characterized by low overall boredom proneness but occasionally succumb to boredom as a result of unchallenging topics and tasks used by the teacher. By the same token, teachers may be generally prone to boredom while also experiencing it on a transitory basis when, for example, they have to strictly follow institutional restrictions and requirements or correct a large number of tests.

> **Reflective Break**
> - Do some of your students exhibit higher boredom proneness than others? What are the main indicators of this experience?
> - Do you see boredom as an emotion that is mainly reflective of personal traits or rather related to the nature of L2 learning tasks and activities? Why?
> - The section has mentioned a number of negative consequences of high levels of boredom proneness. Were you particularly surprised by some of those negative effects? Can you relate them to your own learning and teaching experience?

2.2.2 Degrees of Boredom Intensity

Another important typology classifies boredom according to its intensity. It draws on the dimensions of valence and arousal developed and operationalized by Goetz et al. (2014). Consequently, it refers to this distressing emotion as multiple boredoms, each of which is presented in terms of how un/pleasantly it can be experienced. These different types of boredom are presented below:

- *Indifferent boredom* is a pleasantly and cheerfully experienced state of fatigue, relaxation and withdrawal, which most frequently takes place in students' free time. Those who undergo indifferent boredom display a neutral attitude to the external world, slightly positive valence and low arousal levels.
- *Calibrating boredom* is characterized by higher arousal levels and slightly negative valence. It is a moderately unpleasant state of wandering off-topic thoughts which make students unable and unwilling to concentrate on the task at hand. However, they do not like this situation and would like to change it, although they have no idea how they could achieve it.

- *Searching boredom* is marked by more negative valence and higher levels of arousal than in the case of calibrating boredom. It is experienced in an unpleasant way by restless and at the same time creative students who are dissatisfied with the situation they have found themselves in and who are, therefore, eager to change it, seeking things that could attract their attention.
- *Reactant boredom* is a strongly unpleasant emotion that can be described in terms of negative valence and high arousal levels. It refers to students who desperately look for possibilities of overcoming it, which encourages anger- and aggression-driven behaviors. They usually put the blame for their experience of boredom on different factors, comprising, for example, the teacher, the topic, teaching methods and materials, the subject or the syllabus.
- *Apathetic boredom*, described as an exceptionally unpleasant experience, draws on a combination of very high negative valence and equally low arousal. It is attributed to dissatisfied, helpless or depressed students who exhibit low levels of well-being and satisfaction as well as of positive and negative emotions.

Depending on situational factors, four of the above-described multiple boredoms (i.e., indifferent, calibrating, searching and reactant boredom) can change their intensity moving from one subtype to another. For instance, searching boredom can change into its calibrating counterpart as a result of students' perceived limited control over what transpires in the classroom (Goetz & Frenzel, 2006). While searching boredom may serve as an incentive to discover or accomplish one's goals, indifferent, calibrating, reactant and apathetic boredom may keep students away from their passions, desires and/or interests. In this way, searching boredom may be viewed as the function of a motivating force meant to release a need for meaningful engagement (van Tilburg & Igou, 2011). It should also be indicated that the experience of a particular boredom subtype can be connected with both an individual's personality characteristics and different situations conducive to its emergence (Goetz et al., 2014). Finally, the five types of boredom can also affect teachers. This is because, for example, they can get frustrated by their limited influence on teaching content, pinning the blame on educational authorities (reactant boredom), or, on the contrary, they might try to find creative ways in which they can get out of the straitjacket imposed by the national curriculum or examination requirements (searching boredom).

Reflective Break
- Which type of boredom from the above list do you observe the most often among your students? Can you give specific examples?
- Which of the subtypes of boredom discussed in this section may in fact have a "positive" impact on learning a language? Why?

- When you get bored in your teaching, which of these types of boredom are you most likely to experience? Can you think of a typical classroom situation in this respect?
- Do your students happen to conceal the experience of boredom from you? How do they achieve it? What are the main reasons for such a behavior?
- Have you ever, as an EFL teacher, experienced boredom in your language lessons? When and why did it happen?
- How do you react when you start experiencing boredom in the lesson you teach?
- Which of the subtypes of boredom characterized in this section, if any, did you experience as a language learner? Why did it happen?

2.3 THE PHENOMENON OF AFTER-CLASS BOREDOM

The focus of L2 boredom research has so far been on classroom contexts, with little attention being paid to its after-class counterpart (i.e., *after-class boredom*) (cf. Pawlak, Kruk, Zawodniak, & Pasikowski, 2022a) which, albeit not directly caused by the teacher, can be and in many cases actually is related to what they do in class. At the same time, the phenomenon of boredom experienced outside formal learning settings, usually referred to as *leisure boredom* or *homework-related boredom*, has been fairly extensively described and examined within the scope of educational psychology and sociology.

The umbrella term used in these two scientific disciplines to address individuals' out-of-school work and behaviors is *leisure boredom*, which results from the overall impression that they have too much time for too little to do. Accordingly, leisurely bored students find themselves incapable of intentionally managing and benefiting from their spare time, which leaves their need for arousal unsatisfied. Leisure boredom is often the outcome of emotional and societal problems and has been demonstrated to be linked to weak social networks and absence of or insufficient parental monitoring (Wegner, 2011).

In educational psychology, boredom is viewed as one of homework-related emotions exerting a considerable influence on academic or classroom learning (e.g., Dettmers et al., 2011; Goetz et al., 2012). An important role in the student's perception of homework assignments, including those in L2 courses, is played by their quality, that is, the extent to which they are involving and challenging. More specifically, if a given homework task has been properly adjusted to students' ability and proficiency levels, they will do it with genuine enthusiasm and engagement without recourse to avoidance behaviors. It is notable that students' expectancy beliefs about their ability to complete the task as well as value beliefs about its usefulness and the costs involved have been found to mediate the effects of perceptions of homework quality on the experience of boredom (Trautwein, Lüdtke, Kastens, & Köller, 2006). Homework can thus be seen as an influential, emotionally flavored companion to school learning that is likely to contribute to students' dis/engagement and dis/satisfaction, which depends on whether they positively or negatively perceive its quality. Consequently, this very perception is impacted by the teacher's attempts to connect homework to what is being done in class, design it in such a way that students are not cognitively overtaxed and encourage students to come up with their own task choices (Dettmers et al., 2011). This having been said, it has to be underlined that after-class boredom in L2 learning contexts is by no means limited to homework completion as it may also be affected by self-initiated efforts to improve L2 competence or prepare for tests or exams (cf. Pawlak et al., 2022a). Finally, it should be highlighted that teachers may succumb to after-class boredom as well. While they do not have to complete homework assignments per se, unless they are part of in-service teacher training, they plan their lessons, they mark students' assignments and tests, and they might spend time improving their TL skills. All of these situations might involve a degree of boredom that is not directly linked to what transpires in the classroom.

Reflective Break
- What is your understanding of *after-class boredom*?
- Based on your teaching experience, what symptoms of after-class boredom can you indicate as the most commonly occurring among your students?
- Can you think of ways in which you could make typical homework assignments less boring?
- Have you ever noticed after-class boredom in your own case, whether when preparing your classes or trying to improve your TL skills?

2.4 DIS/ENGAGEMENT AND BOREDOM

Disengagement is one of the essential building blocks of boredom which is known to reduce the quality of student performance and, accordingly, negatively influence the learning process (Fahlman, 2009; Pekrun et al., 2010). Bored individuals are distracted and reluctant to participate in what goes on in class, even though others may derive pleasure and satisfaction from it (Martin, Anderson, Bobis, Way, & Vellar, 2012; Schreck, 2011). Yet again, bored teachers may also display disengagement and take little notice of the effectiveness of the activities they assign in the classroom. Since preventing disengagement is usually associated with combating boredom (Macklem, 2015), it is warranted to pay more attention to it, which, however, would not be possible without first referring to the concept of engagement.

Engagement has become a hot topic and one of the major issues of empirical concern in educational psychology (Sinatra, Heddy, & Lombardi, 2015). It can be specified as "the heightened simultaneous experience of concentration, interest, and enjoyment in the task at hand" (Shernoff, 2013, p. 12), which is conducive to eager participation in it (Appleton, Christenson, & Furlong, 2008). While most educational psychologists agree on the importance of engagement in meaningful learning for all kinds of learners and contexts (Christenson, Reschly, & Wylie, 2012; Pekrun & Linnenbrink-Garcia, 2012; Shernoff, 2013), it has to be stressed that its role is particularly influential in the L2 classroom where the main focus is on the development of communicative competence, which requires exceptionally large amounts of active involvement (Mercer & Dörnyei, 2020). Encouraging student engagement in the face-threatening L2 learning environment may therefore be quite a challenge. One could even argue that achieving this goal requires a high degree of engagement on the part of teachers who should make an effort not only to implement appropriate communicative activities but steer classroom interactions in such a way that students are encouraged to contribute to them.

Engagement is a multifaceted construct as well as an integral part of the learning process and as such it capitalizes on a number of variables comprising effort and prosocial actions (i.e., behavioral engagement), learning strategy use and self-regulation (i.e., cognitive engagement), high levels of enthusiasm entailing low levels of anxiety and boredom (i.e., emotional engagement) and/or deliberate attempts to enhance one's learning experience (i.e., agentic engagement) (Finn & Zimmer, 2012; Mahatmya, Lohman, Matjasko, & Farb, 2012; Veiga, Reeve, Wentzel, & Robu, 2014). This is what connects "the soft skills of engagement" (Schreck, 2011, p. 4) with meaningful learning that accompanies active participation in school-related and/or academic tasks (Mercer & Dörnyei, 2020), which in turn underlies success in L2 learning. Of all the four above-mentioned aspects of engagement, the most essential for the language classroom is the behavioral one since it is directly associated with the actual, here-and-now cultivation and realization of an individual's learning potential (Dörnyei, 2019; Oga-Baldwin, 2019).

A distinction can be made between two dimensions of engagement, namely *internal* and *external*. The former pertains to the amount of time and effort invested by an individual in the learning process, while the latter includes the actions planned and taken at the institutional level to ensure the necessary resources, organize the curriculum and support services meant to encourage participation in activities likely to result in expected outcomes (e.g., persistence and satisfaction) (Harper & Quay, 2009; Kuh, 2009). Although not fully evidenced in SLA research, over a decade ago the notion of engagement attracted the attention of such scholars as

Ellis (2010) with respect to corrective feedback and Svalberg (2009) with regard to language awareness. It is particularly relevant that engagement in the L2 classroom can be approached from the perspectives of engagement with language and engagement with language learning, the former of which was described and operationalized by Svalberg (2009), who offered insights into its cognitive, affective and social facets.

Engagement surely deserves considerable attention and reflection from teachers and researchers, which should not come as a surprise, given that it serves as a behavioral means of actualizing students' motivation that is viewed as essential for optimal learning (Jang, Reeve, & Deci, 2010). Participatory engagement may protect learners' motivation from possible distractions and make them perceive encountered obstacles as worthwhile to face up to and overcome. Since the nature of such engagement is concrete and straightforward, teachers can initiate and regulate it as well as observe how well they have done in this respect (cf. Farrell, 2019). Encouraging active involvement in the L2 classroom is a chance to prevent disruptive behaviors and reduce negative emotions, such as anxiety, frustration and, what is of particular importance given the focus of this book, boredom. While engagement is a manifestation of motivation, boredom is overtly reflective of disengagement which is briefly considered below.

Disengagement represents the flip side of engagement and it can be defined as the learner's withdrawal from the task at hand because of the inability to generate pleasure, enthusiasm, interest and/or satisfaction from it (Henry & Thorsen, 2018; Macklem, 2015). Disengagement is a condition related to amotivation because it involves a complete lack of effort, alienation from one's passions and desires as well as feelings of discouragement from getting involved in the learning environment that is perceived as impoverished (Skinner, Kindermann, Connell, & Wellborn, 2009). Disengagement deactivates positive emotions, increases helplessness as well as negatively influencing self-esteem and self-regulated learning (Lam et al., 2012; Peterson, Maier, & Seligman, 1993). In effect, disengaged students either resort to avoidance behaviors or seek ways to change the frustrating situation, depending on their individual characteristics as well as environmental factors. Once disengaged, students feel stuck in the present, distracted and unwilling to go on doing the task at hand, which altogether contributes to the experience of boredom (Daschmann et al., 2011). Some specialists (e.g., Skinner, 2016; Skinner, Kindermann, & Furrer, 2009) maintain that disengagement in its pure form does not occur too frequently in formal school settings which, due to various institutional restrictions, are not particularly supportive of total non-commitment. This is why, rather than speaking of disengagement that refers to more extreme behaviors, they prefer to use the term *disaffection* which, being marked by disinterest, apathy, resignation and reduced effort, better specifies what may go on in the classroom. Looking at boredom through the prism of disengagement and its weaker variant (i.e., disaffection) may boost our understanding of this complex emotion and allow handling it in a more systematic, psychologically relevant way. Once again, this understanding is by no means confined to learners, because disengagement as well as all of its negative consequences can also afflict teachers when they have to go several times a day over the same set of coursebook tasks or activities or they are discouraged by their students' lack of involvement in those tasks or activities.

> **Reflective Break**
> - What is your understanding of the difference between disengagement and boredom?
> - Does disengagement always have to signal lack of motivation? Why or why not?
> - Can you think of any manifestations of disengagement among your students?
> - Can you think of situations when you became visibly disengaged during the classes you taught? What was your reaction when you realized this?

2.5 DEMOTIVATION, LACK OF INTEREST AND BOREDOM

While at first blush demotivation and lack of interest may, similarly to disengagement, be viewed as the flip side of boredom, on closer inspection their relationship to this negative emotion seems to be more convoluted and intricate. Since these two non-cognitive factors are sometimes confused with boredom (Pekrun et al., 2010), it is warranted to shed light on their characteristics and possible contribution to bored behaviors on the part of learners but also potentially their teachers.

Demotivation pertains to specific external, classroom-related influences and experiences that may culminate in the reduction of the intention to engage in a specific behavior (e.g., practicing speaking skills) or the desire to continue to perform an ongoing activity (e.g., doing a pronunciation activity) in the process of L2 learning (cf. Dörnyei & Ushioda, 2011; Gearing, 2019). It is noteworthy that, as indicated by Dörnyei (1998) as well as Sakai and Kikuchi (2009), the most crucial demotivating force is the teacher with his or her competence, personality, teaching skills and methodology which may, to a greater or lesser extent, impact L2 students' self-regulated learning and intention to persist in pursuing their goals. Although both disengagement and demotivation imply a marginal degree, if any at all, of autonomy, it is demotivation that underlies disengagement which is therefore its consequence at the cognitive, emotional and agentic levels (cf. Martin, 2012). Because, as has already been mentioned above, disengagement is one of the most important determinants of boredom (Fahlman, 2009), demotivation can be seen as mediated by it, which may lead to overall cognitive resource depletion and shallow information processing.

Not surprisingly, demotivation can also affect L2 teachers, which, quite logically, can only further exacerbate the problem of learners' demotivation. However, studies related to this issue are scant. SLA specialists indicate students' attitudes as the main source of L2 teacher demotivation, including, for instance, cell-phone use, refusing to do homework, talking to each other, coming up with negative comments and behaving in a rebellious way (e.g., Sugino, 2010). As for other factors likely to "diminish the motivational basis of [language teachers] behavioral intention or an ongoing action" (Dörnyei, 2005, p. 143), they may comprise teaching materials, working conditions, discrepancies between L2 curriculum and students' actual L2 proficiency levels or human relationships (Addison & Brundrett, 2008; Aydin, 2012; Azad & Ketabi, 2013; cf. Chambers, 1993).

Boredom is also often viewed as resulting from an acute lack of interest which is inseparably connected with distractibility and which exerts a negative influence on task performance (Fisher, 1993; Nett et al., 2010). At this juncture, it should be noted that lack of interest is not merely a counterpart of boredom which is definitely a heavier, more painful and frustrating experience metaphorically referred to as emotional numbness, decay and bankruptcy (Kim, 2013), a monster to be struggled with or one of the plagues afflicting modern world (Spacks, 1995). By contrast, lack of interest and enjoyment is an affectively neutral state with different motivational consequences. Precisely speaking, lack of interest involves the learner's unwillingness to take part in an activity and at the same time reduces their desire to give it up, whereas boredom clearly entails disengagement, which culminates in attempts to withdraw from what transpires in the classroom. Of course, it cannot be denied that lack of interest and boredom are related but in a merely cause-and-effect way where the former leads to the latter (Goetz & Frenzel, 2006; Pekrun et al., 2010).

Reflective Break

- What is the relationship among demotivation, lack of interest and boredom? Can demotivation and lack of interest be simply considered as the flip side of boredom?
- Do you experience demotivation in your L2 classroom and if so, in what situations does it happen?
- What factors influence your demotivation? Are they the same as or similar to those mentioned in section 5?
- What do you do to reduce the impact of this negative phenomenon on your functioning as the L2 teacher?

2.6 L2 TEACHER WELL-BEING AND BURNOUT

It would be a major omission to conclude this chapter without revisiting the concept of *well-being* (see Chapter 1, section 1), this time strictly in relation to L2 teachers. This is because the attitudes, postures, expectations and psychological or emotional states of those teachers may have, as implied in the *crossover theory* (see Chapter 1, section 2.2.), a crucial role to play in their students' perceptions of what transpires in class and of how well they can perform the task at hand. Promoting teacher well-being is inextricably connected with avoiding or minimizing the experience of burnout which therefore also deserves some attention.

Well-being, as a state of equilibrium that results from a balance between an individual's own psychological, social and physical potential, and the challenges that he or she has to face up to, is likely to optimize that individual's functioning at a particular point in his or her career, which may, among other things, refer to the L2 teaching profession and experience (Cummins, 2010; Dodge, Daly, Huyton, & Sanders, 2012). More specifically, the teacher's well-being arises from the dynamic interactions between the ups and downs of his or her teaching practice as well as from how these ups and downs are perceived and approached (Gregersen, Mercer, MacIntyre, Talbot, & Banga, 2020). Going further, well-being draws on the combination of hedonic and eudaimonic perspectives that coincide within the PERMA model (see Chapter 1, section 1), which clearly shows the multidimensional, context-dependent and self-organizing nature of this state. The characterization of L2 teacher well-being would not be complete without considering the role of agency, that is, readiness to proactively change one's surroundings rather than being merely responsive to them (Gao, 2010). It is this agency that, together with unpredictability and interrelatedness, makes it possible to view L2 teacher well-being as one of the complex dynamic systems shaping the reality of the L2 classroom (Larsen-Freeman, 2019; Mercer, 2021).

There are a number of factors that may threaten L2 teacher well-being, including, for example, workload, classroom management problems, a lack of balance between his or her professional and personal affairs, questionable school culture, negative work experience or an insufficient degree of job fulfilment (cf. Dewaele, Chen, Padilla, & Lake, 2019; Skaalvik & Skaalvik, 2011; Sulis, Mercer, Mairitsch, Babic, & Shin, 2021). Unlike in the case of teachers of other subjects, disruptions to language teachers' well-being may be additionally connected with high intercultural demands to be handled in the L2 classroom, extensive emotional labor, or energy-consuming L2 teaching methods and techniques that constantly require creativity and dedication (Borg, 2006; Gkonou & Miller, 2017). Due to their noticeable, usually negative impact on L2 teacher well-being, these factors are known to lead to *burnout*, understood as an interplay of depersonalization, emotional exhaustion and personal inefficacy (Maslach, 2015; Maslach & Leiter, 2016). All of this contributes to the teacher's feeling of being overwhelmed by the affective burden of responsibilities and commitments, which may, in turn, result in denial, anger, aggression and/or withdrawal as one of the indicators of boredom (see Chapter 2, Sections 2.2., 4; Chapter 3, section 1.5).

The extent to which L2 teachers can manage to enhance their well-being, pulling its trajectory towards a positive state likely to prevent, delay or reduce the consequences of burnout, depends on, for example, their agentic power, resilience to cope with adversity, ability to accept the situation they find themselves in, irrespective of how difficult or frustrating it may be, and to adapt to new, often unexpected circumstances or willingness to seek instrumental support from others (Kostoulas & Lämmerer, 2020; MacIntyre, Gregersen, & Mercer, 2020). Notably, an L2 teacher's well-being can be influenced by his or her boredom not only negatively but also in a positive way. It is true of course that this negative emotion can in many cases result in teacher passivity, helplessness and resigned responsiveness. However, there also situations in which boredom may in fact trigger agentic eagerness to look for best options to solve the problems encountered in the L2 classroom and beyond (Wilson et al., 2014; cf. Goetz et al., 2014; Greenier, Derakhshan, & Fathi, 2021).

Reflective Break
- What factors do you think pose a real threat to L2 teacher well-being? Are there any others that you would like to indicate and comment on next to those mentioned in the above section?
- Do you perceive yourself as a burned-out L2 teacher and if so, what makes you think so?
- In your opinion, is burnout connected with boredom? Is this the case with your own L2 teaching experience and if so, in what respect?
- What options to promote L2 teacher well-being do you regard as the most important and/or effective? Did you happen to resort to them in your own teaching practice and on what occasions was it the case?

CONCLUSION

This chapter has portrayed boredom as a neglected, superficially understood, under-investigated and underappreciated construct (Lewis, Haviland-Jones, & Feldman Barrett, 2008), which is particularly true of L2 learning contexts (Chapman, 2013; Li et al., 2023). It has been highlighted that, regardless of its inconspicuous and elusive nature, boredom is a harmful and aversive emotion and, as such, it may negatively impact students' perceptions of the learning environment (Pekrun et al., 2010) as well as teachers' instructional practices. Without doubt, boredom is among the most distressing experiences afflicting the modern world; hence it occupies an important place in human behavior and mentality (Spacks, 1995). It may be a relatively pleasant or extremely unpleasant experience, depending on the degree of valence and arousal, which is connected with individuals' decision whether or not to search for ways of combating it (Goetz et al., 2014). Additionally, the relationship between boredom and other ID factors, such as disengagement, demotivation and lack of interest, has been commented on and so have the concepts of well-being and burnout. The following chapter will seek to account for the experience of boredom in light of different theoretical perspectives, zooming in in particular on its causes as well as potential solutions to its occurrence.

Chapter 3

Perspectives on Boredom, its Causes and Solutions

INTRODUCTION

In view of the fact that boredom is one of the most frequently experienced academic emotions, both in content classes and in L2 education, there is a clear need to better understand its underlying causes as this can serve as a springboard for the generation and implementation of strategies that can be employed to minimize the likelihood of the occurrence of this negative emotion or reduce its detrimental effects on the learning process. While one might be tempted to argue that such understanding is primarily a scholarly exercise and is thus mostly relevant to theorists and researchers, this could not be further from the truth. In fact, it is of paramount importance that L2 teachers on the ground fully grasp the reasons for students' bored behaviors indicative of their withdrawal, distraction and off-topic thoughts which are likely to result in poor performance and low attainment. This is because such awareness can better equip them to prevent this negative emotion and effectively deal with it when it arises in the classroom but also potentially when assigning homework. Moreover, it can help them better understand why they may experience boredom themselves in some situations and come up with ways in which the negative effects of this debilitating emotion can be ameliorated. For these reasons, this chapter aims to highlight multiple causes of boredom against the background of several relevant theories that have been proposed in the field of educational psychology and have also been employed as a point of reference in studies on L2 boredom. These theoretical positions elaborate on various factors that contribute to the emergence of this negative emotion, determine its nature as well as intensity. The discussion of such theoretical issues is accompanied by suggestions on how L2 teacher awareness of the contributors to student boredom can be raised and/or enhanced. The explanations of boredom are subsequently used for the purpose of suggesting possible coping strategies that could help L2 teachers adequately address this aversive emotion as experienced by their students and, whenever possible, attempts are also made to show how such strategies might apply to teacher boredom.

3.1 CAUSES OF BOREDOM

The theories and models presented below shed light on a constellation of boredom-provoking factors and circumstances in which some students tend to tune out and resort to avoidance strategies, thus remaining passive and disengaged during the activities from which they are unable to generate pleasure, interest and/or satisfaction. Even though these theoretical positions have not been proposed for this purpose, they can also shed some light on the causes of teacher boredom. These antecedents of boredom are either externally or internally oriented since, on the one hand, the aversive emotion in question is shown to be connected with the type and quality of environmental input, while, on the other, it is portrayed as stemming from individual perceptions and appraisals of what transpires in class (Barnett & Klitzing, 2006; Westgate & Wilson, 2018).

3.1.1 Insufficient Stimulation

The under-stimulation model posits that insufficient stimulation is the root reason for the occurrence of boredom that results from excessive exposure to repetition and at the same time a scarcity of challenge (Larson & Richards, 1991). This in turn leads to under-arousal that is experienced in situations when students feel uninterested, unexcited and/or fatigued (Vogel-Walcutt et al., 2012). Consequently, a lack of involving tasks, that is, those that would be varied, open-ended and slightly above learners' current level of communicative competence in the L2, may reduce their desire for change as well as willingness to establish and persistently accomplish new goals, thus negatively impacting their motivation to learn and the quality of learning per se (Pawlak et al., 2020a; cf. Pekrun et al., 2010). To give an example, when a relatively advanced L2 learner is instructed to perform controlled activities focusing on grammar structures and vocabulary items with which he or she is familiar, it is somewhat inevitable that boredom will sooner or later set in, with the caveat that, as elucidated in the previous chapter, it can take on more or less deleterious forms. By the same token, teachers assigning those activities are also likely to succumb to boredom as not only are they obviously familiar with the responses but sometimes have to use the same tasks several times in a row on a single day.

3.1.2 Imposed Tasks

The forced-effort model implies that boredom can be experienced as a result of having to perform a task that, although on the whole uninteresting, requires immoderate investment of effort (Hill & Perkins, 1985; Perkins & Hill, 1985). In such situations the teacher acts as controller determined to take charge of what goes on in the classroom, which only adds to students' frustration and helplessness. This feeling of being in no position to make one's own choices has been labeled by Perkins and Hill (1985, p. 231) *subjective monotony* which may somewhat naturally lead to boredom. Not surprisingly, when students are expected to work under pressure and participate in tasks that they consider not worth the effort, the levels of their dissatisfaction and disengagement will inevitably increase (Derakhshan, Kruk, Mehdizadeh, & Pawlak, 2021; Farrell, Peguero, Lindsey, & White, 1988; Pekrun et al., 2010). For example, the experience of boredom may be intensified when learners are forced to check the meaning of a huge number of words and phrases that they see as irrelevant to how they expect to use the TL in the future. While teachers are responsible for the choice and implementation of classroom activities, they themselves may be forced to do things that are mandated, require a considerable amount of effort, but may bring little satisfaction. This is the case with marking essays knowing full well that many students may not even bother to look at the corrections.

- How do your students react to your attempts to control the L2 learning situation? Are they bored and if so, what are the symptoms of this emotion?
- What do you understand by the notion of *freedom of choice* in the L2 classroom? In what sense and to what extent do you encourage your students to benefit from it?
- Do you think *freedom of choice* minimizes your students' experience of boredom? What in their behaviors and/or attitudes observed in such situations tells you that they are less bored?

3.1.3 Difficulty in Regulating Attention

According to the attentional theory of boredom proneness, boredom is brought about by an individual's inability to self-regulate attention and therefore to activate the amounts of cognitive resources necessary for engaging in a task that can be viewed as potentially promising or rewarding (Eastwood, Cavaliere, Fahlman, & Eastwood, 2007; LePera, 2011). More specifically, if the task at hand does not arouse sufficient interest, students are compelled to generate self-sustained attention, which may lead to a decrease in motivation and meaning, and, at the same time, to an increase in boredom (Cheyne, Carriere, & Smilek, 2006; Hunter & Eastwood, 2016). Poor attentional control is linked to working memory deficits, which contributes to students' susceptibility to unrelated mind-wandering thoughts that may easily trigger boredom. If, however, they are exposed to more demanding tasks with some degree of novelty and challenge, these off-topic thoughts are suppressed in working memory, as a consequence of which student engagement and willingness to participate are on the increase. (cf. Kane & McVay, 2012; Pawlak & Biedroń, 2021). Importantly, the theory in question stresses that boredom in terms of failure of attentional processes usually afflicts individuals who, rather than trying to understand their own interests, values and/or expectations, tend to blame external factors for difficulties in attending to their learning environment (Damrad-Frye & Laird, 1989; Eastwood et al., 2007, 2012). As an example, when performing a reading task, the content of which might be unappealing, a learner might not be able to allocate sufficient attentional resources to it as a result of becoming excessively preoccupied with lexical items that he or she might not know. L2 teachers are also likely to be confronted with problems with attentional control when monitoring repetitive, uninteresting tasks, which can trigger boredom and perhaps prevent them from finding optimal ways of conducting instruction (e.g., failure to appropriately respond to learners' errors).

Reflective Break

- Do your students have problems with sustaining attention? How is it manifested?
- What are the main contributors to your students' attentional difficulties? How do you cope with this issue?
- Are your students aware of their attention deficits? Does this frustrate or demotivate them? How do they demonstrate it? Do they try to do anything about it?
- Do you ever have problems with maintaining attention in the lessons you teach? When does it happen and how do you react in such situations?

3.1.4 Difficulty in Managing Emotions

The emotion theory posits that boredom may be caused by limited ability to identify, understand, reflect on and communicate one's own feelings and/or thoughts, which suggests that bored individuals are externally oriented and therefore incapable of facing up to various problematic situations including contexts in which L2 learning might occur. It is noteworthy that this difficulty may be associated with some of the symptoms of alexithymia (i.e., a lack of emotional awareness), especially those pertaining to deficits concerning the processing of negative emotions (Parker, Prkachin, & Prkachin, 2005). The emotion theory underlines that readiness to describe, express and differentiate emotions can be a strong predictor of internally oriented thinking, thus positively impacting students' engagement with task completion (Rieffe & De Rooij, 2012). The main implication of this approach to boredom is that teachers are advised to raise their students' emotional awareness, which may help them cope with their feelings and therefore become more effective L2 learners (cf. Bielak & Mystkowska-Wiertelak, 2020). In the context of learning an L2, a learner might manifest boredom when performing a communicative task because he or she is not able to constructively respond to the feedback on his or her mistakes offered by other group members. Clearly, inappropriate emotional control can also affect L2 teachers, with the effect that, for example, a lack of learners' involvement or their disruptive behavior may trigger highly negative emotions (e.g., anger or frustration), which in turn might cause boredom.

Reflective Break

- Do you talk to your students about the role of emotions in L2 learning? If so, do you encourage them to identify their own emotions?
- Do you teach your students to distinguish between positive and negative emotions? How do you accomplish it?

> - What emotions do your students most frequently experience in the L2 class-room? In what situations do your students experience these emotions and how are they manifested?
> - What steps would you like to take to help your students process emotions in the L2 classroom?
> - Do your emotions negatively affect the way in which you teach? How do you manage them? Can you give a specific example?

3.1.5 Control-Value Appraisals

The control-value theory (CVT) of achievement emotions stipulates that achievement emotions, including, among others, boredom, anxiety, enjoyment or hope, are triggered when students feel that they can or cannot control the activity they are supposed to perform and when they perceive it as subjectively (un)important to them (Pekrun, 2006). In other words, control appraisals and value appraisals constitute the two proximal determinants of these emotions (Pekrun et al., 2011; Tulis & Fulmer, 2013). To be more precise, control appraisals refer to students' personal agency beliefs regarding a particular task or activity as well as its outcomes, and as such they comprise self-efficacy, self-concept, causal attributions and outcome expectancy. Value appraisals pertain to the subjective importance and meaning attached by students to the task or activity they are instructed to perform and its outcomes (Pekrun, Frenzel, Perry, & Goetz, 2007; cf. Simonton & Garn, 2020).

In more practical terms, students' expectations that they can successfully complete the task in hand can enhance their perception of having control over this task and its outcomes, which is likely to reduce the experience of boredom. This negative emotion can as well be minimized if students are interested in English and appreciate the very opportunity to deal with it on various occasions or if they value the instrumental utility of academic study or the good grades they receive, which may be conducive to the accomplishment of future goals, such as getting a well-paid job or a scholarship, or moving to another country (Li, 2021; Putwain et al., 2018).

The CVT also stresses the link between control-value appraisals of activities, tests and exams, on the one hand, and success or failure, on the other. For instance, if students receive exhaustive feedback on the exam that they have failed, this may help them make positive control-value appraisals of their ability to re-sit it, which may in turn lower dissatisfaction levels, motivating them to avoid another failure. At this juncture, it is worthwhile to highlight that, according to the CVT, teachers' and students' emotions draw on reciprocal causation, which implies, for example, that the former's boredom may influence the latter's experience of this aversive emotion. In line with the crossover theory (see Chapter 1, section 1.1.3., Hatfield et al., 1994; cf. Gkonou & Miller, 2021), reciprocal causation goes two ways as students who are withdrawn, distracted or disappointed with the teacher's instruction, materials, attitudes or behaviors can as well contribute to his or her disengagement and dissatisfaction. By the same token, the experience of boredom, disengagement and dissatisfaction on the part of the teacher is likely to trigger similar feelings in the case of his or her students. Finally, in line with the tenets of CDST (Larsen-Freeman, 2016, 2019), the CVT posits that the co-development of teacher-student emotions is an ongoing, unpredictable process that can assume different forms and vary in duration, depending on the quality of teacher-student relationship or what transpires in the classroom.

Reflective Break

- Do you encourage your students to take control over (some of) the tasks and activities in the L2 classroom? To what extent do you give them this opportunity? Provide one or two examples of such situations and/or activities.
- Based on your observations, how do your students react to activities which allow them to take responsibility for their work and decisions related to the learning process? Do these activities, in your view, really prevent the experience of boredom?
- What are your ways of providing L2 students with feedback on task completion or test/exam results? What aspects of L2 performance do you concentrate on?
- In your opinion, what strategies can help L2 students reflect on self-perceived control over and value of the tasks they are exposed to? What are the advantages of such reflections?
- Are there any aspects of the teaching process over which you feel you have little control or which you believe to be of limited value? Please provide an example and justify.

3.1.6 Boredom as an Impulse for Action

The dimensional model addresses boredom in terms of both its activating and deactivating potential (Pekrun et al., 2010). More specifically, while boredom is most frequently referred to as a low-arousal emotion associated with general passivity, tedium and helplessness likely to result in lowered performance, it may also activate students in their attempts to combat this aversive situation. Consequently, trying to sustain attention and control anger that has been triggered by the need for change and more or less effective efforts to achieve this goal may be attributed to searching and reactant boredom (see Chapter 2, section 2.2.), thus leading to arousal behaviors. In light of this, the model in question shows that alongside its undesirable and detrimental effects, boredom can also be viewed as a point of departure for taking the initiative, which is motivated by eagerness to find something more promising or involving to do (Bench & Lench, 2013; Goetz et al., 2014). To give an example, a learner who is extremely bored because of a very long reading activity, and whose boredom might intensify as the task progresses, might try to combat this aversive emotion by focusing on some new lexical items in the text or might be very eager to get engaged in the following activity even if it is not extremely appealing in and of itself but still represents a so-much-needed opportunity for change. The dimensional model can also be extended to L2 teachers. For instance, the teacher who has just conducted two or three almost identical classes replete with repetitive activities might feel an irresistible urge to change something about one more class to be taught in the same way to reduce his or her own boredom. This might result in a more creative approach to the attainment of the same instructional goals and diminishing the danger that students will fall victim to boredom as well.

> **Reflective Break**
> - Based on your L2 teaching experience, do you perceive your students' boredom as a deactivating or activating emotion or perhaps both?
> - On what occasions and in what way does the experience of boredom activate your students and when does it deactivate them? Do they withdraw from what transpires in class or do they persevere in working on the task at hand?
> - What emotions accompany your students' boredom and how do they affect this experience?
> - Can you think of a situation in which the occurrence of boredom prompted your students to become engaged in a subsequent activity or task?
> - How does your students' activating and deactivating boredom impact your emotions and attitude to L2 teaching?
> - Can you think of a situation in which your own boredom led you to think of ways to make your L2 instruction more creative and engaging?

3.1.7 Allocation of Mental Resources

According to the menton theory of engagement and boredom, boredom is experienced when there is a surplus of mental resources, measured in mental energy units unevenly distributed within a cognitive system, known as *mentons*, which remain unused as a consequence of underchallenging task settings (Davies & Fortney, 2012). In other words, the task which is not involving enough does not occupy excess mentons, which is likely to culminate in student boredom. However, if the task is overchallenging, boredom may also occur as the minimum amount of mentons required for its completion is not available to students. An important implication of this theory is that it is necessary for teachers to keep student arousal at an optimal level that should be neither too high nor too low. For instance, in a listening or reading activity perceived by students as boring, excess mentons can be used by simultaneously visualizing a story they have been listening to or reading, another option being mind-mapping or merely doodling (cf. Andrade, 2010). Finally, it is also worth considering how a shortage of mentons could be compensated for, a good example being the provision of feedback, peer teaching or questions for clarification. For instance, a communicative task that is overly challenging in cognitive terms as it requires learners not only to use the TL but also to engage in thinking and reasoning (e.g., making decisions on the basis of the stimulus material provided) can be alleviated by teacher assistance with new vocabulary or cooperation with peers, which can free the mentons necessary to successfully complete it. While the theory has not been proposed to illuminate such phenomena, teachers can also face problems with appropriate allocation of their mental resources. On the one hand, when they have to supervise repetitive, predictable activities, the unused mentions can generate boredom. On the other hand, when they strive to monitor communicative activities in the classroom, the available mentons my turn out to be insufficient to pay attention to all aspects of the interaction, which may lead to the feeling of being overwhelmed and result in boredom as well.

> **Reflective Break**
> - Are your students' reactions to particular L2 activities similar or different? Why do you think they are similar (or different)?
> - Do your students happen to be bored as a result of both underchallenging and overchallenging activities? What are the symptoms of boredom experienced in these two learning situations? Provide a few examples of such activities and comment on how your students react to them.
> - What are the criteria that you use for preparing activities to be implemented in your L2 classroom? What measures do you take to ensure the right level of challenge in these activities?
> - Can you think of situations in which the tasks you attempted to implement in the classroom proved to be so challenging that you felt overwhelmed and powerless to properly monitor and respond to them?

3.1.8 Insufficient Cognitive Engagement

The meaning and attentional components (MAC) model indicates deficits in meaning and attention as the main proximal causes of boredom, with those factors functioning independently of each other (Westgate & Wilson, 2018). To be more precise, this aversive emotion is shown to occur when there is insufficient cognitive engagement with the task (i.e., the attentional component) and when students do not attach enough value to this task that would make it worth completing (i.e., the meaning component). In other words, boredom stems both from the inability (deficits in attention) and unwillingness (deficits in meaning) to participate in assigned tasks, which implies that avoiding or combating this negative experience requires meaningful engagement that can be experienced when individuals are focused on the task and eager to do it. In line with the menton theory (Davies & Fortney, 2012) that was described above, Westgate and Wilson (2018) maintain that boredom can be brought about not only by understimulation but also by overstimulation, both of which are inseparably connected with a lack of balance between cognitive demands of the task and an individual's mental resources.

The MAC Model, however, goes further since it proposes that boredom may stem from external activity as well as from internal thought. The former refers to mind wandering and off-topic thoughts that characterize students who are unable to replace an uninvolving activity with a desirable alternative. By contrast, the latter concerns intentional thinking or thinking for pleasure that is typical of students who are able to deliberately focus on their own thoughts while performing a boring task (Bench & Lench, 2013; Seli, Cheyne, Xu, Purdon, & Smilek, 2015). Importantly, even though students are capable of intentional thinking, they may not succeed in escaping boredom, which can be the case with meaningless thought content, such that is not valued and unrelated to task goal(s) (Alahmadi et al., 2017). A decrease in the experience of this aversive emotion may therefore depend on a more pronounced relationship between thought content and the task in hand, which needs to be perceived as both valuable and meaningful (van Tilburg, Igou, & Sedikides, 2013). Meaningfulness can also be related to the extent to which the task in hand is applicable to real-life contexts since learners' awareness of its potential usefulness may genuinely encourage them to complete it (cf. Fahlman, 2009). The MAC Model also stresses the role of strategy use in reducing cognitive demands posed by the task and enhancing the enjoyment of its performance (Westgate, Wilson, & Gilbert, 2017). Clearly, meaningfulness and value are also important for L2 teachers, who may easily succumb to boredom when those attributes are not present. One could stipulate that also in this case, reliance on appropriate coping strategies might be instrumental in alleviating this aversive emotion.

Reflective Break

- Do you prepare alternative activities for your students in your classes? Provide one or two examples of situations in which you found them useful when it comes to reducing the experience of boredom.
- Do you encourage intentional, task-related thinking in your L2 classroom? Do you give your students time to reflect on the assigned task while completing

it? Do these intentional thoughts make them more engaged and willing to participate in this task?
- In your opinion, what conditions should be fulfilled to make an L2 activity meaningful? Do you think that a lack of meaning can culminate in boredom? Have you observed it in your classes and if so, on what occasions did it happen?
- How do you understand meaningfulness and value in your own teaching?
- Do you raise your students' awareness of the opportunities for coping with boredom in L2 learning? Briefly characterize these opportunities and explain how you take advantage of them during your classes.

The description of the different antecedents of boredom provided above alongside their theoretical explanations clearly shows how complex, pervasive and perplexing this emotion can be. Against the backdrop of these theoretical positions, it is much easier to understand the problematic nature and detrimental impact of boredom on the language learning process which, due to its uniqueness, requires high levels of engagement, self-regulation, attentional control and/or reasonably dosed challenge. Sufficient understanding of the mechanisms underpinning boredom can also help L2 teachers pinpoint the reasons why they might be susceptible to this aversive emotion themselves. Finally, and perhaps most importantly, all these theories and models have the potential to equip the teacher with ideas for pedagogical interventions intended to alleviate the aversive experience of boredom among their students but also to help them find ways of dealing with their own boredom. Such issues are elaborated on in the remaining part of this chapter.

3.2 BOREDOM-COPING OPTIONS IN THE L2 CLASSROOM

As has been pointed out above, the theories and models discussed in the preceding section can give L2 teachers insights into the reasons why their students get stuck in a bored state and thus withdraw from what goes on in their immediate L2 learning environment. After all, anyone who has been involved in the business of L2 teaching would like to avoid situations in which uninvolved students are impatiently checking the time on their smartphones or, even worse, start whispering to their desk mates or, which would be a really egregious problem, decide to openly state how boring the lesson is. Similarly, most teachers would probably be overjoyed if they could better understand the reasons for their own boredom so that they can minimize this typically unpleasant experience. Teacher readiness to realize that boredom is a distinct and intricate emotion with numerous, often unpredictably overlapping antecedents may be a starting point for reflecting on possible solutions likely to deal with it in an effective manner. Looking for ways of addressing L2 boredom is all the more important, given that related studies are few and far between when compared to the work in educational psychology (e.g., Daniels et al., 2015; Eren & Coskun, 2016; Nett et al., 2010, 2011). The following subsections briefly outline the strategies that L2 practitioners can fall back upon in this respect. While, due to the nature of the available empirical evidence, the bulk of the suggestions is related to coping with learner boredom, we have also attempted to point out how specific strategies can be applicable to L2 teachers.

3.2.1 Raising Awareness of the Experience of Boredom

A noteworthy idea and at the same time a good point of departure for helping students but also teachers come to grips with their experience of boredom would be to raise their awareness of this perplexing emotion (the emotion theory – Eastwood et al., 2007, 2012). As a first step, it is essential to ensure opportunities to define boredom and discuss with students as well as teachers its multifarious manifestations, with a focus on its ramifications and impact on their involvement and the quality of their work. Also, both learners and teachers can be encouraged to look into this state in retrospect, considering different situations in which they have felt dissatisfied, distracted or withdrawn (cf. Parker et al., 2005).

Importantly, the experience of boredom can be situated in the context of other, not only negative but also positive emotions (e.g., anxiety, anger, enjoyment, curiosity, hope), which will give students and teachers a wider perspective on the process of L2 learning and teaching, thus enhancing their understanding of the difficulties that they may encounter in the L2 classroom and behaviors in response to such unwanted or unexpected circumstances. It should be noted that L2 boredom can or even should be discussed and intentionally reflected upon in relation to particular tasks and activities that are considered uninteresting as opposed to others from which more enjoyment and/or meaning can be derived (cf. the MAC Model of boredom and cognitive engagement; Westgate & Wilson, 2018). In fact, intentional reflection can be viewed as a mechanism underlying mindfulness (i.e., the ability/ readiness to concentrate on and acknowledge one's own internal as well as external experience; e.g., Brown & Ryan, 2003; Flook, Goldberg, Pinger, Bonus, & Davidson, 2013), which has been shown to be negatively associated with attentional difficulties (the attentional theory of boredom proneness; Eastwood et al., 2007), and as such it may ameliorate the experience of boredom and improve self-regulation (LePera, 2011). As a result, a deliberate comparison between boredom- and engagement-generating activities has the potential to enable students and teachers to gain a deeper insight into their own goals, needs and mindsets. By answering questions about their preferences and expectations in connection with the reason(s) for which they attribute little value to a particular task or activity and/or appraise it as being out of their control, both sides (i.e., learners and teachers) may view themselves as capable of overcoming the aversive emotion of boredom (the control-value theory of achievement emotions; Pekrun, 2006). Likewise, those of them who are inclined to exchange ideas concerning boredom can participate in socially shared regulation of this emotion, which is likely to help them refocus and approach a given activity from a new, previously overlooked angle (Järvelä, Järvenoja, Malmberg, & Hadwin, 2013). In sum, quite paradoxically, talking about boredom based on their own hands-on experience may positively energize students and teachers, contributing to the development of engagement and curiosity towards what awaits them in the L2 classroom.

Reflective Break
- How would you like to introduce the topic of boredom to your students? What questions would you like to ask to elicit information about their perceptions of this phenomenon? What emotion vocabulary would you like to familiarize your students with?
- Admitting boredom might be challenging for L2 teachers. How would you encourage your own colleagues to talk about this negative experience? Can you think of the resources you could use or questions you could ask?
- Find an L2 text dedicated to the experience of boredom, adjust it, if necessary, to your students' L2 proficiency level and demonstrate how you would use it in the classroom. What text-related tasks would you propose to arouse your students' interest in the phenomenon of boredom?
- What boredom-related topics would you like to ask your students to write about?

3.2.2 Identifying Boredom-Coping Profiles

In order to probe into L2 learners' experience of boredom, together with its sources, types and manifestations, it is reasonable to observe how they respond to L2 instruction and assigned tasks with the aim of identifying their coping profiles and comparing them with those indicated in related studies. Nett et al. (2010) categorize students into three groups depending on how they handle boredom, labeled *evaders*, *criticizers* and *reappraisers*. *Evaders* can be characterized by adopting cognitive and behavioral avoidance strategies enabling them to give up the task in hand and look for something more involving to do, which is symptomatic of searching boredom. As for *criticizers*, they resort to behavioral approach strategies, thus displaying a clearly disapproving, accusatory attitude to boredom manifested by their attempts to pin the blame for this unpleasant condition on everyone or everything (e.g., the teacher, peers, teaching methods, materials, beliefs or the topic) but themselves, which can be associated with reactant boredom. Finally, *reappraisers* are individuals who mainly deploy cognitive approach strategies and therefore do their best to persevere with the task and resist wandering thoughts, no matter how boring. The reason for being active and positive about what transpires in class is that they believe that it might bring them closer to goal achievement, which they perceive as worthy of the effort and unpleasantness. Consequently, reappraisers are ready to revisit the task with self-sustained attention and a broader value system allowing for re-engaging with its content as well as a more comprehensive view on its goals and implications (cf. Nett et al., 2011; Weinerman & Kenner, 2016). Similarly to evaders, reappraisers can be described as experiencing searching boredom (see Chapter 2, section 2.2.), although in this case it is connected with eagerness to continue doing the task initially considered boring rather than switching to something else. To relate these profiles to the L2 classroom, when confronted with boredom-inducing language learning tasks and activities, evaders are likely to switch to some other activity, whether it is related to L2 learning or not, criticizers will in all likelihood be quite vocal about their disapproval of what they are expected to do, while reappraisers are likely to persevere in completing the task trying to focus on elements that might be beneficial to their L2 learning.

Although to is not easy to apply this classification to L2 teachers, who do not have the opportunity of just opting out or openly complaining when confronted with boredom (although some of them might in fact do this in front of their students), their reactions can also be described using some of the aforementioned labels. For example, some practitioners might not simply resign themselves to what the curriculum and the coursebook require them to do, thus trying to find more interesting alternatives when their learners are engaged in the performance of repetitive and therefore boring activities (i.e., evaders). By contrast, others might decide to carefully monitor these activities and their outcomes in the hope that their feedback and suggestions will help students make more progress in learning the TL (i.e., reappraisers).

Reflective Break
- What are your students' boredom profiles? Are they similar to Nett et al.'s distinction?
- How do your students manifest boredom and how do they react to this experience?
- Do some of the profiles dominate others and why do you think this is the case?

- Which of the profiles presented in this section best describes your own response to boredom that you experience in your teaching? Please provide one or two examples from your teaching practice.

3.2.3 Overcoming the Experience of Boredom

Once L2 student boredom-coping profiles have been identified, it is warranted to introduce strategies that could lead learners to come to grips with this aversive emotion. To begin with, it is important to assist students in taking volitional control over the task at hand by encouraging them to (re)state its goal or spell out reasons that could make it worth completing (Bartels, Magun-Jackson, & Kemp, 2009). Put differently, choosing goals that they find effective, important and/or inspiring, rather than merely relying on those established by the teacher, may motivate students to maintain effort, as a result of which they will see themselves as decision-makers freed from a boredom-specific sense of powerlessness (cf. the forced-effort model; Hill & Perkins, 1985). An interesting idea would be to provide opportunities for goal-oriented self-talk triggered by intentional thought revolving around a boring activity that can be made more involving if the student's attention is focused on its most relevant or stimulating aspects (Westgate & Wilson, 2018). This could be accomplished, for example, by having students read a difficult L2 text for gist before having them focus on its formal properties or all possible plot twists and turns. Trying to alter students' perceptions of things done in the L2 classroom with a promising or interesting goal in mind may therefore contribute to a decrease in boredom levels (Daniels et al., 2015; cf. the under-stimulation model; Larson & Richards, 1991).

There are also interesting boredom-coping interventions which can be related to the tenets of positive psychology with its emphasis on capitalizing on one's strengths and re-directing negative emotions (see Chapter 1, section 1; cf. Seligman, 2011; Yeager, Fisher, & Shearon, 2011). One example could be enhancing students' awareness of the role of imagination and positive thinking in picturing themselves as successful, fulfilled and/or self-satisfied individuals. In other words, the emotion of boredom can be alleviated every time learners attempt to mentally (re)capture past moments of well-being and add them to their current L2 learning experience. Recalling past achievements is likely to prevent students from thinking about potential pitfalls and failures, which may in turn orient them towards more active participation in what transpires in class (Heiss, Ziegler, Engbert, Gropel, & Brand, 2010). Another interesting possibility of fostering a positive mindset and confidence in one's own self-efficacy or abilities can be the adoption of the *persona technique* that invites individuals to assume the identity of another person. This creates proximity to someone else, which may help L2 learners overcome psychological barriers and distance themselves from aversive emotions and circumstances (Brans, Koval, Verduyn, Lim, & Kuppens, 2013; Larsen-Freeman, 2000; cf. Khajavy, MacIntyre, & Hariri, 2020). For instance, a bored L2 learner might be encouraged to put himself/herself in the shoes of a native speaker or his/her favorite movie/book character from an English-speaking country. Such a change of identity could motivate learners to look at the task in hand from a more optimistic perspective of someone who feels at ease as an L2 user and is therefore more willing to search for inspiration, surprise or novelty.

Yet another boredom-coping strategy is encouraging cooperation and active learning by partially delegating the responsibility for what transpires in the classroom to students (Mennim, 2017). This can be achieved, for example, by arranging peer teaching sessions with the purpose of engaging students in the exchange of thoughts and ideas. Such an approach may work particularly well for L2 learners whose boredom is caused by a paucity of novel and/or challenging stimuli (Davies & Fortney, 2012; Larson & Richards, 1991) resulting from having finished a given task ahead of others. The opportunity to share their knowledge with classmates may increase bored students' arousal, alertness and concentration, while at the same time contributing to their sense of higher accomplishment and psychological well-being (cf. Ainley, 2010; Seligman, 2011). Allowing students to interact in a meaningful and open-ended way may help enhance their attentional control (Eastwood et al., 2007; Westgate & Wilson, 2018) as well as stirring their enthusiasm.

L2 student boredom levels can also be reduced by organizing lessons around a range of open-ended and close-ended activities intended to practice different target language skills and subsystems. Only then is it possible to escape the boredom-provoking routine and unchallenging learning contexts overly supervised by the teacher (cf. the forced-effort model; Hill & Perkins, 1985; the under-stimulation model; Larson & Richards, 1991). Exposing students to a greater variety of activities may result in interchangeably or simultaneously fostering analytical thinking (e.g., explicit reflection on grammar rules), creative thinking (e.g., discovery learning involving trial and error, coming up with new ideas or using old ones in new and imaginative ways) and practical thinking (e.g., making connections between L2 tasks and real-world situations). In effect, students who are encouraged not only to think in terms of concepts and words but also to create vivid mental images, self-express or seek novelty and meaning in what they are expected to do in class will be less likely to experience boredom (cf. Gardner, 2004; Pawlak, 2018, 2020b; Sternberg & Sternberg, 2012)

Boredom-coping strategies can also build on the fact that students need a socially constructed relationship with L2 learning material in general and the task at hand in particular. Thus, it is essential to ensure that they do not hesitate to ask the teacher for clarification of a new topic, grammar rules or vocabulary items, which may result in repetition, provision of extra examples, explicit explanations or additional practice opportunities. Equally importantly, it is crucial to let students know that they are welcome to either directly or indirectly appeal for peer help (Brown & Heekyeong, 2015), which does not only apply to situations when they have to work in pairs or small groups. Realizing that there are various ways to compensate for their lack of knowledge or inadequate TL proficiency, learners may be better prepared to reframe the activity so that it can be perceived as more attractive or involving and look ahead with anticipation of future challenges rather than obstacles (Heiss et al., 2010; cf. Oxford, 2014). As a consequence, the danger of the occurrence of boredom can be diminished and its intensity can be reduced.

While boredom-reducing strategies described in this section are primarily intended for L2 learners, some of them could be employed by L2 teachers to combat their own boredom. One example could be discussing with colleagues coursebook activities that can be viewed as boring and repetitive, trying to collaboratively decide on their valuable aspects but also perhaps thinking of ways in which they could be tweaked or enriched to make them more engaging to the teachers themselves. Another possibility is to occasionally recall all the rewarding aspects of being an L2 teacher (e.g., the opportunity to constantly meet new people and confront novel challenges), those that may have been decisive in choosing this occupation in the first place. Teachers could also make sure to include as much variety as possible in their classes and be on constant lookout for creative, imaginative ways of teaching the same content (e.g., a specific grammar structure) in slightly different ways, which might alleviate boredom when the same instructional objectives have to be met in several learner groups on one day.

Reflective Break

- Do you think it is warranted to react to L2 student boredom? When are such interventions necessary?
- Do you encourage your students to (re)state and articulate their own goals for L2 activities? Is there a discrepancy between your and your students' goals? Does this help them cope with boredom? Provide one or two examples in this respect.
- Think about a topic and/or grammar rule that you would like to cover in your L2 classroom. How would you introduce it (them) to two different age groups of your choice? What measures would you take to make this topic and/or grammar rule involving for either of these groups?
- In your opinion, can students escape boredom trying to positively think about L2 activities which they initially perceived as uninteresting? Can this negative emotion be alleviated by attempting to understand why these activities are appreciated and enjoyed by their classmates?

- Do you organize peer teaching sessions in your classes? On what occasions does this happen? Do your students enjoy peer teaching? How is their enjoyment demonstrated?
- Are the L2 tasks you expose your students to intended to activate different types of thinking? Are your students more bored as a result of repetitive tasks than those alternately or concurrently fostering the three types of thinking mentioned above? What are your observations in this respect?
- Do you let your students know that they can ask you for clarification? Are their behaviors indicative of such a need? Do your attempts at clarification contribute to their arousal? Provide one or two examples in this respect.
- What other measures, among those mentioned in section 2.3. as well as those that have not been referred to above, can be useful in addressing L2 student boredom?
- Find one or two coursebook activities that you often use but perceive as mundane and boring. Together with your colleagues, discuss how these activities could promote L2 learning and consider the ways in which they could be adjusted to make them more engaging.

3.3 L2 TEACHER CHARACTERISTICS IN RELATION TO L2 STUDENT BOREDOM

While explicitly showing students how they can address their experience of boredom in the L2 classroom is undeniably important, L2 teacher mindset and personality can by no means be overlooked or underestimated in this respect. For one thing, it is the teacher's passion about the material and the subject taught that comes to the fore as a factor which may decrease student boredom (Exeter et al., 2010). This is in line with the tenets of the crossover theory (see Chapter 1, section 2.2.), which focuses on the phenomenon of emotional contagion as resulting from the tendency to orchestrate one's feelings, expressions or postures with those displayed by another person (e.g., Bakker, 2005; cf. Kruk & Zawodniak, 2018). It is equally crucial that the practitioner brings into the classroom a diverse repertoire of alternative activities in case some of the students find themselves over-challenged or under-challenged by the tasks in hand (the menton theory of engagement and boredom; Davies & Fortney, 2012; cf. Pekrun & Stephens, 2009). In addition, it is worth affording students a greater degree of freedom of choice. This can be achieved, for example, by enabling them to decide who they would like to work with or what aspects of the task they would rather pay more attention to (Gregory, Allen, Mikami, Hafen, & Pianta, 2014), solutions which obviously require open-mindedness, flexibility and readiness to listen to learners' voices. Equally importantly, it is essential for teachers not to place any of their students at a disadvantage, meaning that learners should be encouraged to indicate what poses difficulties to them or makes them confused, in which case feedback can be provided (McCann & Turner, 2004). Offering positive affective feedback, which reflects the teacher's appreciation of his/her students' effort and/or diligence, may positively impact their self-esteem and shape the perception of themselves as successful L2 users, which is likely to translate into their willingness to sustain attention and complete tasks originally viewed as uninvolving. The experience of boredom may also be minimized as a consequence of giving students the possibility of self-correcting by, for instance, using such corrective feedback techniques as clarification requests, metalinguistic clues, repetition or elicitations (cf. Lyster, Saito, & Sato, 2013; Van Ha, Murray, & Mehdi Riazi, 2021). Indicating that the student's utterance was erroneous, rather than providing him or her with a ready-made form, may make him or her more attentive, curious and eager to discover what has gone wrong with their L2 production. A valid argument could be made that following some of these guidelines would have the effects of reducing not only students' but also teachers' boredom, thus killing the proverbial two birds with one stone.

L2 student boredom may also be effectively addressed by creating a pleasant, non-threatening classroom environment (CE) that, owing to its reliance on congenial interpersonal relationships based on mutual respect and emotional support, could be conducive to fostering positive emotions seen as the catalyst of involvement (Patrick, Kaplan, & Ryan, 2011). A noticeable aspect of CE is positive teacher communication comprising interactive behaviors, clarity, care, humor and immediacy (i.e., the state of perceived physical or psychological closeness and involvement with other people), all of which are likely to contribute to L2 learner engagement with the activities and material covered in class (Andersen, 1999; Derakhshan, Eslami, Curle, & Zhaleh, 2022a). Specifically, the teacher's sensitivity and responsiveness to students' needs, ideas and problems as well as avoidance of judgmental behaviors, as is the case with the techniques of providing corrective feedback mentioned above, may help learners approach the task at hand with more openness and focus (Khajavy, MacIntyre, & Barabadi, 2018; Li et al., 2021). Also, the teacher's sense of humor and ability to engage in appropriate jocular behavior may positively impact the L2 classroom climate, thus facilitating the performance of tasks and increasing their attractiveness (Muñoz-Basols, 2005; Pawlak, Derakhshan, Mehdizadeh, & Kruk, 2021). However, such an open-ended, insightful approach to students' L2 learning experiences and expectations would not be feasible or at least would be very hard to come by without teachers' familiarity with the principles underlying cognitive and affective development. This naturally underlines the importance of participating in various teacher training courses devoted to such topics as, for example, innovative methods/techniques, recent advances in cognitive and educational psychology, trait emotional intelligence, L2 assessment or L2 classroom management (Aubusson, 2008; McNamara, Murray, & Jones, 2014; Richards & Farrell, 2005). Whether the ability to create a welcoming classroom climate and build good rapport with students derives from some kind of formal training, constitutes an inborn gift or is the result of accumulated experience, it can also be instrumental in reducing boredom on the part of teachers. This is because the prospects of the occurrence of this negative emotion are likely to be decreased when teachers can engage students in friendly conversations in the TL about everyday issues, crack jokes with them or negotiate the most propitious ways of attaining instructional goals.

Reflective Break

- Do you offer your students choices? In what circumstances does it happen? What are your students' expectations in this respect?
- Do you ever try to decide together with students what instructional practices would be the most beneficial or what homework assignments would best respond to their needs?
- What types of corrective feedback do you expose your students to? In your opinion, is the use of explicit correction more boredom-provoking than encouraging self-correction? Provide one or two examples in this respect.
- Try to relate the crossover theory to your teaching experience.
- What other teacher-specific features that may have a role to play in ameliorating L2 student boredom would you like to add?
- What is your understanding of positive L2 classroom environment? Which of its characteristics do you perceive as important in combating L2 student experience of boredom?
- Do you participate in teacher training courses and, if so, could you enumerate some of them? In what way do they improve your teaching skills? How do these courses relate to the attractiveness and innovativeness of your L2 instruction?

CONCLUSION

The present chapter has discussed L2 boredom from a broadly-conceived cause-and-effect perspective, providing insights into the most influential theories aimed at highlighting various antecedents of this academic emotion and demonstrating how these theories can be capitalized on in the language classroom. Consequently, it has attempted to show why on some occasions students feel more bored than on others, why it is important to raise their awareness of boredom in connection with other negative as well as positive emotions and why students should learn how to communicate their emotional states to other people. Whenever feasible, an effort has been made to demonstrate how the various theoretical accounts of boredom can apply to L2 teachers. Emphasis has also been placed on the diverse strategies that can be employed to minimize the danger that boredom will occur or reduce its deleterious effect. Notwithstanding the impact of appropriately addressing boredom on the quality of L2 instruction or the well-being of individuals involved in this process, attention has also been paid to the teacher's mindset and personality as potential contributors to the experience of this emotion. All things considered, it has to be underscored that boredom occupies a significant place in L2 learning and teaching and thus it has to be overtly named, understood and attended to. More insights in this respect will be provided in the last three chapters of this book in which the findings of the research project will be presented and discussed, the need for reflective practice with respect to L2 boredom will be highlighted, specific guidelines on dealing with L2 learner and teacher boredom will be proposed, and a handful of awareness-raising activities will be offered.

Chapter 4

Researching L2 Boredom in L2 Learning and Teaching

INTRODUCTION

The first three chapters of this book have been devoted to an overview of the role of emotions in L2 learning and teaching as well as, more specifically, the definition and conceptualization of the construct of boredom, theoretical explanations of its occurrence and the ways in which it can be combated in educational settings, including L2 instruction. Although some empirical studies have inevitably been referred to in these three chapters, no attempt has been made thus far to provide a comprehensive overview of empirical investigations that have specifically focused on different aspects of boredom that can be experienced in various contexts. The bulk of the existing empirical evidence in this respect comes from the domain of educational psychology, where the study of boredom was initiated (e.g., Daniels et al., 2015; Daschmann, Goetz, & Stupnisky, 2014; Dettmers et al., 2011; Mann & Robinson, 2009; Taxer & Frenzel, 2015), but such investigations are not directly relevant to the focus of this book. For this reason, the present chapter is confined to the discussion of research that has specifically targeted boredom in L2 learning and teaching. While such empirical inquiry is still in its infancy and therefore evidently limited in volume and scope, the number of pertinent studies has increased exponentially in the last two or three years (cf. Kruk & Pawlak, 2022, for an overview of some of the related research), which surely warrants a brief overview of the main research foci, existing gaps, methodological choices as well as the main results.

This is exactly the purpose of the present chapter, which has been divided into four main parts. At the outset, an attempt is made to explain why research into L2 boredom is of relevance to teachers, a group of readers for which this book is primarily intended. Subsequently, emphasis will be placed on the main foci of empirical investigations into this aversive emotion, both such that are being currently pursued by specialists and such that yet have to be explored, which will allow identification of evident research gaps. This will be followed by a succinct discussion of research designs and tools that can be used to illuminate issues related to L2 boredom. The last part of the chapter will provide an overview of a selection of studies representing the dominant research foci, briefly commenting on their aims, methodology and the main findings. Several important issues need to be highlighted at this juncture. First, the overview is not meant to be exhaustive and is confined to the most recent studies published in the last several years. Second, studies examining boredom manifested by both L2 learners and teachers have been included, with the crucial caveat that the latter are still few and far between. Third, chronological order is followed when examples of studies representing different research foci are provided. Fourth, a critical evaluation of the existing body of empirical evidence in terms of its foci and scope is deferred until the conclusion to this chapter.

4.1 WHY SHOULD L2 TEACHERS BOTHER WITH RESEARCH INTO BOREDOM

Although the question posed in the title of this section may seem to be overly provocative, it is fully warranted to ask it for several reasons. Generally speaking, much has been written about the gap between the worlds inhabited by theorists and researchers, on the one hand, and classroom teachers, on the other (e.g., Ellis, 1997; Erlam, 2008; Medgyes, 2017; Nassaji, 2012; Sato & Loewen, 2022). SLA specialists are primarily concerned with developing theories about how L2 learning proceeds in different contexts and in some cases also how this process can be aided by instruction. They subsequently set out to test the theoretical assumptions in empirical studies which typically single out very specific instructional options with little regard for others and give little attention as to how different techniques and procedures can be combined to result in more effective L2 learning. Other researchers may be driven by particular theories to a much lesser extent and strive to describe and understand the teaching and learning practices in various groups. By contrast, L2 teachers are mainly focused on making the instruction they provide as effective as possible in the contexts in which they have to function, taking into consideration the existing curricula, examination requirements, local conditions and other exigencies. This means that they are not really interested in the theoretical assumptions justifying the practices in which they engage and their main concern is that these practices actually work even if this means combining approaches that some SLA specialists may view as irreconcilable. While it might seem at first blush that despite different priorities pursued by both groups, there is room for their agendas to converge, this does not happen very often, although it is certainly possible. One of the main reasons for this blatant lack of communication is that researchers are obliged to publish their work and their papers have to meet rigorous academic standards, which is why this kind of research is difficult to access for teachers and pedagogical implications, if they are formulated at all, may be just squeezed in somewhere at the end, let alone the fact that they frequently have little practical relevance. As a result, teachers view SLA research as something that is beyond their reach and they do not see how its results could assist them in providing more effective instruction, with the effect that they seldom read research reports. The problem is further aggravated by the fact that readable summaries of the findings of existing studies are hard to come by.

Arguably, the interaction between theorists, researchers and teachers may prove even more problematic in the case of empirical investigations into L2 boredom. For one thing, just like journal editors who had to deal with the first submissions reporting studies on this negative emotion, many teachers may just raise their eyebrows in disbelief and ask themselves why they should pay attention to something that is so obvious and pervasive. Some of them might even argue that when learners feel bored in the classroom, they have only themselves to blame and many teachers might be reluctant to admit their own boredom as something that would reflect badly on their classroom practices as well as themselves as language teaching professionals. This having been said, there are surely practitioners who might find L2 boredom research to be highly relevant, perhaps much more so than research in other areas (e.g., working memory, personality, developmental sequences in teaching grammar), not least because they are willing to admit that this negative emotion may have had a detrimental impact on their L2 learning and also has the potential to derail their current instructional practices. The problem is that existing studies of L2 boredom may have little to offer to teachers and thus be seen as irrelevant. First, as the overview offered later in this chapter will demonstrate, most of the available studies have focused on this negative phenomenon as experienced by L2 learners rather than teachers. Even though this is understandable and reflects overall trends in research on ID factors in SLA, such an emphasis is short-sighted, not least because of the close link between emotions that learners and teachers experience in the classroom, a simple truth highlighted by the crossover theory (Hatfield et al., 1994). Second, most of the empirical investigations conducted thus far have focused on the causes and manifestations of boredom or reasons for the changes in the intensity of this emotion over time rather than the effects of pedagogical interventions or strategies that can be applied to alleviate it. While such a focus is fully warranted in this nascent field, many interested teachers may wonder what they are supposed to do with information of this kind, on condition that it is communicated to them in an accessible way. Third, some of the most recent research has drawn upon advanced statistical procedures to explore links between boredom and other academic emotions, sometimes longitudinally (e.g., Dewaele et al., 2022; Kruk, Pawlak, Elahi Shirvan, Taherian, & Yazdanmehr, 2022a). Although such attempts can be regarded as groundbreaking and laudable by fellow researchers, they cannot really be appreciated by L2 teachers who are bound to struggle to identify links to their own instructional practices.

While all the issues mentioned above are undoubtedly valid, there are many important reasons why research into boredom should be of interest to practitioners and why they should not simply decide to skip the remainder of the present chapter. First and foremost, as has been emphasized several times earlier in this book, the awareness of the causes of boredom, whether in the case of L2 learners or teachers, is of paramount importance since it can pave the way for effective implementation of strategies that can be drawn on to prevent this aversive emotion, decrease its intensity and ward off at least some of its negative consequences. In other words, it is not really feasible to combat boredom if its antecedents in different contexts are not fully grasped, appreciated and accepted. Equally important is the fact that the causes of this negative emotion and the solutions that can be implemented to ameliorate it are similar in the case of teachers and learners, and thus, the insights gained from existing, admittedly limited, research can be beneficially capitalized upon in different ways. After all, an argument could be made that successfully dealing with some of the triggers of boredom among learners may also lead to a decrease in its intensity among teachers. For example, students' active engagement in the task set by the teacher which can manifest itself, among others, in a flurry of questions or a whole-class discussion, is more than likely to effectively prevent teachers from easily getting bored. Another reason why practitioners should engage with research on L2 boredom is the fact this ID factor is amenable to some kind of external manipulation, such as the employment of adept pedagogical interventions or reliance on appropriate coping strategies. In other words, unlike such variables as working memory, aptitude, personality or learning styles but similarly to motivation (Lamb, 2019) or learning strategies (cf. Chamot & Harris, 2019), there is clear potential to adopt appropriate strategies to avoid the occurrence of boredom or to minimize its negative consequences, once again, both in the case of learners and teachers. Last but not least, the implementation of such strategies is something that L2 teachers can easily do in their own classrooms with little concern for academic rigor (i.e., inclusion of control groups, the use of pre- and posttests). In simpler terms, this is an area where teachers have the opportunity to engage in action research, seeking solutions that could make L2 instruction more effective in their own local contexts (cf. Banegas & Consoli, 2020). It is our hope that in the face of all the arguments offered above, L2 teachers who happen to be reading this book will decide to proceed to the next section which is devoted to the discussion of the main foci of research into L2 boredom.

> **Reflective Break**
> - Have you ever read articles written by SLA specialists? If yes, briefly comment on the one that you have recently read. If not, explain why.
> - Can you list five areas that, in your opinion, SLA researchers should investigate? Please justify your choices.
> - Do you think that there is merit to investigating L2 boredom? Why or why not?
> - What should research on boredom try to uncover in the first place? Please justify your opinion.
> - What is your opinion about action research, such that aims to solve problems that teachers face in their classrooms? Have you ever undertaken such research? Why or why not?

4.2 MAIN FOCI OF RESEARCH INTO BOREDOM IN L2 LEARNING AND TEACHING

Figure 1 diagrammatically illustrates the main foci of empirical investigations of boredom in L2 learning and teaching. Before these foci are characterized in more detail, several caveats are in order. First, the figure includes both research directions that are currently being pursued by specialists (e.g., causes and manifestations) and such that, in the view of the present authors, hold considerable promise for a better understanding of the role of this negative emotion and are thus in need of empirical investigation in the near future (e.g., examination of L2 boredom with respect to TL skills and subsystems). Second, despite the attempt to be as comprehensive as possible, one could probably envisage other potential lines of inquiry, which could be linked, for instance, to the theoretical lens adopted by researchers (e.g., CDST) and the methodological apparatus that specific theories and models advocate. Likewise, it is certainly possible to add further levels of granularity by, for example, looking at the causes of boredom in terms of the effects of specific tasks, topics, student groupings, lesson stages, pedagogical objectives, etc. Third, the current and potential areas of empirical inquiry indicated in Figure 1 are meant to apply to both learners and teachers, although it is warranted to assume that some of them may be more relevant to students (e.g., the effects of interventions aimed at reducing the intensity of boredom). Fourth, many existing studies but also such that still await being undertaken may aim to simultaneously examine several issues. A good case in point are empirical investigations of the changes in the levels of boredom over time which typically do not stop at tracing such fluctuations over different timescales but also seek to pinpoint their causes, which might involve gaining insights both into contextual issues and individual learner characteristics.

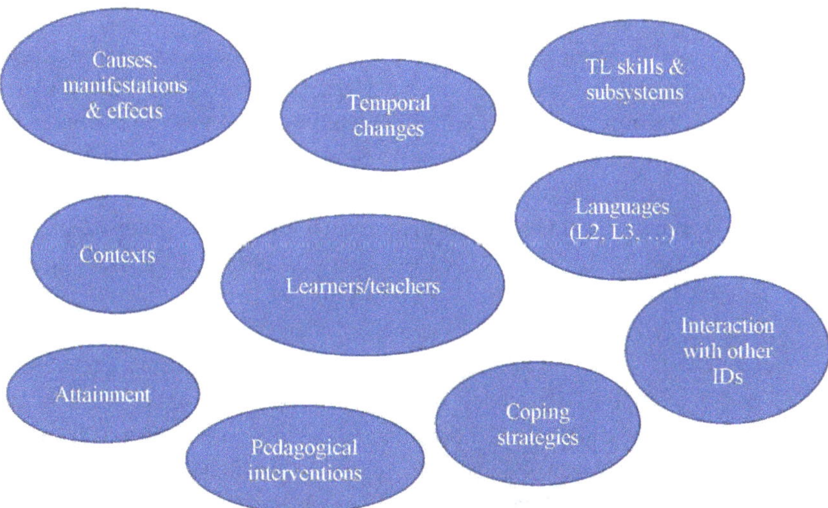

Figure 1 Current and potential foci of research on L2 boredom

As can be seen from Figure 1, research on boredom in L2 education can concentrate on both learners and teachers, with these groups being examined in separate or single studies. As the overview of the available empirical evidence later in this chapter will clearly demonstrate, the vast majority of investigations have targeted different aspects of boredom experienced by L2 students, while teacher boredom has been blatantly neglected, having been the focus of just a handful of studies (e.g., Dumančić, 2018). This also applies to investigations that would set out to juxtapose learner and teacher perspectives. When it comes to the (potential) areas of inquiry included in Figure 1, close examination of the available body of research allows the following observations:

- on the whole, the main emphasis has been placed on the identification of the causes, symptoms, and effects of boredom (e.g., Nakamura et al., 2021; Zawodniak et al., 2021); attempts have also been made to reveal its factor structure in different contexts (e.g., Li et al., 2021; Pawlak et al., 2020b);
- there are quite a few studies that have focused on temporal changes in the intensity of boredom during single lessons, sequences of classes or longer timespans, sometimes providing crucial insights into the multifarious triggers of such fluctuations (e.g., Elahi Shirvan, Yazdanmehr, Taherian, Kruk, & Pawlak, 2021; Kruk & Zawodniak, 2020; Pawlak et al., 2020c, 2020d);
- research into L2 boredom can be conducted in a wide variety of contexts which can be defined in a general or more specific manner: national contexts, different educational levels and thus also disparate age groups (e.g., university,

secondary school, primary school), different types of programs (e.g., university programs for students majoring in a given L2, English-medium instruction [EMI], content and language integrated learning [CLIL], computer-assisted language learning [CALL]), online teaching vs. face-to-face instruction, or in-class and after-class boredom; only some of these contexts have been taken into consideration, often in isolated studies; only several national contexts have been involved, mainly Poland, Iran and China (e.g., Derakhshan, Kruk, Mehdizadeh, & Pawlak, 2022b; Kruk, 2016; Li & Wei, 2022); mostly university L2 students, in particular English majors, have been participants of boredom-related studies (e.g., Pawlak et al., 2020a); face-to-face (e.g., Pawlak et al., 2020c, 2020d) as well as online contexts (e.g., Pawlak et al., 2021) have been targeted, the latter mainly due to the COVID-19 pandemic; there are studies that have looked at L2 boredom in CALL contexts, especially in virtual worlds (e.g., Kruk, 2021b); the occurrence of boredom in other settings is a terra incognita and, to the best of our knowledge, after-class boredom has been investigated in just a handful of published studies (Pawlak et al., 2022a; Pawlak, Kruk, Csizér, & Zawodniak, 2023);

- research exploring links between L2 boredom and other ID factors is limited (e.g., Pawlak et al., 2022b) and researchers have mostly confined themselves to examining links between boredom and other frequently investigated emotions, such as anxiety or enjoyment (e.g., Dewaele et al., 2022);
- just a couple of studies have investigated boredom in an L2 other than English, mainly German, even fewer have compared its causes or intensity as a function of the L2 being taught and learned (e.g., Kruk & Zawodniak, 2020; Yazdanmehr, Elahi Shirvan, & Saghafi, 2021), and there has been no attempt to explore boredom in the case of multilingual learners;
- there is only extremely scant empirical evidence on coping strategies that can be used to combat the experience of boredom (e.g., Derakhshan et al., 2022b; Pawlak et al., 2021);
- very few studies have attempted to link boredom levels to TL attainment (e.g., Pawlak et al., 2020b, 2022a) but this variable has been operationalized in terms of grades or self-assessment rather than actual performance of TL tasks (i.e., controlled or spontaneous);
- to the best knowledge of the present authors, there are few studies that would have looked specifically at boredom in relation to particular TL skills and subsystems (e.g., reading, writing, grammar, pronunciation) or such that would have verified the effectiveness of pedagogical interventions specifically designed to combat this negative emotion.

Reflective Break
- In your opinion, which of the areas included in Figure 1 are in most need of investigation? Why?
- Do you think that the causes and symptoms of boredom may differ in face-to-face teaching and online instruction? Why or why not?
- Are there reasons to believe that the intensity of boredom may differ depending on the language being learned? Why do you think this might be the case?
- Do you think that the causes of boredom experienced during L2 lessons and in L2 learning outside the classroom are likely to differ? Why?
- In your opinion, does the experience of boredom depend on the TL skill (e.g., reading) or subsystem (e.g., grammar) being practiced? Why or why not?

4.3 HOW CAN L2 BOREDOM BE RESEARCHED

In-depth discussion of the methodology of research into L2 boredom falls beyond the scope of this book, which is primarily intended for teachers. For this reason, the discussion in the present section is not meant to be exhaustive and only focuses on the main approaches to exploring various facets of this negative emotion that can be used for this purpose. We are convinced that awareness of such basic methodological considerations is crucial to be able to better appreciate empirical investigations of boredom in L2 learning and teaching, some representative examples of which are provided later in this chapter. It will also be instrumental in better understanding the design and findings of the research project that will be reported in Chapter 5. Familiarity with the fundamentals of how boredom can be empirically explored may also come in handy for practitioners wishing to gain insights into this aversive emotion in their own classrooms, whether with respect to their learners or themselves, and perhaps take steps to alleviate it.

As is the case with research into other ID factors in SLA, the study of L2 boredom can be undertaken from the macro-perspective or the micro-perspective (cf. Pawlak, 2020a; Pawlak & Kruk, 2022). When the *macro-perspective* is embraced, the main goal is to establish general patterns and/or relationships between boredom and other variables in specific populations. In most cases, studies falling into this category are quantitative in nature, the data are collected by means of carefully developed and validated tools, usually questionnaires including Likert-scale items (e.g., a 5-point scale) from large samples of participants (not only learners but also teachers), and advanced statistical procedures are employed to analyze such data (e.g., factor analysis, structural equation modeling, correlations, regression analysis). One example is the study by Pawlak et al. (2020a), which identified factors underlying boredom and investigated their importance as a function of general boredom proneness and attainment. Another is the research conducted by Li and Wei (2022), who examined how anxiety, boredom and enjoyment predicted L2 achievement over time. General patterns can also be established with the help of qualitative research, where open-ended queries or interviews can be utilized, on condition that data are obtained from large numbers of informants, as was the case in the study carried out by Derakhshan et al. (2021), who examined sources of boredom and strategies applied to cope with it. By contrast, the *micro-perspective* aims to illuminate L2 boredom in a situated manner, focusing on its experience in a given context (e.g., a learner group, one teacher, an L2 class or a sequence of such classes, a specific learning task), often also seeking to examine the dynamic changes in this emotion over different timescales (e.g., minutes, weeks, months) as well as the reasons for such changes. The main concern here is thus seeking greater understanding of the nature and functioning of this negative emotion, and sometimes shedding light on its interaction with other ID factors including emotions, rather than pinpointing some overall trends. As a consequence, research embracing the micro-perspective usually relies on mixed methods, with a combination of quantitative and qualitative data being collected by means of different tools (e.g., self-ratings, immediate reports, interviews, observations, questionnaires) and the analysis often integrating these two approaches as well. A number of such studies have been conducted in the Polish contexts (e.g., Kruk, 2016, 2021b; Pawlak et al., 2020d) and some examples will be presented in more detail in the following section. On the whole, it would seem that if teachers would like to examine learners' or their own boredom, the micro-perspective would be a natural option as they would in all likelihood be interested in why this phenomenon occurs in a specific context rather than in general tendencies in large samples.

A very different research design is needed when the aim is to investigate the effects of coping strategies or pedagogical interventions implemented with the purpose of preventing L2 boredom or reducing its intensity. Although, as signaled in section 2 of this chapter, specialists have yet to embark on such intervention-based studies, they seem to be of particular relevance to practitioners wishing to try out different solutions to this negative phenomenon in their own classrooms or to engage in more structured action research (Banegas & Consoli, 2020). When the rigorous requirements of academic research are adhered to, empirical investigations of this kind should involve an experimental group, where some kind of treatment (e.g., intervention) takes place, preferably over an extended period of time (e.g., several weeks or even months), and a control group, in which regular instruction is followed. Both groups would need to take a pretest, an immediate posttest following the intervention to determine if it has been effective, and, preferably, also a delayed posttest to establish if the effects, if any, are retained over time. In this case, the tests would simply involve the administration of a questionnaire that would tap into factors underlying L2 boredom and their levels, such as the *Boredom in Practical English Classes – Revised* (BPELC-R) questionnaire (Pawlak et al, 2020b; see section 4 in this chapter). Statistical procedures (e.g., *t*-tests, analysis of variance) would then be employed to check if the differences between groups and between different measurement times are significant. It is also possible to enrich insights into the effectiveness of the intervention through interviews or open-ended items that would be administered before, during and after the treatment. While ensuring high quality research is crucial for researchers, many of the requirements listed here would perhaps be irrelevant for teachers willing to experiment with various ways of reducing boredom. It is understandable, for example, that, unless they are conducting a research project for a degree, they are unlikely to need a control group, delayed posttests or inferential statistics. Although they would be advised to draw on the BPELC-R inventory or a similar questionnaire, they could easily evaluate the effect of their interventions by regularly observing their students or themselves, holding group interviews, asking learners to express their opinions in more or less formal ways or engaging in introspection on their own instructional practices.

Reflective Break

- In your own words, how would you explain the main difference between the macro- and micro-perspective in research on L2 boredom?
- Do you agree with the assumption that studies based on the micro-perspective are likely to be more useful to teachers than those adopting the macro-perspective? Why or why not?
- Can you think of ways in which the findings of studies seeking to establish general tendencies concerning boredom and its links to other ID factors could be beneficial to L2 teachers?
- Looking at the classes you teach, what pedagogical interventions could you use to reduce your students' boredom? How would you know if they have been effective or not?
- If you decided to use strategies to prevent or reduce your own boredom, how could you determine if they are working or not?

4.4 EXAMPLES OF STUDIES ON BOREDOM IN L2 LEARNING AND TEACHING

The present section includes examples of empirical studies that have sought to offer insights into different aspects of L2 boredom. In each case, a short label is added to demonstrate which of the lines of inquiry represented in Figure 1 a given study roughly corresponds to, with the caveat that some of these empirical investigations might have simultaneously pursued several objectives and their description may be somewhat arbitrary reflecting its main focus. Many of the research directions included in the figure are not represented here for the simple reason that no relevant studies have been conducted thus far. The examples are presented in chronological order and all of them include brief information about the main goals, participants, methodology and the main findings. Reflective Breaks are also added in each case to stimulate reflection on the issues that each study set out to examine.

Kruk and Zawodniak (2017): Causes and Changes of L2 Boredom

Main Goals

The study investigated the relationship between general boredom proneness and L2 boredom as well as sources of the negative emotion of boredom in the L2 classroom.

Participants

The sample consisted of 174 Polish first-, second- and third-year English majors (125 females and 49 males, aged 19–44).

Methodology

The data were gathered by means of three research instruments: (1) the *Boredom Proneness Scale* (Farmer & Sundberg, 1986), (2) the *Boredom in Practical English Language Classes Questionnaire* (which was a modified version of the *Boredom Proneness Scale* consisting of 28 items related to boredom experienced in learning the English language) and (3) a description of boredom-evoking situations in the L2 classroom.

Main Findings

Quantitative analysis showed a significant, positive correlation between general boredom proneness and the experience of this aversive emotion in the L2 classroom as well as a growing tendency to experience the negative emotion in question over time (i.e., it was higher in the case of second- and third-year students in comparison to first-year students). Qualitative analysis revealed that L2 boredom was triggered by repetitiveness and monotony of the language activities performed during English classes, a mismatch between the level of challenge and respondents' L2 proficiency, their language teachers (e.g., their lack of involvement, excessive teacher talk, personality), class components (e.g., listening, reading and writing classes), topics covered during classes (e.g., uninteresting and useless topics) and modes of work imposed on students (e.g., pair work and individual work).

> **Reflective Break**
> - In your opinion, can teacher talk contribute to L2 student boredom? What experiences do you have in this respect?
> - Do you give priority to (a) particular mode(s) of work (i.e., individual, pair, group, whole-class) in your L2 classroom and if so, why is this the case? Do your students find some of these modes more boredom-provoking than others? How can you explain it?

Dumančić (2018): Causes and Effects of Teachers' Boredom, and their Coping Strategies

Main Goals

The study was guided by four objectives: (1) to uncover the causes of boredom, (2) to examine the most frequent indications of boredom, (3) to investigate boredom-coping strategies and (4) to identify the impact of teacher boredom on instructional quality.

Participants

38 Croatian teachers of English as a foreign language working at the primary and secondary school level took part in the investigation.

Methodology

The data were gathered thorough an online open-ended survey comprising two parts. The first part included general information related to the participants. The second part encompassed five items intended to explore issues concerning teacher boredom. They were based on other instruments aimed at measuring L2 student boredom (Chahkandi, Rasekh, & Tavakoli, 2016; Kruk & Zawodniak, 2018). The collected data underwent content analysis which comprised several stages, that is, reading the data, highlighting pertinent passages, coding and clustering the identified cases into categories.

Main Findings

Seven main causes of boredom were identified: (1) teaching content (e.g., grammar-related), (2) subject matter (e.g., uninteresting lessons and topics), (3) students (i.e., their behavior, motivation, knowledge), (4) tasks and activities (e.g., repetitive, undemanding), (5) student assessment (i.e., taking tests and grading learners), (6) teaching aids and materials (e.g., textbooks, the lack of multimedia in the L2 classroom) and (7) teaching methods (i.e., the use of methods that learners disliked, repetitive use of the same methods). Manifestations of teacher boredom were grouped into five categories: (1) cognitive (e.g., drifting away, loss of concentration, wishing for a lesson to be finished), (2) expressive (e.g., yawning, postures), (3) motivational (i.e., loss of enthusiasm or interest, the desire to change an activity), (4) an absence of visible signs of boredom (i.e., some teachers did not express boredom in front of students) and (5) no experience of boredom. The boredom-coping strategies employed by the respondents were categorized into eight groups: (1) the introduction of different tasks and/or activities, (2) the use of physical activity (e.g., stretching, walking), (3) engaging students (e.g., making a lesson more conversational), (4) suppression (i.e., not showing emotions to students), (5) cognitive change (i.e., imagining being a student and having to attend lessons), (6) attention deployment (i.e., diverting oneself from feeling boredom), (7) playing music and (8) no desire to regulate (i.e., accepting emotions and not modifying them in any way). The respondents failed to report any deleterious effects of their boredom on the quality of their instruction.

Reflective Break

- In your opinion, is student assessment likely to generate L2 student boredom? Is this the case with your students and if so, in what circumstances does it happen? What can be done by the teacher to make student assessment less boredom-provoking?
- Does any of the above-mentioned five categories of manifestations of teacher boredom refer to some of your behaviors in the L2 classroom? Can any other English teachers that you know be characterized in terms of one or two of these categories? Why do you think are these categories the same as/different from yours?
- Which of the eight boredom-coping strategies discussed by Dumančić (2018) do you consider the most effective in the L2 classroom? Is/Are there any that you have never thought about but would like to adopt in your teaching practice?
- Is there a relationship between your boredom and the instructional quality of your work as an EFL teacher? What aspects of the instructional quality of your work are most negatively affected by your boredom?

Kruk and Zawodniak (2020): Causes and Changes of Boredom in English and German

Main Goals

The study comparatively investigated changes in boredom levels over the course of a semester and from one semester to another with regard to learning L2 (English) and L3 (German) as well as reasons for such changes from a retrospective perspective.

Participants

The sample consisted of 30 Polish university students (21 females and 9 males; average age: 22.43) majoring in English (L2) and learning German (L3) as an additional language.

Methodology

The students filled out the *Language Learning Boredom in Retrospect Questionnaire* (LLBR) in which they were requested to look back upon their experience of boredom in learning English and German over the period of three semesters at university, with the first semester making up the initial point for their reflections. In addition, the students were asked to indicate the intensity of this aversive emotion at three points in time (i.e., start, middle, end) regarding each of the three consecutive semesters.

Main Findings

Quantitative analysis demonstrated that regardless of the language they studied, boredom levels were the lowest at the very start and the highest at the end of every semester. Changes in boredom levels detected from one semester to the next differed to some extent as a function of L2 and L3. More specifically, the participants experienced the least and the most boredom in learning L2 throughout the first and the second semester, respectively, while in learning L3 the experience of boredom was the lowest in the first semester and it reached its peak in the third one. The analysis also identified some sources of boredom in learning the two languages. As for L2, three boredom-prompting factors were identified: (1) lesson-related (e.g., repetitiveness, uninvolving content, predictability of classes), (2) teacher-related (e.g., lack of involvement, the same teaching methods/techniques, monotonous voice) and (3) other (e.g., class time, the weather). With respect to L3, four factors responsible for boredom were distinguished: (1) lesson-related (e.g., uninteresting topics, repeatability of the material, the level of difficulty of language activities), (2) reluctance to learn German, (3) people-related (e.g., too demanding teachers, peers) and (4) other (i.e., class time and its length).

> **Reflective Break**
> - In your view, has the experience of your students' boredom in L2 classes changed over a longer period of time? More specifically, how does the present intensity of this distressing emotion compare to how it used to be experienced at the very beginning of the EFL learning process?
> - Does your students' boredom in L2 learning differ from how they experience it in L3 learning? If you are not able to answer this question, talk to your students about their boredom in the L2/L3 classroom and briefly report the results of this inquiry.

Pawlak, Zawodniak and Kruk (2020d): Changes in L2 Boredom in a Sequence of Classes

Main Goals

The study investigated differences in the levels of boredom and factors responsible for them throughout four English classes. In addition, the study explored differences in the experience of this negative emotion among individual students and its causes.

Participants

Two parallel, intact groups of Polish university students majoring in English (Group 1: $N = 13$ and Group 2: $N = 10$).

Methodology

The data were gathered by means of the following instruments: (1) a background questionnaire (used to obtain demographic information concerning the participants), (2) a semi-structured interview (employed to provide more insights into L2 boredom and its intensity), (3) lesson plans (they were used to offer detailed information regarding the conducted classes) and (4) an in-class boredom questionnaire encompassing four parts: (i) the first part was completed by the participants at the start of a class and included students' names and the date of a given class, (ii) the second part was filled out as the class was in progress and comprised a boredom grid, that is, a self-rated measure of boredom (on a 7-point scale: 1 – minimum, 7 – maximum), on which the learners indicated the intensity of their boredom in real time at 5-minute intervals, (iii) the third part contained a semantic differential scale (example items: *dull* vs. *exciting*; *unsatisfying* vs. *satisfying*; *monotonous* vs. *absorbing*) which was completed towards the end of a given class and (iv) the fourth part required the students to write a short paragraph about their experience of boredom during a particular class.

Main Findings

The findings showed that the experience of boredom underwent changes in its intensity within an individual activity, a whole class and from one class to the next. These changes were attributed to the type of language activity, monotony, repetitiveness, opportunities to interact with peers, the stage of a class, or some individual learner characteristics and dispositions. The results also demonstrated that the patterns of boredom exhibited by individual students substantially deviated from those observed for the two groups of learners. In addition, they were affected by internal and external variables that tended to undergo variation over time.

> **Reflective Break**
> - Recall a situation when your students' boredom fluctuated within the same activity. What do you think were those fluctuations caused by?
> - In your opinion, what individual learner characteristics can contribute to the experience of boredom in the L2 classroom?
> - Think about one or two of your students whom you found bored during a particular activity, a whole class or from one class to another. What "bored" behaviors did they display and how did they compare to other students' behaviors?

Pawlak, Kruk, Zawodniak and Pasikowski (2020b): Factor Structure of L2 Boredom in Poland

Main Goals

The main aims of the research project were to uncover factors underlying the experience of L2 boredom, to investigate the mediating effects of boredom proneness and attainment, and to develop and validate an L2 boredom scale for measuring the negative emotion in question among advanced language learners.

Participants

The study involved 107 Polish students majoring in English (80 females and 27 males; average age: 21.45).

Methodology

The students were requested to fill out the *Boredom Proneness Scale* (BPS; Farmer & Sundberg, 1986) and the *Boredom in Practical English Language Classes* (BPELC) questionnaire, which was a modified version of a similar instrument used by Kruk and Zawodniak (2017). The items included in these two questionnaires and end-of-the-year examination grades made it possible to divide participants into two groups: (1) students who were less and more susceptible to boredom and (2) high and low-achievers.

Main Findings

Exploratory factor analysis allowed identification of two factors underlying boredom: Factor 1: disengagement, monotony and repetitiveness, and Factor 2: lack of satisfaction and challenge. Factor 1 and Factor 2 were associated with two fundamental facets of L2 boredom: *reactive* (calibrating, indifferent and apathetic boredom) and *proactive* (searching boredom). Independent-samples *t*-tests demonstrated for both factors that the participants who were generally more prone to boredom were also significantly more likely to experience this aversive emotion. It was also revealed that low-achievers were significantly more prone to experience boredom than high-achievers in the case of Factor 1 but not Factor 2. This finding was attributed to greater likelihood that successful learners can persevere in the face of uninteresting, unengaging and insufficiently stimulating activities and tasks. The researchers also speculated that the fact that lack of satisfaction and challenge was unrelated to attainment could indicate that more and less successful students were equally likely to abandon routines and boring language activities on condition that more attractive tasks are implemented. Most importantly, the analysis resulted in the development of a new data collection instrument, namely, the *Boredom in Practical English Language Classes – Revised* (BPELC-R).

Reflective Break

- Do you perceive the two factors identified by Pawlak et al. (2020b) as equally important in shaping your students' experience of boredom or is any of them more influential than the other? Are there any other factors that in your opinion contribute to your students' boredom?
- Do those of your students who are low-achievers tend to experience boredom more intensely than their more successful classmates? Provide one or two examples in this respect.

Coşkun and Yüksel (2021): Factor Structure of L2 Boredom in Turkey

Main Aims

The main aims of the study were to adapt the BPELC-R scale (Pawlak et al., 2020b) for the Turkish high school EFL context, to reveal participants' level of boredom and to determine whether the reported boredom levels differed in relation to gender, grade level and selected academic track (e.g., science, foreign languages).

Participants

The sample comprised 680 Turkish high school EFL students (461 females and 219 males) between 14 and 17 years of age and their English proficiency ranged from A2 to B2 according to the *Common European Framework of Reference for Languages.*

Methodology

The data were collected by means of the BPELC-R scale and subjected to exploratory and confirmatory factor analysis. Statistical tests were used to establish significance of the differences revealed between different groups of participants.

Main Findings

The analysis showed that the level of boredom experienced by the students was medium. The most common causes of boredom turned out to be monotonous lessons and the participants' dissatisfaction with them. In addition, the study revealed significant differences in boredom levels with regard to grade level and selected academic track. Specifically, the experience of boredom increased with grade level and the students who chose the foreign languages track manifested less boredom in English classes when compared with the learners who selected the science track. The study allowed validation of the BPELC-R scale for the Turkish high school EFL context and the development of the *Boredom in English Language Classes Scale* consisting of 21 items.

> **Reflective Break**
> - Do you think there is a relationship between L2 students' gender and the level of boredom? What are your observations in this respect?
> - Are more advanced students likely to experience more boredom and, if so, how can it be explained?

Dewaele and Li (2021): Links Between Perceived Teacher Enthusiasm, Boredom, Enjoyment and Engagement

Main Aims

This mixed-methods study investigated relationships between perceived teacher enthusiasm, the positive emotion of enjoyment and the negative emotion of boredom as well as social-behavioral learning engagement in the Chinese educational context.

Participants

A large sample of Chinese university EFL learners ($N = 2,002$) took part in the study. They came from 11 universities in mainland China and were enrolled in different programs.

Methodology

The data collection instruments included a composite online questionnaire and an online interview. The questionnaire comprised four 7-point Likert scales related to: (1) perceived teacher enthusiasm, (2) foreign language enjoyment, (3) boredom and (4) engagement. The online interviews were conducted with nine students who were asked to provide information on their teachers' enthusiasm and its effect on their learning of the TL.

Main Findings

Quantitative analysis showed that: (1) perceived teacher enthusiasm exerted both a direct and indirect impact on social-behavioral learning engagement, (2) the positive emotion of enjoyment and the negative emotion of boredom were related to teacher enthusiasm positively and negatively, respectively and (3) the two emotions mediated the effect of perceived teacher enthusiasm on students' engagement. Qualitative analysis of the interview data confirmed the role of teacher enthusiasm and positive classroom atmosphere as direct sources of engagement which led to heightened enjoyment and effort as well as diminished boredom. In addition, lack of teacher enthusiasm was found to be a source of disengagement, lack of enjoyment and solidarity with peers as well as frequent yawning as a result of boredom.

Reflective Break
- What do you understand by L2 teacher enthusiasm?
- Do you perceive enthusiasm as one of your characteristics as an L2 teacher?
- How can the teacher create a positive classroom atmosphere that could be conducive to a decrease in students' experience of boredom?

Kruk (2021b): Changes in One Student's L2 Boredom in a Virtual World

Main Goals

This mixed-methods case study examined the causes of and changes in the experience of boredom in the virtual world Second Life (SL), both during single sessions and from one session to the next over one semester.

Participants

There was a single participant in this study. It was a female Polish university student who was majoring in English as a foreign language.

Methodology

The data were collected by means of four instruments: (1) A background questionnaire providing demographic information about the participant. (2) The *Learning Style Survey* (LSS; Cohen, Oxford, & Chi, 2002), which is a self-report questionnaire intended to assess learning style preferences; it comprised 11 dimensions (e.g., visual, auditory and tactile/kinesthetic, deductive and inductive) and 23 subscales (e.g., "How I use my physical senses"). (3) A session log which consisted of three parts: (i) session date, (ii) a self-report grid where the participant marked her boredom level on a 7-point Likert scale (1 – minimum, 7 – maximum) three times during a session (i.e., at the start, in the middle and at the end) and (iii) a description of the visit to SL. Finally, (4) a semi-structured interview conducted at the end of the semester (i.e., after the last session in SL) which aimed to yield additional insights into L2 boredom during visits to SL.

Main Findings

The results revealed the dynamic character of boredom since changes in its level were observed both throughout a single session and from one visit to another. These fluctuations were triggered by, for example, encountering the same interlocutors, limited discussion topics, monotonous chats, group discussions, conversations that were not conducive to linguistic development or meeting aggressive SL users. It was also found that the student's preferred learning styles (e.g., she turned out to be an introverted learner) played a part in her experience of boredom during her attempts to use the TL in SL.

> **Reflective Break**
> - Do you encourage your students to practice English during visits to Second Life or any other virtual environments? If so, invite one student to provide a description of his or her visit to such environments and then ask him or her a few additional questions, as was the case with the semi-structured interview conducted in Kruk's (2021b) study. What did the student under examination reveal about his or her virtual experience? In what aspects was it a boring experience and to what extent did he or she enjoy it?
> - If, however, you have not so far taken this L2 learning option into account, would you like to consider it in the future? In your opinion, could your students' visits to SL make their experience of boredom in L2 learning less aversive and/or intense than it is right now? Why do you/do you not think so?

Li (2021): Causes of L2 Boredom from Learners' and Teachers' Perspectives

Main Goals

In order to investigate control-value appraisals as antecedents of boredom in learning English, Li (2021) drew on the control-value theory (CVT) of achievement emotions (Pekrun, 2006; Pekrun et al., 2010).

Participants

The sample consisted of 2,002 Chinese EFL university students who were requested to fill out a questionnaire tapping into value and control appraisals and the experience of boredom in learning the English language. In addition, 11 students and 11 English teachers took part in an interview in order to provide more insights regarding the occurrence of boredom in the L2 classroom and its causes.

Methodology

The items included in the questionnaire were responded to with the help of a 7-point Likert scale (1 – strongly disagree, 7 – strongly agree), based on existing tools (e.g., Frenzel, Pekrun, & Goetz, 2007; Putwain et al., 2018).

Main Findings

Correlational and regression analyses showed that different control-value appraisals predicted the emotion of boredom distinctively or interactively. Specifically, it was demonstrated that boredom was negatively predicted by perceived control and value. It was also revealed that, generally, the more competent language learners, or those who valued the learning of the English language more, tended to be less bored than their less competent peers. Qualitative analysis of interview data corroborated the quantitative findings as well as uncovered more intricacies concerning the link between control-value appraisals and boredom. It was indicated that learners experienced boredom when feeling under- or over-challenged. Based on these results, the researcher hypothesized the existence of upper and lower boundaries for the negative impact of control-value appraisals on boredom.

Reflective Break
- Do you agree that both insufficient and excessive control over what goes on in class may predict L2 student boredom? Which of these two situations is more common in the L2 classroom? Provide one or two examples in this respect.
- Which L2 activities do your students perceive as particularly valuable? Do these activities really prevent them from experiencing boredom?

Nakamura, Darasawang and Reinders (2021): Causes of Boredom

Main Goals

The study set out to uncover the antecedents of L2 boredom at the university level in Thailand.

Participants

The sample comprised 25 second-year Thai university students (9 females and 16 males; 20–21 years of age) attending an English oral communication course.

Methodology

The data were gathered by means of an online semi-structured questionnaire, which asked participants to think about and describe a situation in which they felt boredom in the classroom, and a set of focus group interviews with five students, who were requested to comment on their experience of this negative emotion during an English class they had just attended. A modified form of constant comparative analysis was employed.

Main Findings

The analysis revealed nine thematic factors as causes of boredom, which were further supported by interview findings. The first factor was named *unfavorable appraisals of the task* since it was related to such issues as uninteresting, unimportant or novelty lacking activities. The second factor was labeled *activity mismatch* as it concerned the participants' negative perceptions of a particular situation. The third factor was referred to as *lack of comprehension* and involved such issues as the content and TL features offered in the coursebook and other materials, teachers' explanations and requirements of various language tasks. The fourth factor was named *physical fatigue* as it concerned tiredness and sleepiness. The fifth factor was *insufficient L2*, which involved participants' deficiencies in their L2 knowledge which got in the way of understanding L2 input or engaging in task performance. The sixth factor was labeled *task difficulty* and mostly pertained to debates. The seventh factor was called *negative behaviors of classmates* and involved such negative phenomena as disruptiveness or lack of engagement. The eighth factor was named *lack of ideas* since it stemmed from inadequate content to share in a given task. Finally, the ninth factor was *input overload* and it was related to the participants' perception of receiving too much input (e.g., when reading long passages of texts).

Reflective Break
- Which of the nine indicators of boredom identified in Nakamura et al.'s (2021) study do you regard as deserving special attention? Briefly justify your point of view.
- Do you have the impression that some of these factors have so far been neglected by teachers in their attempts to alleviate L2 students' experience of boredom? Why is it so?
- Think about those factors that are new to you and try to come up with options for minimizing their boredom-provoking influence on L2 students' performance.

Pawlak, Derakhshan, Mehdizadeh and Kruk (2021): Learners' and Teachers' Perspectives on Causes of Boredom and Coping Strategies

Main Goals

The empirical investigation sought to determine which class mode (i.e., online vs. physical classes) and course type (i.e., content-based vs. skills-based courses) were more boring for L2 learners and teachers. It also aimed to explore coping strategies employed to combat boredom in online English classes.

Participants

The sample consisted of 34 Iranian EFL teachers (15 females and 19 males; aged 30–55) and 256 Iranian EFL university students (181 females and 75 males; aged 18–51).

Methodology

The data collection instruments included two open-ended, online questionnaires (one for students and one for teachers) as well as a series of semi-structured interviews conducted with students and teachers who expressed their consent to take part in them. Qualitative analysis of the gathered data was conducted through the MAXQDA software

Findings

The majority of teachers and students regarded online classes as more boring than traditional (i.e., in-person) ones. While teachers deemed skills-based and content-based courses as equally boring, most students were of the opinion that content-based online courses were more boredom-evoking because of their lecture-type character. In addition, the teachers had a range of beneficial coping strategies in their toolbox. These strategies were categorized into five groups: (1) increasing students' engagement (e.g., trying to initiate vigorous discussions, making classes more interactive, introducing controversial topics), (2) developing teacher-student interpersonal relationships (e.g., telling jokes, using humor), (3) improving teaching style (e.g., making instruction more related to real life, increasing creativity, using online resources), (4) adjusting learning tasks (i.e., alternating between receptive and productive tasks as well as between teacher-centered and learner-centered tasks) and (5) miscellaneous (e.g., helping students in looking for personal enrichment programs, giving students frequent break time). The boredom-coping strategies used by students were divided into two categories: (1) facilitative strategies (i.e., being active and attentive, adjusting the lifestyle and having a positive attitude) and (2) debilitative strategies (i.e., tuning out of class, tolerating not knowing what to do).

Reflective Break
- Do you agree with the Iranian EFL teachers examined by Pawlak et al. (2021) that skills-based and content-based courses are equally boring? Justify your opinion.
- What do you think about online classes as compared to their traditional counterpart? Which of them are more boredom-provoking and why?

> • Are you familiar with all boredom-coping strategies adopted by the teacher-participants in Pawlak et al.'s (2021) research project? Which of them and for what reason would you recommend to other teachers?

Zawodniak, Kruk and Pawlak (2021): Causes of Boredom

Main Goals

The aim of this qualitative study was to explore factors accountable for boredom in English classes experienced by students majoring in English enrolled in different levels of a three-year BA program at a university in Poland.

Participants

The sample consisted of 115 first-, second- and third-year students (85 females and 30 males who were on average 21.30 years of age).

Methodology

The participants were requested to write a paragraph about their experience of boredom during their intensive English course encompassing classes related to the practice of the TL skills and subsystems. Qualitative analysis consisted of some of the stages described by Dörnyei (2007).

Main Findings

The factors responsible for the experience of boredom were divided into five main categories, some of which contained several subcategories. The first category, *language tasks*, included the following subcategories: task difficulty (boredom caused by too easy and/or too difficult tasks), task repetitiveness (boredom induced by similar, conventional and mundane tasks), task monotony (i.e., boredom influenced by tasks perceived as lacking in variety and taking too much time to complete) and task topics (e.g., boredom generated by uninteresting or too challenging topics). The second category, *the teacher*, encompassed four subcategories: lack of involvement (i.e., boredom caused by insufficiently prepared and unengaged teachers), scant explanations (i.e., boredom triggered by inadequate teacher explanations), excessive teacher talk (i.e., boredom evoked by teachers who dominated classroom interaction) and (negative) characteristics of the teacher (i.e., teacher behavior and personality). The third category was named *modes of class organization* and concerned ways in which the students were requested to work in class (e.g., individual work, pair work). The fourth category was labeled *class components* and was related to specific foci of the classes in which the students experienced boredom (e.g., reading, phonetics). The last category, that is, *other*, included a number of boredom-generating factors, such as practicing specific language structures, tiredness, classes scheduled late in the afternoon or problems with the use of classroom equipment.

> **Reflective Break**
> - Take another look at the teacher category and its subcomponents. Which of them do you think are the most influential contributors to your students' boredom?
> - Look back upon your experience as an L2 learner and think about the sub-components of the second category that used to shape your own boredom. Put simply, which behaviors displayed by your teacher's behaviors, reactions and/or personality traits were the most boredom-provoking? How does this compare to your experience as an L2 teacher?

Kruk, Pawlak, Elahi Shirvan, Taherian and Yazdanmehr (2022a): Causes of Boredom

Main Goals

The study employed an interpretive approach to uncover individual learners' perspectives on L2 boredom.

Participants

The sample consisted of 37 EFL Iranian learners (26 females, 11 males; aged 17–33) in two private language learning institutes.

Methodology

The investigation relied on Q methodology, a method which includes elements of qualitative and quantitative research approaches. The data were gathered in accordance with the tenets of this approach (Watts & Stenner, 2003) and the following steps were followed: defining a research question, developing a Q set, distributing Q sorts among the participants, performing statistical analyses and interpreting the results.

Main Findings

Three various accounts of L2 boredom were uncovered, analyzed and discussed with the help of factor arrays and qualitative analysis of interview data. The three factors revealed three prototypical perspectives regarding sources of boredom experienced in online EFL classes: (1) teacher-induced boredom, which concerned, among others, unsupportive role of the teacher, his or her failure to offer students necessary challenge or variety, inadequate student monitoring, inability to set clear goals, unfriendly behavior, lack of care, overreliance on repetition and memorization, and dependence on outdated teaching techniques, (2) student-induced boredom, which was related to students' passivity in classes, feeling like doing nothing, feeling at a loose end and the impression of not making progress in learning the target language and (3) activity-induced boredom, where boredom emerged when participants were instructed to perform unchallenging, uninteresting, repetitive language tasks or activities that required memorization as well as when students could not understand the goal of an activity or when there was a mismatch between the task and their proficiency level.

> **Reflective Break**
> - How does L2 student boredom in the traditional learning environment compare to this emotion as experienced in COVID-19-induced online classes? In which of these two distinct situations can the emotion of boredom be viewed as more common and intense? How can this be explained?

Li and Wei (2022): Effects of Boredom and Other Emotions on L2 Attainment

Main Goals

Drawing on the control-value theory of achievement emotions (Pekrun, 2006), the study was undertaken to investigate the independent and joint predictive effects of enjoyment, anxiety and boredom on L2 achievement over time.

Participants

Participants were 954 EFL junior secondary school learners from rural China (358 females and 596 males, aged 11–17).

Methodology

The data collection instrument was a questionnaire consisting of two parts: (1) background information (e.g., age, sex, socioeconomic status and onset age for learning English) and (2) three scales concerning the three emotions under investigation: a short version of the *Foreign Language Classroom Anxiety Scale* (Horwitz et al., 1986) used by Dewaele and MacIntyre (2014), the *Chinese Version of Foreign Language Enjoyment Scale* (Li et al., 2018), the *Foreign Language Learning Boredom Scale* (Li et al., 2021). The questionnaire data and the achievement data were gathered at four different points in time: Time 1 (T1) – in the middle of March, Time 2 (T2) – one week after T1, Time 3 (T3) – five weeks after T1 and Time 4 (T4) – nine weeks after T1. Structural equation modeling was used to analyze the data.

Main Findings

The three emotions under investigation at T1 predicted English achievement at T2 and T3 independently; however, it was only the positive emotion of enjoyment that predicted achievement at T4. Furthermore, when combined, enjoyment was the strongest and most durable predictor of attainment over time (i.e., T2–T4), followed by the negative emotion of anxiety predicting achievement at T2 and T3 negatively. Finally, the aversive emotion of boredom lost its predictive power through T2–T4 in its entirety.

Reflective Break
- How do the emotions of enjoyment, anxiety and boredom relate to your students' L2 achievement? More specifically, which of these ID factors is the best indicator of success and which best predicts failure? What does your teaching experience tell you about it?
- Do those of your students who are high-achievers experience more or less boredom, enjoyment and anxiety than low-achievers? How do they manifest and cope with boredom compared to low-achievers?

Pawlak, Kruk, Zawodniak and Pasikowski (2022a): Factor Structure of After-Class Boredom

Main Goals

This quantitative empirical investigation was conducted in order to identify factors shaping after-class boredom, to investigate the degree to which the intensity of boredom is influenced by general boredom proneness and attainment, and to develop and validate a scale related to the experience of boredom in after-class settings. The construct of after-class boredom was operationalized as a negative emotion that individuals experience when they engage in L2 learning in their own time outside of the educational context to complete homework assignments, to prepare for their classes or simply to practice and use the TL of their own accord.

Participants

The study was conducted with 107 English majors enrolled in BA and MA programs at a Polish university. There were 80 females and 27 males, who were on average 21.45 years of age.

Methodology

The participants completed the *Boredom Proneness Scale* (BPS; Farmer & Sundberg, 1986) and the *Boredom in Learning English Outside of School Questionnaire* (BLEOS). Using the BPS and end-of-the-year examination grades, the participants were grouped into those more and less susceptible to boredom as well as into high- and low-achievers. Exploratory factor analysis was used to identify the factor structure of after-class boredom and independent-samples *t*-tests were employed to determine whether differences between groups were statistically significant.

Main Findings

Three factors underpinning after-class boredom were identified: Factor 1: unwillingness to learn English and inability to find (interesting) tasks, Factor 2: lack of creativity, focus and involvement, and Factor 3: altered time perception, underused language abilities and monotony. The causes of boredom encompassing these three factors were explained in terms of the attentional theory of boredom proneness (Eastwood et al., 2007), the emotion theory (Eastwood et al., 2007), the dimensional model (Pekrun et al., 2010), the forced-effort model (Hill & Perkins, 1985) and the concept of leisure boredom (Wegner, 2011). The participants who were generally less prone to boredom reported experiencing less after-class boredom in connection with the three factors. No significant differences were found between more and less successful students in relation to any of the three factors. Most importantly, the analysis allowed the development and validation of the BLEOS, that is, a scale related to the experience of boredom in after-class settings.

Reflective Break
- Drawing on the emotion theory (Eastwood et al., 2007, see Chapter 3, section 1.4.), discuss with your students after-class situations in which they experience boredom. Based on their comments, do you perceive the three factors identified by Pawlak et al. (2022a) as equally impacting students' after-class boredom or is any of them more influential than the other two?
- In your opinion, is in-class boredom likely to affect after-class boredom? Can it work the other way round as well? Provide one or two examples in this respect.

Pawlak, Zarrinabadi and Kruk (2022b): Boredom, Self-Assessment and Other ID Factors

Main Goals

This quantitative study aimed to shed light on the interrelationships of such ID factors as enjoyment, anxiety, boredom, L2 grit and self-perceived proficiency as well as their indirect impact on motivated learning behavior.

Participants

The sample included 238 Iranian EFL majors comprising 76 males and 162 females whose age ranged from 18 to 36.

Methodology

The data were collected by means of a six-part online questionnaire intended to measure motivated behavior (Taguchi, Magid, & Papi, 2009), enjoyment (Mahmoodzadeh & Khajavy, 2019; cf. Dewaele & MacIntyre, 2014; Peixoto, Mata, Monteiro, Sanches, & Pekrun, 2015), anxiety (Dewaele & MacIntyre, 2014, cf. Horwitz et al., 1986), boredom (Pawlak et al., 2020b), L2 grit (Teimouri, Plonsky, & Tabandeh, 2020) and perceived competence. Confirmatory factor analysis and path analysis were used.

Main Findings

Complex interactions were revealed between the ID factors under examination, some of which were unexpected. For example, motivated behavior was found to be significantly positively impacted by anxiety, a possible explanation being that the latter may have played a facilitative role in the face of a challenging university program demanding large amounts of effort and dedication from those students who are determined not to fail their exams. There was also an indirect relationship between enjoyment and L2 motivation which was mediated by L2 grit. At the same time, anxiety was shown to exert a negative indirect influence on motivated behavior, through the mediation of one of the components of L2 grit, namely, consistency of interest (CI). Another interesting finding was the positive indirect CI-mediated association between boredom and motivated behavior. The researchers suggested that in some circumstances L2 students' negative emotions may act as an incentive to pursue their L2 learning goals and engage with the task at hand, even though they perceive it as uninteresting.

Reflective Break
- Do you think it is possible for boredom and anxiety to positively influence the L2 learning process? Is this the case with your students? In what situations do these emotions lose their detrimental effect?

CONCLUSION

The present chapter has touched upon several key issues related to researching the negative emotion of boredom in L2 learning and teaching. In particular, it has attempted to illustrate the importance of such empirical investigations for teachers, it has outlined the lines of inquiry that L2 boredom research has pursued or should follow in the future, it has discussed some basic issues concerning the methodology of such research and it has provided examples of selected studies into L2 boredom, succinctly presenting their goals, participants, methodology and main findings. Looking at the existing empirical evidence, it is indisputable that considerable progress has been made in the study of different aspects of L2 boredom within the space of just a few years. More specifically, such research is now conducted in different national contexts, populations other than university students, particularly English majors, have started to be included and languages other than English have begun to be considered. In addition, the foci of relevant studies have been extended from the initial preoccupation with the causes of boredom to include coping strategies, to investigate this emotional state in relation to teachers, to explore its occurrence in L2 learning outside the classroom, and to relate it to other emotions and individual difference factors. This said, it should be emphasized that these developments are often limited to one or two studies (e.g., teacher boredom, after-class boredom, coping strategies employed to combat this aversive emotion) and some areas remain terra incognita, a good case in point being pedagogical interventions aimed to prevent or reduce boredom. This observation certainly applies to teachers' perspectives on this negative emotion, both with respect to how they view boredom manifested by learners and how they try to counter it, but also in relation to the reasons why they succumb to boredom themselves and the actions they take to minimize its effects. These are the issues that were investigated in the research project that will be reported in Chapter 5.

Chapter 5

Boredom in the L2 Classroom: Listening to Teachers' Voices

INTRODUCTION

The four previous chapters have provided an overview of key issues related to the theme of this book, that is, the role of emotions in L2 education, definitions of boredom and theoretical accounts of its causes as well as empirical research into boredom in L2 learning and teaching. By contrast, Chapter 5 focuses on the design and findings of the study which aimed to explore boredom in L2 classroom learning from the perspective of the teacher. In the first part, the rationale for the study, its aims and research questions will be discussed. This will be followed by the description of methodological issues, including the participants of the study, the tools that were employed to gather the data, the procedures of their administration as well as ways in which the data were analyzed. Subsequently, the results of the study will be presented in accordance with the research questions, with the findings being considered separately for quantitative and qualitative data. The research questions will also provide a point of reference for the discussion of these findings in the last part of the chapter. Finally, the limitations of the research project will be outlined and insights stemming from the study will be offered.

5.1 AIMS AND RESEARCH QUESTIONS

The present study aimed to shed light on the role of the negative emotion of boredom in the L2 classroom, adopting the perspective of foreign language teachers. Specifically, it was intended to determine how L2 teachers view boredom experienced by their learners and what strategies they employ to ameliorate it. It also looked at how teachers themselves are affected by this negative phenomenon, what actions they take to combat this aversive emotion and how their boredom changes during the classes they teach. More specifically, the study set out to provide answers to the following research questions:

RQ1:   What is the participants' overall proneness to boredom?

RQ2:   What are the causes and manifestations of boredom experienced by L2 learners in English lessons in the eyes of the language teachers and how does this negative emotion manifest itself?

RQ3:   What efforts to reduce student boredom do language teachers undertake?

RQ4:   What are the causes and indicators of boredom experienced by L2 teachers during English lessons?

RQ5:   What do L2 teachers do to combat the boredom they experience during their English classes?

RQ6:   Is there a relationship between boredom as experienced by students and teachers?

RQ7:   How does boredom experienced by teachers change during a language lesson and from one lesson to another?

5.2 PARTICIPANTS

The participants were 106 Polish teachers of English as a foreign language, 96 of whom were females and 10 were males. They worked at schools representing different educational levels across Poland. More specifically, 61 (57.55%) teachers worked in elementary school, 43 (40.57%) in secondary school and two (1.89%) were employed in the private sector of education, teaching English in private language schools. On average, the participants were 36.49 (SD = 7.44) years of age. Their average experience in teaching English as a foreign language equaled 12.43 years (SD = 7.40). To be more precise, 18 participants (16.98%) had been teaching English for less than five years, 30 (28.30%) between 5 and 10 years, 44 (41.51%) between 11 and 20 years and 14 (13.21%) for more than 20 years. As for the participants' qualifications for teaching English, 85 (80.19%) had a MA degree, 18 (16.99%) held a BA degree and three (2.83%) declared having a PhD. The vast majority of the teachers (91.50%) reported attending a variety of workshops, webinars and postgraduate courses in order to develop their professional qualifications. Importantly, two of those participants, that is, two female teachers referred to as Teacher 1 and Teacher 2, provided additional data that allowed insights into the dynamics of boredom over time. They both were teachers of English in Polish secondary schools. Teacher 1 held a PhD in applied linguistics and her experience in teaching English equaled 29 years. Teacher 2 had an MA degree and her experience in teaching English amounted to 18 years.

> **Reflective Break**
> - It was very difficult to convince teachers to take part in this study and we had hoped for a greater number of participants. What do you think could have been reasons for such a situation? Would you be willing to help with data collection in this study? Why and why not?

5.3 DATA COLLECTION INSTRUMENTS

The data were gathered by means of two instruments: the *Teacher Boredom Questionnaire* (TBQ; see Appendix 1) and a lesson report (see Appendix 2). What follows is a description of the research instruments utilized in the study:

- The TBQ comprised three parts:

  - ▸ Part One elicited the respondents' consent and demographic information (i.e., sex, age, education, type of school they worked in, work experience, professional development).

  - ▸ Part Two included the *Boredom Proneness Scale* (BPS, Farmer & Sundberg, 1986); BPS aims at assessing the participants' overall tendency to experience boredom in different situations; the scale consists of 28 statements based on a 5-point Likert scale (1 – *disagree strongly* and 5 – *agree strongly*); example items are as follows: "Time always seems to be passing slowly", "I am seldom excited about my work", I often find myself with nothing to do – time on my hands;" the internal reliability of the BPS was satisfactory as determined by calculating Cronbach alpha on the basis of the data collected for the present study ($\alpha = .86$).

  - ▸ Part Three encompassed 11 open-ended questions; the first six questions prompted the participants to reflect upon their perceptions regarding their students' experience of boredom in the L2 classroom; the following queries were utilized for this purpose: (1) *Have you observed any feelings of boredom in learning English during English lessons among your students? How were such feelings manifested? What could have caused them? Please provide examples and explain them.* (2) *Are your students bored the most at the beginning, middle or end of a lesson? Why is this the case?* (3) *During what types of activities (e.g., practicing specific language skills, language subsystems, tasks, forms of work) are your students the most likely to get bored? Why is this the case?* (4) *What is your reaction when you see students who are bored with English lessons?* (5) *How do you try to reduce the experience of boredom among students during English lessons? Please provide examples and explain.* and (6) *If your students are bored during English lessons, do*

> *you feel responsible for it? Why or why not?*; the remaining five questions were related to the respondents' own experience of boredom in the English classes they taught; these queries were the following: (1) *Do you feel bored while conducting English lessons? If so, what are the symptoms and causes of this negative experience? In what situations does it occur most often? Please provide examples and explain.* (2) *In your opinion, what factors are responsible for making you feel bored while conducting English lessons? Why?* (3) *If you experience feelings of boredom while conducting English lessons, how do you try to deal with this aversive emotion?* (4) *Over the years of your work as an English teacher, have you been experiencing more or less boredom? What have you been doing to reduce the intensity of boredom?* and (5) *Do you see a relationship between your feeling bored while conducting English lessons and your students' boredom? How is it manifested? Provide examples.*

- The lesson report consisted of three parts:

  ▸ Part One requested the following information: the name of the teacher, the grade taught, the date of the lesson and its topic; this part of the report was filled out at the very start of a lesson.

  ▸ Part Two included a boredom grid in which the participating teachers were asked to self-rate the levels of their own boredom as well as the perceived levels of student boredom on a scale from 1 (minimum) to 5 (maximum) every five minutes during a lesson; in this part, the teachers were also requested to provide detailed information about the modes of classroom organization, forms of work as well as the tasks and language activities performed throughout a lesson, taking the five-minute intervals as a point of reference; this part of the lesson report was completed by the teachers as a particular lesson was in progress.

  ▸ Part Three required the participating teachers to write a short narrative about the manifestations of observed boredom among the students as well as their feelings of boredom experienced while conducting a given lesson; The teachers were asked to respond to the following prompts: *What were the causes of boredom among your students? What were you going to do to prevent the feeling of boredom from occurring among your students during the next lesson? What caused the feeling of boredom you experienced when conducting the lesson? What did you intend to do to prevent the feeling of boredom from accompanying you during the next lesson?*; this part of the report was completed by the teachers after each lesson.

The TBQ was disseminated online through *Google Forms* with the help of the present authors' networks of professional contacts. It was filled out anonymously at the participants' convenience and no time limitations of any kind were imposed. It should be pointed out at this juncture that both the TBQ and the lesson report were delivered in Polish, the teachers' mother tongue, and the participants were given a choice as to the language they wished to rely on in their responses to the open-ended items. This was done in order to avoid potential misunderstandings or misinterpretations and to facilitate the ease of expression. Importantly, the research instruments utilized in the present study were piloted with a group of nine English teachers, who were not participants of the present investigation. This resulted in changing the wording of some of the questions to increase their clarity and the likelihood that they could produce the kind of data that would illuminate the issues of interest to the present study. With respect to ethical issues, it should be noted that the teachers were informed about the nature and objectives of the study, and they were asked to give their consent to provide the data. They were also ensured that their anonymity would be preserved and that their responses would not be made available to anybody in the school in which they were employed. Efforts were made to handle the data with ultimate care and to ensure that they were available only to the three researchers who are the authors of this book.

> **Reflective Break**
> - Can you try to answer some of the open-ended questions included in the TBQ for yourself? If possible, share them with a colleague and briefly compare and discuss your answers.
> - Can you try to make a lesson report that was described above for one of your lessons in its entirety or in part? Was it easy or difficult to indicate the levels of boredom when the lesson was in progress? What causes of your students' boredom and your own boredom did you observe? What can you do to prevent this negative emotion in both cases?

5.4 DATA ANALYSIS

The data were analyzed quantitatively and qualitatively. More detailed information about the steps that each of these analyses involved is provided in the following subsections.

5.4.1 Quantitative Analysis

The data gathered through the *Boredom Proneness Scale* (i.e., the second part of the TBQ), some parts of the TBQ and the boredom grids included in the second part of the lesson report underwent quantitative analysis. The procedure involved in the main determining the mean (M) values (i.e., arithmetical averages) and standard deviation (SD) values (i.e., showing how much individual data are dispersed in relation to the mean) for the Likert-scale items in the BPS (Farmer & Sundberg, 1986) as well as the self-ratings of the teachers' and students' boredom as the classes under investigation were in progress. The level of the teachers' overall proneness to boredom was interpreted according to the range of mean scores included in Table 1 (cf. Wattana, 2013). In the case of the open-ended queries, the frequencies of specific categories of responses which emerged from qualitative analyses were established.

Table 1 The interpretation of mean scores for the overall level of boredom proneness

Range of mean scores	Interpretation
4.50–5.00	**Very high** level of boredom proneness
3.50–4.49	**High** level of boredom proneness
2.50–3.49	**Neutral** level of boredom proneness
1.50–2.49	**Low** level of boredom proneness
1.00–1.49	**Very low** level of boredom proneness

5.4.2 Qualitative Analysis

The teachers' responses to the questions posed in the third part of the TBQ were thematically and inductively analyzed. This procedure was in compliance with the five-step data analysis model proposed by Gao and Zhang (2020). The first step consisted of cleaning the original data. The data were read in order to check their consistency, eliminate irrelevant responses and correct evident errors such as, for example, incorrect spelling and/or grammar. It should also be noted that some of the respondents did not provide their answers to some of the questions at all, which, in the experience of the present authors, is common when open-ended queries are used. The second step comprised coding the data. At this stage, the data were read recurrently and open codes were created. The third step involved generating themes. In this step, the open codes were compared and grouped under related themes. The fourth step entailed categorizing the themes. At this phase, the themes were divided into groups and higher-order umbrella terms were generated for them. The final step involved producing a detailed report of the analyzed data. When it comes to the two last items included in the questionnaire, which aimed to tap into the teachers' opinions on whether there exists a relationship between boredom experienced by teachers and learners during English lessons and which part of a lesson period (i.e., start, middle or end) is the most boredom-provoking for their students, the answers supplied by the teachers were thoroughly read and tallied.

To improve the credibility of our research project, all the stages of the data analysis were done jointly by two of the authors of the present book. In order to further strengthen the study's confirmability, the entire data together with the produced codes and themes were audited by an outside researcher, a specialist in the field of applied linguistics with a publication record on emotions in L2 learning and teaching. All areas of disagreement were resolved though discussion and compromise.

> **Reflective Break**
> - Which of the research instruments used in this study do you find the most suitable for collecting data in your teaching context? Why?

5.5 FINDINGS

In order to enhance readability, the findings are roughly presented in accordance with the order of the seven research questions formulated for the present investigation.

5.5.1 The Participants' Overall Proneness to Boredom

The first research question (RQ1) concerned the teachers' overall proneness to boredom. The analysis of the aggregate responses to the BPS for the entire sample ($N = 106$) and interpreted according to Wattana (2013) showed that the teachers' tendency to experience boredom in different situations can be considered low ($M = 2.22$). This is not surprising in view of the fact that the average responses of 76 (71.5%) participants were in the range of 1.50–2.49, with the mean of 2.02. It should also be noted that there was little individual variation in the experience of boredom as indicated by the value of standard deviation ($SD = .48$). Table 2 includes detailed information about the teachers' general proneness to boredom.

Table 2 The mean and standard deviation values for the teachers' overall proneness to boredom

	Number of participants	M (SD)	Overall proneness to boredom
	0	—	Very high
	3	3.63 (.06)	High
	23	2.78 (.22)	Neutral
	76	2.04 (.27)	Low
	4	1.43 (.05)	Very low
Overall	106	2.22 (.48)	

5.5.2 The Experience of Boredom Among Language Learners in English Lessons in the Eyes of English Teachers

The next two research questions (RQ2 and RQ3) dealt with the experience of boredom among language learners in English lessons from the perspective of the English language teachers who participated in the present study. Based on the thematic analysis of the data obtained by means of the first six questions in Part Three of the TBQ, four broad categories emerged: (1) *triggers of boredom*, (2) *indicators of boredom*, (3) *who/what is to blame?* and (4) *attempts to reduce student boredom*. These categories are diagrammatically presented in Figure 2.

As for the first category, *triggers of boredom* (183 references in total), one of the most frequently mentioned causes of this negative emotion among language learners in the opinion of the respondents concerned the practice of *language skills*, in particular reading, writing and listening as well as *language subsystems*, especially with respect to the practice of grammar structures (26 references in total for both of these subcategories). To be more specific, language activities related to practicing reading (21 references), writing (8 references) and listening (7 references) skills were seen as the most likely to induce boredom. According to the respondents, this was mostly due to the quality and type of exercises included in coursebooks, students' problems with concentration and their insufficient TL knowledge dating back to instruction in secondary school, all of which directly affected their comprehension of the issues covered during English lessons. In addition, the respondents pointed to the practice of English grammar as the most boring activity for their students (51 references). This was mainly due to grammar activities contained in coursebooks as they were described by the teachers as "conventional", "dull" and "repetitive", involving for the most part different types of controlled practice (e.g., gap filling, paraphrasing). Besides, difficulties that the students experienced in learning English grammar and their unwillingness to focus on this TL subsystem were also regarded as factors triggering boredom among their learners. Such issues are illustrated in the following comments:[1]

- Too much text ... when reading an article students get bored with such activities.
- Performing exercises in books, especially grammar ones.
- Working with the text is relatively monotonous. The text must be read with understanding and the texts are quite long.
- Working with a text and listening tasks. The students with the biggest backlog or attention problems are the most bored.

---

1   These and other excerpts are translations of the participants' responses.

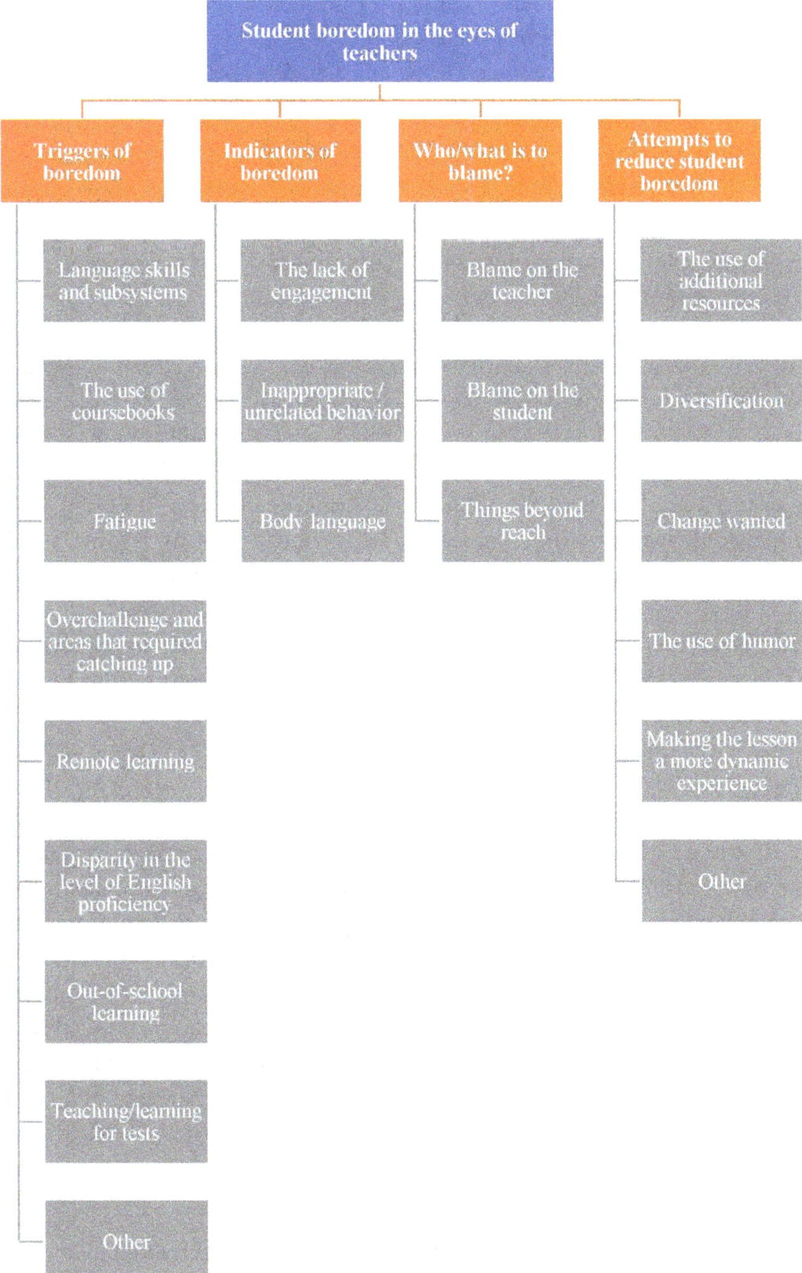

Figure 2 Causes of student boredom from the perspective of English teachers

- As a rule, students do not like to learn grammatical structures and perform routine exercises from the coursebook.
- When solving written exercises in the coursebook or on worksheets, especially in grammar. I find these tasks monotonous for students, especially because many students have difficulty understanding English grammar.

The use of coursebooks constituted another major trigger of boredom (17 references). This is because coursebooks were perceived by the respondents as containing similar, predictable and uninteresting content (i.e., similar dialogs, uninspiring texts, repetitive exercises). Yet another cause of boredom was simply related to students' *fatigue* which might have been the outcome of scheduling issues or time of day (11 references). Other factors responsible for student boredom identified in the data concerned *overchallenge* and *areas that required catching up* (10 and 8 references, respectively). While the former concerned excessive amounts of difficult material to be covered during the language course and overloaded core curriculum with respect to L2 education, the latter involved students' "gaps in knowledge" resulting from their previous language learning experiences and could be related to the fact that, similar to other school subjects, most of L2 education in the last year had been held online. This brings us to the next trigger of boredom which was *remote learning* induced by the COVID-19 health crisis, which was mentioned by eight respondents as a substantial cause of this aversive emotion. The fact that the pandemic resulted in the closure of schools and mandatory reliance on distance learning had a number of negative consequences, such as limited contact with teachers and peers, reduced opportunities for more spontaneous interactions in the TL as well as a number of technical problems. Six respondents ascribed student boredom to a *disparity in the level of English proficiency* represented by students comprising a single group/class, four teachers attributed the aversive feeling of boredom afflicting their students during English lessons to *out-of-school learning*, in particular private lessons in which students in advance covered the same language issues as in the classroom, and three participants related the feelings of boredom to *teaching/learning for tests*. Apart from these main triggers of boredom, individual respondents also mentioned *other* causes of this negative phenomenon. These included boring topics, organizational issues (e.g., checking attendance) and overall overstimulation as important causes of student boredom. What follows are examples of excerpts which illustrate some of the issues mentioned by the teachers:

- No interesting content in the coursebook.
- Mainly during lessons conducted with the use of the coursebook. Unfortunately, I have not yet found the one in which the practice of a language skill would be interestingly planned and motivating for students.
- Sometimes this is because it is the last lesson.

- The material is quite difficult for most students, so there is boredom.
- The reason may be that the curriculum is overloaded, there is a lot to learn, boredom is visible especially in weaker students who do not keep up and after some time they give up and do not even try to understand the issues discussed in lessons.
- Yes, especially during the online learning. I think this is because of technical problems and the lack of contact with peers.
- Sometimes. This is due to the varied proficiency levels represented by students. Those who are more talented, despite getting extra work, finish much earlier than those who need more time and additional teacher guidance.
- I believe that this is due to the ubiquitous trend of private lessons, lessons in language schools, etc. In such lessons, the core curriculum is very often covered in advance (it also happens that tutors use the same coursebooks as the schoolteachers, discuss topics beforehand and often do homework assignments for students or take ready-made tests with them). I also observed a few students who used two notebooks during English lessons – one contained solved exercises during private lessons.

When it comes to the second category identified in the analysis, that is, *indicators of boredom* (42 in references in total), the most frequently mentioned symptom of boredom (22 references) was labeled *the lack of engagement* because it was related to a number of instances in which language learners displayed signs of insufficient attention, interest, involvement or willingness to actively participate in English lessons. The second most often mentioned indicator of boredom (13 references) was referred to as *inappropriate/unrelated behavior* as this concerned such unacceptable and/or irrelevant to English lessons behaviors as talking with peers about things unconnected with the focus of the class, playing with smartphones, looking through the window or daydreaming. The third indicator of boredom mentioned by the participants (7 references) was labeled *body language* and included such indications of boredom as yawning, facial expression, gestures or sighs. The following excerpts provide examples of the issues raised:

- Yes, no desire to do exercises.
- Less involvement in the lessons.
- Lack of attention to what is happening in the lesson.
- Some students start to disturb the lesson, play with various objects, sometimes they daydream.
- Yes, they are doing something different than they should (usually they talk or play with their smartphones).
- Looking at the window
- Checking the time on the phone.

Another category identified in the current analysis, that is, *Who/what is to blame?* (107 references in total), included the following three subthemes: (1) *blame on the teacher*, (2) *blame on the student* and (3) *things beyond reach*. As for the first theme (*blame on the teacher* – 66 references), the participants felt responsible for evoking the feelings of boredom among their students by not being able to plan an interesting lesson which would capture their students' attention and stimulate their engagement in the topics or activities performed. The teachers also blamed themselves for the lack of ideas for "interesting activities" and "not adjusting activities to students' level of proficiency". In addition, the respondents pinned the blame on themselves for "not putting enough effort in preparing a good lesson" or "not being well prepared for a lesson". Importantly, all the teachers explained such situations in terms of insufficient time they had at their disposal to prepare the lesson, a problem that was only aggravated but the necessity of conducting the classes online. Such issues are also evident in the following excerpts:

- I feel embarrassed, I blame myself for not being able to interest my students.
- That I should try harder and do my best. The way students deal with English largely determines my attitude towards work and students.
- Bored students – it is a sign that I should have planned the lessons much better.

When it comes to the second theme (*blame on the student*, 23 references), boredom experienced by language learners in English lessons was attributed by the teachers to the students themselves. According to the teachers, the feelings of boredom among their learners resulted from the lack of cooperation on the part of students despite teachers' efforts to get them involved, students' failure to prepare for their lessons, their personality and simply fatigue on a particular day. It should also be noted that, in the respondents' point of view, language learners representing lower TL proficiency were generally more susceptible to experience boredom in the L2 classroom. Some of the issues related to the theme *blame on the student* are exemplified in the following excerpts:

- These are usually weaker students who do not give priority to the English language.
- Those who are bored are usually unprepared for lessons. In some classes the same students are always bored. These students are hard to get interested in anything.

As regards the last theme (*things beyond reach*, 18 references), some of the teachers who took part in the study also mentioned the obligation to implement all the requirements included in the core curriculum as a source of student boredom. This was evident in such statements as: "I am responsible for the implementation of the core curriculum", "I often feel helpless in the face of having to follow an overloaded core curriculum" and "I have no influence on everything that is included in the curriculum. They have to understand that sometimes they have to do less pleasant things".

The last category, that is, *attempts to reduce student boredom*, pertained to strategies that the teachers participating in the present study employed in order to reduce the feelings of boredom among their students during the English lessons they taught (189 references in total). These were grouped into six themes and included (1) *the use of additional resources,* (2) *diversification,* (3) *change wanted,* (4) *the use of humor,* (5) *making the lesson a more dynamic experience* and (6) *other.* The first theme, that is, *the use of additional resources,* had the highest number of references (70). The resources the teachers reported using in order to reduce the feelings of boredom among their students were mostly based on digital technology and included authentic materials found on the Internet, links to a variety of language activities (e.g., vocabulary and grammar), movie clips, online games and multimedia presentations as well as the creation of new materials by means of computer software/applications. The following comments demonstrate some of these issues:

- I am trying to diversify my lessons with digital materials.
- My students are always eager to perform tasks during lessons with the use of smartphones.
- I use platforms where I can introduce an element of competition: Kahoot, Quizizz, Quizlet.
- I am trying to introduce multimedia presentations and short educational movies.
- I often use videos, songs and TV series on a given topic in order to best convey the knowledge and get students interested in the topic.

The second theme, *diversification,* was referenced by 46 participants. The teachers most frequently mentioned the use of a wide range of language activities, the application of different teaching methods and techniques as well as varied modes of work (e.g., individual, pair-work). Illustrative examples pertaining to this theme follow:

- I introduce different teaching methods. I change strategies.
- Each of my students is activated and I choose the most diverse methods and exercises so that the English lessons are attractive to them.
- I use various methods and forms of work. I often try to surprise my students with something new. I try to individualize work during lessons.

As far as the third theme is concerned, that is, *change wanted* (38 references), it referred to the teachers' willingness to amend the flow of a lesson "right away" and/ or "next time" by making an interactive decision (cf. Richards & Lockhart, 1996) in order to boost students' interest and involvement and thus diminish the feeling of the negative emotion of boredom among the students. The following excerpts provide examples of the issues raised:

- I have to change the activity immediately. I have to interest them now.
- What I can do next time to make an exercise not boring.

The fourth and fifth themes, that is, *the use of humor* and *making the lesson a more dynamic experience* (each with 12 references), comprised the use of jokes, funny topics and tasks as well as the employment of "short" and "quick" activities as well as such that require "movement" on the part of students, respectively. These themes are illustrated by the following comments:

- I try to start talking on an interesting and cheerful topic. I tell a joke.
- I change my voice to make my students laugh.
- I introduce short, quick, activating exercises.
- ... and in lower grades I do several tasks that require a lot of movement. For example, I use the TPR method.

Finally, the last theme, namely, *other* comprised a number of strategies employed by individual teachers (11 references). In order to alleviate the experience of student boredom, some of the participants, for example, "made gestures", drew on "the element of surprise" during a lesson, told their students "interesting facts about English", tried to establish "good rapport with [their] students", as well as "praised" or "awarded" their students in order to sustain their interest in English lessons.

> **Reflective Break**
> - Do you find the causes of student boredom presented in this subsection surprising? Why?
> - Are the causes of student boredom identified in this study similar or different from your teaching context?
> - What other cases of student boredom can you think of? Please explain.

5.5.3 The Experience of English Teachers' Boredom During English Lessons

RQ4 and RQ5 dealt with the experience of boredom among teachers while conducting English lessons. Based on the thematic analysis of the data, three broad categories emerged: (1) *triggers of boredom*, (2) *self-perceived indicators of boredom* and (3) *dealing with boredom*. These themes are diagrammatically presented in Figure 3 together with the subcategories they comprised.

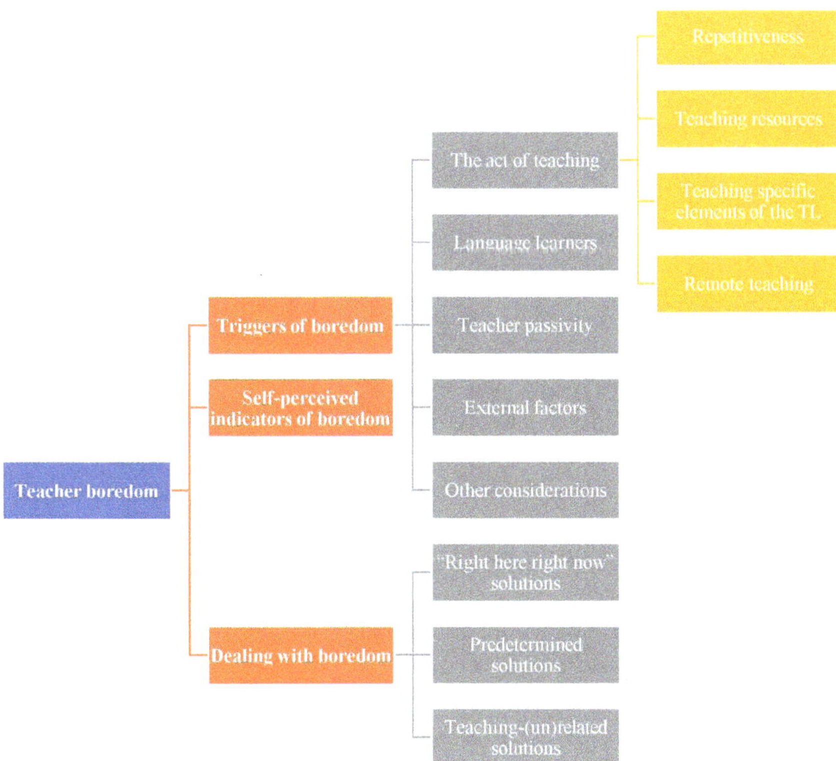

Figure 3 Causes of teacher boredom

As far as the first category is concerned (i.e., *triggers of boredom*, 186 references in total), it comprised five themes: (1) *the act of teaching*, (2) *language learners*, (3) *teacher passivity*, (4) *external factors* and (5) *other considerations*. The most important source of boredom among the teachers who participated in the study was the *act of teaching* itself (81 references in total). This theme included four subthemes: (1) *repetitiveness*, (2) *teaching resources*, (3) *teaching specific elements of the TL* and (4) *remote teaching*. The first subtheme (i.e., repetitiveness, 44 references) was related to teaching the same issues (e.g., topics, language aspects) in several lessons and/or covering the same things in different groups of students by means of the same teaching materials. This is something that typically happens when the schedule is constructed in such a way that the teacher meets several groups at the same level in a row on a given day. As for the teaching resources (i.e., the second subtheme, 15 references), the most boredom-inducing, in the opinion of the respondents, was the coursebook, which they regarded as "dull", "not very interesting" and "run-of-the-mill" as well as containing "conventional activities", "boring texts" and "rare vocabulary". The third subtheme (i.e., teaching specific elements of the TL, 14 references) was associated with the experience of boredom while teaching English grammar, "teaching for exams", and the necessity of teaching various language aspects not related to students' interests, mainly because they are included in the core curriculum. Finally, the fourth subtheme (8 references) involved online or remote teaching imposed by the COVID-19 pandemic and relating to sanitary restrictions. The following excerpts provide examples of some of the issues raised:

- If I feel bored, it is usually because of the content of the coursebook.
- Monotony of tasks, several lessons in a row on the same topic.
- Extensive grammar issues to-be repeated and worked on.
- Repeating the same content over and over again as well as covering the same topic in another group.
- Repeatability of types of tasks due to the preparation of students for exams.
- If I conduct the same lessons three times in a row, then yes. How much is enough?
- Yes, if I have to use the same materials over and over again.
- Yes, sometimes I experience boredom if there are several lessons in a row at the same level and the material is repeated.
- Very typical grammar exercises. Work with repetition drills. No element of surprise.
- I think it is very boring to keep doing the required exam tasks repeatedly.
- The need to implement the core curriculum (focused on grammar and teaching for the exam).

The second most pronounced cause of boredom identified in the responses to the open-ended questions concerned *language learners* (60 references). The respondents experienced boredom when teaching students who were uninvolved or uninterested as well as learners who were simply "not willing to cooperate" with them. The teachers also felt bored when working with "calm" and "weak students" or in situations when they had to teach English to students who represented lower levels of TL proficiency. Such issues are exemplified in the following excerpts:

- I get bored when I see my students' lack of commitment.
- Lack of interest on the part of students during the lesson.
- Lack of student involvement.
- ... when the class is extremely calm, I sometimes face the challenge of not becoming bored.
- It happens to me from time to time, especially when I teach at a lower level.
- I usually feel bored when teaching classes with poor language students.

- Classes are different. This feeling happens most often in intellectually weak groups.

Teacher passivity, external and *other considerations* constituted another three sources of teacher boredom (15, 6 and 24 references, respectively) that emerged from thematic analysis. Teacher passivity was related to classroom situations in which students were requested to work on their own. These typically involved writing tasks (e.g., writing an essay or an email), sitting tests and doing a set of activities in workbooks. External and other factors were not, or only weakly, linked to the teaching of English in the classroom and comprised references related to "the weather", "a sleepy day" or "time of day" in the case of external factors as well as bureaucracy, staff meetings and "last lessons" in the case of other factors. Illustrative in this regard are the following excerpts:

- Most often, I personally feel bored during lessons in which my students write tests.
- When students work with their workbooks. Then I do little.
- Most often I am bored when my students work individually or in pairs, because then I do not speak and the production is on the part of the students.
- Afternoon time.
- Sometimes it is the weather. The constant lack of the sunlight makes me feel I do not feel like doing anything.
- Sometimes it is also a sleepy day and students work slowly.
- Bureaucracy and meaningless staff meetings.
- When students' work pace is very slow.
- It happens sometimes, especially during my final lessons.

When it comes to the second category, that is, *self-perceived indicators of boredom* (27 references in total), it pertained to the participants' self-identified physical and psychological symptoms such as, for example, fatigue, lack of energy and/or concentration on a given day. The category also encompassed the teachers' mentions of "impatience", "lack of motivation" and "a feeling of failure" as self-perceived indications of boredom in the classroom. Importantly, such indicators were typically regarded as more transient rather than permanent. The excerpts that follow illustrate some of these issues:

- Fatigue, too many lessons and duties.
- Sometimes. The lack of concentration during routine exercises, e.g., warm-ups, questions at the beginning of a lesson.
- It happens but rarely. I wait when a lesson is over.
- It starts with a feeling of helplessness but in extreme cases it turns into frustration.

As far as the third category is concerned, that is, *dealing with boredom*, it was related to the teachers' ways of mitigating this negative emotion in the language classroom when conducting English lessons (101 references in total). As can be seen in Figure 3, the solutions to confront the phenomenon of boredom during English lessons were classified into three themes: (1) *"right here right now" solutions*, (2) *predetermined solutions* and (3) *teaching-(un)related solutions*. As regards the first theme (i.e., "right here right now" solutions), it had the highest number of references (49). The solutions that the teachers tried to employ the most often in order to cope with the negative emotion of boredom concerned the issue of changing the activities used, either language-related (e.g., the change of a language exercise) or language-unrelated (e.g., the introduction of short physical exercises), blending in or taking part in activities performed by learners as well as acting spontaneously, for example, by improvising. Individual respondents also mentioned the use of humor ("I tell a joke"), asking colleagues for "help" and "walking around the classroom". The following excerpts illustrate some of the points presented above:

- I sometimes use a different exercise when the course of the lesson is boring for me.
- I become active by asking students additional questions (not necessarily related to the lesson) or I make a break for a short period of gymnastics, movement games, etc.
- I try to do language activities together with my students and it helps me get rid of boredom.
- Due to the fact that I feel bored when students work individually or in pairs, I try to observe what they do, check their books, help and praise them.
- I pull myself together, improvise and come up with an extra assignment.
- I try to change something during the lesson, be creative.

When it comes to the second theme, that is, *predetermined solutions*, it pertained to measures involved in designing an English lesson (41 references). To deal with the feeling of boredom in the classroom, the respondents referred to searching for "new ideas", selecting interesting teaching materials and language tasks, as well as utilizing digital technologies. They also attempted to introduce more variety into their lessons by implementing more plays and games, they used different locations for conducting English lessons (e.g., a school library) and they did not slavishly rely on the coursebook as the only source of the teaching materials. Such issues are exemplified in the following excerpts:

- I plan games or activities that must involve everyone. It also makes me feel committed and boredom fades away.

- I plan to carry out a lesson outside the classroom, for example, in the school library.
- I look for new ideas for English lessons on online forums.
- I try to choose proper materials and exercises so that they are not boring for me or my students.
- I'm not clinging to the coursebook.
- I use the available multimedia resources that diversify my lessons and my work.
- I plan to work on multimedia boards and that's why I don't get bored.

Finally, the third theme comprised ways of tackling the aversive feeling of boredom in teaching-(un)related circumstances and it was mentioned 11 times. The comments in this category referred to such coping strategies as "filling in the register", "drinking a cup of favorite coffee" and "trying to keep myself busy". One teacher thought about planning another lesson and another one mentioned the activities she planned to be performed in her free time at home:

- While the students are working, in the meantime, I try to figure out the scenario for the next lesson in my head, by reading, for example, texts that are in the coursebook and which are interesting to me.
- I plan to go to bed when I come home and then I plan some physical activities.

Reflective Break
- Do you find the causes of teacher boredom presented in this subsection surprising? Why? Why not?
- Do you think the causes of teacher boredom are similar to your teaching context or different?
- What other causes of teacher boredom can you think of? Please explain.

5.6 THE RELATIONSHIP BETWEEN TEACHER AND STUDENT BOREDOM

RQ6 was related to the relationship between teacher and student boredom in the L2 classroom. The analysis of the data showed that the respondents were almost equally divided with respect to this issue, with 52 and 54 teachers providing an affirmative and negative response, respectively. The teachers who claimed to observe the relationship between teacher and student boredom in English lessons remarked that they experience boredom when their students become "not active, withdrawn, less concentrated" and "less involved" in lessons as well as when they show "no motivation" and "no enthusiasm" for learning English in the classroom. They also indicated that when they succumb to boredom while conducting their lessons, the students start to reveal signs of "no reaction", "no cooperation" and they are "unwilling to do some activities". Such moments were also frequently accompanied by students' physical symptoms and behaviors typical of boredom: "I can see that my students start to yawn and look at the clock".

> **Reflective Break**
> - Do you find the relationship between teacher and student boredom surprising? Why?

5.7 FLUCTUATIONS IN THE EXPERIENCE OF BOREDOM IN ENGLISH LESSONS

When it comes to RQ7, conclusions in this regard can be based on two sources: (1) one of the items in the questionnaire asked the teachers to indicate which part of an English lesson period (i.e., start, middle or end) was the most boredom-inducing for their students, and (2) the lesson reports submitted by the two teachers who volunteered to provide relevant data. The results in this section are presented in the order of these two sources.

As can be seen in Figure 4, only nine teachers (8.49%) regarded the beginning of a lesson as the most boring for their students. This, in their opinion, was due to such activities as checking attendance and checking homework assignments (four and two references, respectively). 33 (31.13%) teachers pointed to the middle of a lesson as the time when their students were the most likely to succumb to boredom. These participants mostly attributed the experience of this negative emotion among their students to monotonous and dull coursebook activities, problems with comprehension of the issues covered during lessons, students' diminished interest and motivation as well as their tiredness. The majority of the respondents (45 individuals or 42.45%) indicated the end of a lesson as the most boring period for learners, mainly because of fatigue, reduced motivation and concentration, or simply anticipation of the upcoming break. The following comments illustrate some of these points:

- At the beginning of a lesson the most, when checking attendance.
- At the start of lessons when students present their homework and they are asked about the tasks they prepared at home.

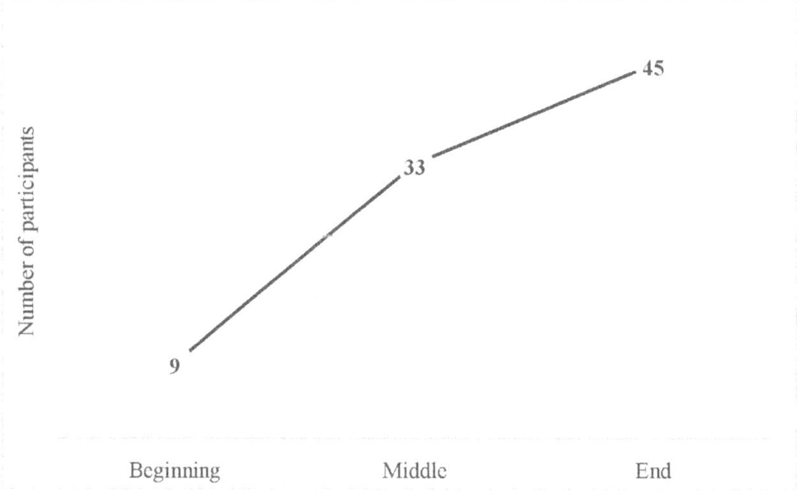

Figure 4 The most boredom-generating parts of an English lesson for language learners in the eyes of the teachers

- In the middle when performing tedious tasks.
- In the middle of a lesson motivation and willingness to do activities go down. In contrast, at the start of a lesson my students have energy and when they see that a lesson is coming to an end as well.
- I think in the middle of a lesson because they are a bit tired at that point.
- It usually starts towards the end of a lesson. Then their interest and concentration decrease.
- It's at the end of lessons. I think they are usually tired by then.

The second source of data shedding light on fluctuations in the level of boredom were the lesson reports completed by two participants, that is, Teacher 1 and Teacher 2. These reports allowed insights into changes in the intensity of teacher and student boredom during English lessons as well as from one lesson to another based on the analysis of the data obtained through boredom grids and short narratives. Table 3 and Table 4 provide a description of the lesson plans designed by the two teachers. These lesson plans focused on the topics, the activities applied and approximate time in which they were performed.

Table 3 A description of lessons conducted by Teacher 1

Lesson no. and topic	Activities	Time (minutes – approx.)
Lesson 1: English in practice (part 1)	Organization and word formation: prefixes and suffices	1–5
		6–10
		11–15
	Exercises: prefixes	16–20
		21–25
	Speaking: describing pictures	26–30
	Listening: suspending a student	31–35
	Speaking: Should the school suspend the student? (discussion)	36–40
	Multiple-choice activity and conclusion	41–45
Lesson 2: English in practice (part 2)	Organization and word formation (a brainstorming activity)	1–5
	Word formation (revision: parts of speech)	6–10
	Completing a table with missing parts of speech	11–15
		16–20
	Language activities	21–25
		26–30
		31–35
		36–40
	Conclusion	41–45
Lesson 3: Describing a person (part 1)	Organization	1–5
	A sample description of a person - reading and translating	6–10
		11–15
	Preparing a list of words useful for the description of a person	16–20
		21–25
	Vocabulary activities	26–30
	Writing a description of a person	31–35
		36–40
	Conclusion	41–45
Lesson 4: Describing a person (part 2)	Organization	1–5
	Revision of vocabulary (a brainstorming activity)	6–10
		11–15
	Discussing strategies needed for writing an essay	16–20
		21–25
	Vocabulary and grammar activities useful for writing a description	26–30
		31–35
	Describing a person: workbook exercises and conclusion	36–40
		41–45

(Continued)

Table 3 (*Continued*)

Lesson no. and topic	Activities	Time (minutes – approx.)
Lesson 5:	Organization	1–5
The judiciary	Presentation of new vocabulary	6–10
	Speaking activities	11–15
	Describing words (a guessing game)	16–20
	Speaking activities – discussing Aesop quotes	21–25
	Working with a text containing thematic vocabulary	26–30
		31–35
	Practicing new vocabulary and conclusion	36–40
		41–45
Lesson 6:	Organization	1–5
Passive voice (part 1)	Passive voice: general rules	6–10
		11–15
	Passive voice: detailed rules	16–20
		21–25
	Grammar activities (transformation)	26–30
		31–35
	Grammar activities (translation) and conclusion	36–40
		41–45
Lesson 7:	Organization	1–5
Passive voice (part 2)	Passive voice (revision of usage and rules)	6–10
	Watching a video clip showing the passive voice rules	11–15
	Working with a text containing passive voice sentences	16–20
		21–25
	Grammar activities related to the passive voice	26–30
		31–35
		36–40
	Conclusion	41–45

Table 4 A description of lessons conducted by Teacher 2

Lesson no. and topic	Activities	Time (minutes – approx.)
Lesson 1: How to post a comment?	Organization	1–5
	What and how can be posted as a comment on a website? (discussion)	6–10
	Reading and translating an online comment	11–15
	Working with a text (analyzing vocabulary and doing an exercise related to general rules concerning posting comments)	16–20
		21–25
	Practicing writing online comments	26–30
		31–35
		36–40
	Conclusion	41–45
Lesson 2: Central Park: listening comprehension	Organization	1–5
	What do you know about Central Park? (a brainstorming activity)	6–10
	Central Park - more information about Central Park from the coursebook	11–15
	Completing sentences with numbers (pair-work)	16–20
	Checking the activity by listening to a recording	21–25
	Listening activity (multiple choice)	26–30
	Listening to another text about Central Park and doing an accompanying activity. Checking the answers.	31–35
		36–40
	Conclusion	41–45
Lesson 3: Reported speech: orders and questions	Organization	1–5
	Introduction to reported speech (orders)	6–10
		11–15
	Reported speech - orders (exercises, pair-work)	16–20
	Checking the answers (self-evaluation)	21–25
	Introduction to reported speech (questions)	26–30
		31–35
	Reported speech - questions (exercises)	36–40
	Conclusion	41–45

(Continued)

Table 4 (*Continued*)

Lesson no. and topic	Activities	Time (minutes – approx.)
Lesson 4:	Organization	1–5
Reported speech: affirmative sentences	Revision of rules (a brainstorming activity)	6–10
		11–15
	Doing exercises – pronouns and adverbs of time and place (pair-work)	16–20
	Checking the answers (self-evaluation)	21–25
	Doing exercises – introductory verbs (pair-work)	26–30
		31–35
	Checking the answers (self-evaluation)	36–40
	Conclusion	41–45
Lesson 5:	Organization	1–5
E-books	E-books (short discussion)	6–10
	Reading a text and performing a set of exercises	11–15
		16–20
		21–25
	Answering a set of questions	26–30
		31–35
	Doing a gap-filling exercise	36–40
	Doing a gap-filling exercise and conclusion	41–45

Teacher 1

The mean levels of teacher and student boredom during each lesson as well as the teacher's overall self-reported levels of the experience of boredom and her perception of boredom experienced by the students were generally low and comparable since they equaled 1.95 and 1.97, respectively (see Figure 5 and Table 5). In addition, the highest overall levels of this negative emotion were reported by the participant in Lesson 3 and Lesson 6 (each 2.56). In contrast, the lowest general levels of teacher boredom were found in Lesson 1 and Lesson 2 (each 1.33). When it comes to the highest overall levels of boredom perceived by the teacher among the students, they were found in Lesson 5 and Lesson 6 (each 2.56). Conversely, Lesson 1 and Lesson 2 were perceived by the participant as the least boring for her students (each 1.33).

Table 5 Overall means (*M*) and standard deviation (*SD*) values for boredom experienced by Teacher 1 and her perception of boredom experienced by the students during English lessons

	Lesson 1	Lesson 2	Lesson 3	Lesson 4	Lesson 5	Lesson 6	Lesson 7	Overall
				M (*SD*)				
Teacher	1.33 (.50)	1.33 (.50)	2.56 (.53)	2.00 (.71)	2.33 (.87)	2.56 (.53)	1.56 (.53)	1.95 (.55)
Students	1.33 (.50)	1.33 (.50)	2.22 (.44)	2.22 (.83)	2.56 (.88)	2.56 (.53)	1.56 (.53)	1.97 (.55)

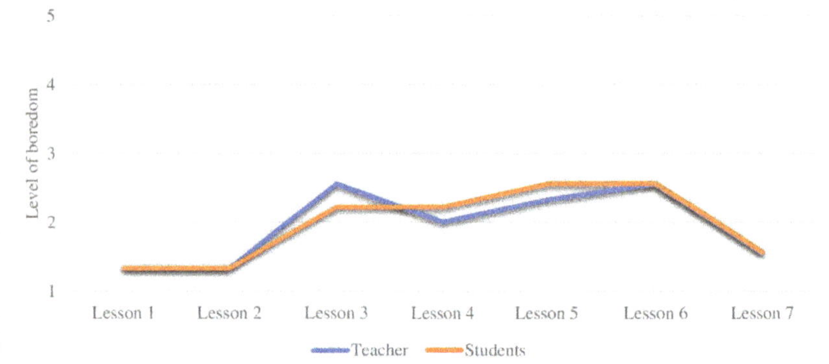

Figure 5 The experience of Teacher 1 boredom and her perception of boredom experienced by the students during English lessons

As far as self-reported levels of boredom experienced by the teacher and her perception of this aversive emotion among her learners during Lesson 1 are concerned, the feelings of boredom were only present, albeit on a very low level (i.e., 2 points), during the first 15 minutes of the lesson, that is, the part concerning the explanation of the rules related to the addition of prefixes and suffixes to English words (see Figure 6). The teacher commented: "There was virtually no time for boredom. The students were disciplined as they found the topic important. Lots of different activities".[2]

Figure 7 shows that during Lesson 2 boredom, whether it was self-reported by the teacher or perceived among the students, was only present between minutes 11–20, when the students were asked to complete a table with missing parts of speech, and at the very end of the lesson in question (i.e., minutes 41–45), in its wrap-up phase, when the teacher summarized the main points of it and set the homework assignment. The teacher remarked: "I have not observed any major problems with

---

2   These and other excerpts are translations of the comments made by the two teachers (i.e., Teacher 1 and Teacher 2).

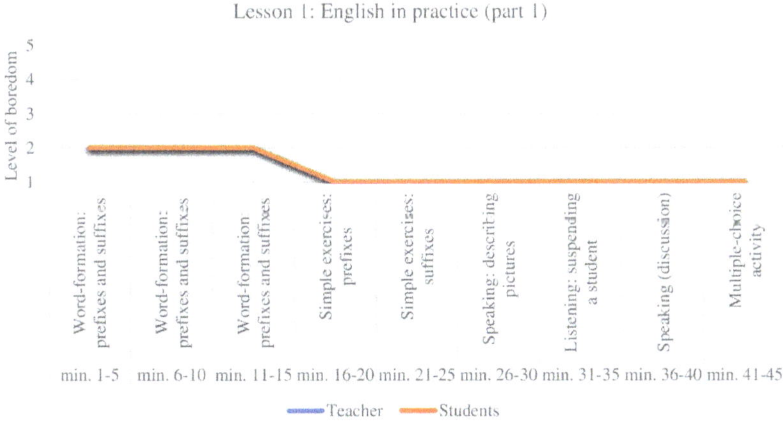

Figure 6 Teacher and student boredom during Lesson 1

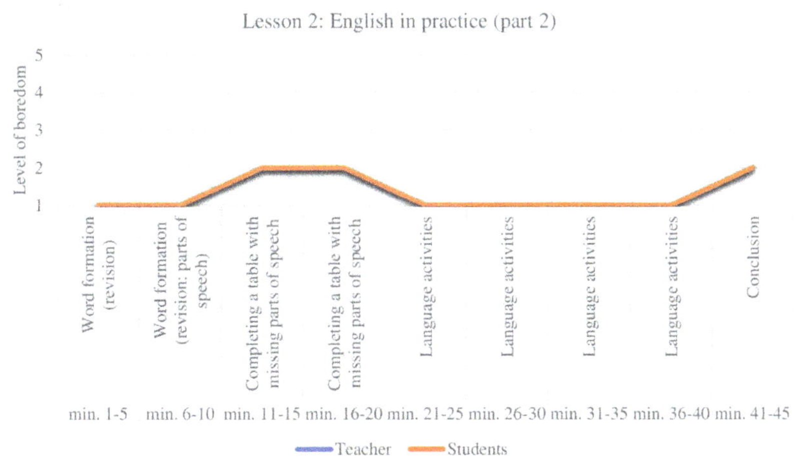

Figure 7 Teacher and student boredom during Lesson 2

my students being bored. They were focused and tried to keep up. Time pressure made students work efficiently".

As can be seen in Figure 8, the level of self-reported experience of boredom by the teacher was the highest for the most part of Lesson 3, that is, in minutes 16–40. This negative emotion accompanied the teacher during language activities in which the students worked individually and were requested to come up with a list of words needed for the description of a person, they performed a vocabulary exercise

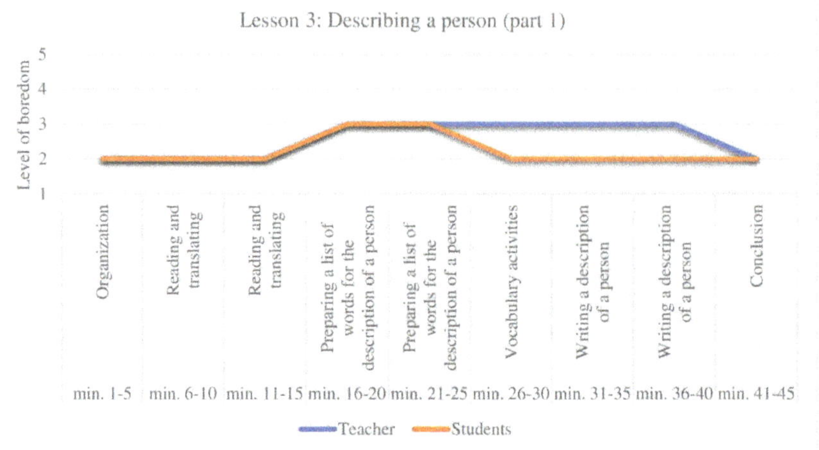

Figure 8 Teacher and student boredom during Lesson 3

and then they wrote such a description. This stands in contrast to the experience of boredom observed by the teacher among her students. This is because the learners seemed to be bored as much as their teacher only in minutes 16–25, that is, during a task in which they worked on a list of words needed for the description of a person. The teacher commented: "The students were reluctant to participate in the preparation of the word list. They would prefer to get a ready-made word list. The teacher was more bored than the students when they did the vocabulary exercises. It was difficult to remedy this by doing something else as this could be misunderstood by the students".

When it comes to Lesson 4, the teacher observed that her students turned out to be somewhat more bored than she was throughout most of the first half of the lesson (i.e., minutes 6–25), although the difference was minute and amounted to only one point (see Figure 9). This was the time when the students were requested to revise vocabulary from the previous lesson and discuss strategies needed for writing an essay. The situation changed during the subsequent 10 minutes (i.e., minutes 26–35) in which the teacher's self-reported experience of boredom was slightly higher than the feeling of this negative emotion perceived by the teacher among her students (a difference of 1 point). During that time the students performed a series of exercises focused on grammar and vocabulary. The last 10 minutes of Lesson 4 were devoted to exercises from the workbook related to the description of a person and no boredom, either on the part of the teacher or the students, was recorded at that time. The highest levels of boredom found in the lesson in question were commented upon by the teacher in the following way: "The students reached their highest level of boredom during the revision of vocabulary and the discussion

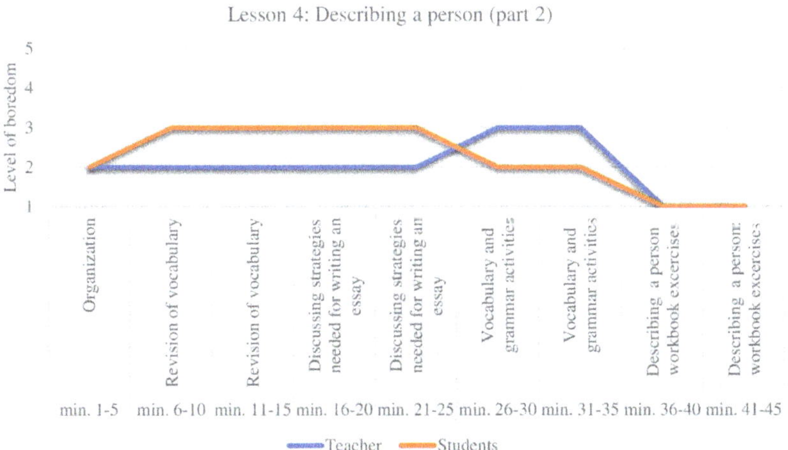

Figure 9 Teacher and student boredom during Lesson 4

of the strategies needed to write an essay. Maybe next time I will use group work. The teacher reached the highest level of boredom during vocabulary and grammar exercises. It is difficult for me to find a solution to the situation for the future".

In contrast to the previous lessons, the beginning of Lesson 5 dedicated to organizational issues saw the students slightly more bored (3 points) when compared with the teacher (2 points) (see Figure 10). Next, the intensity of this negative emotion increased by one point in the case of the students and two points in the case

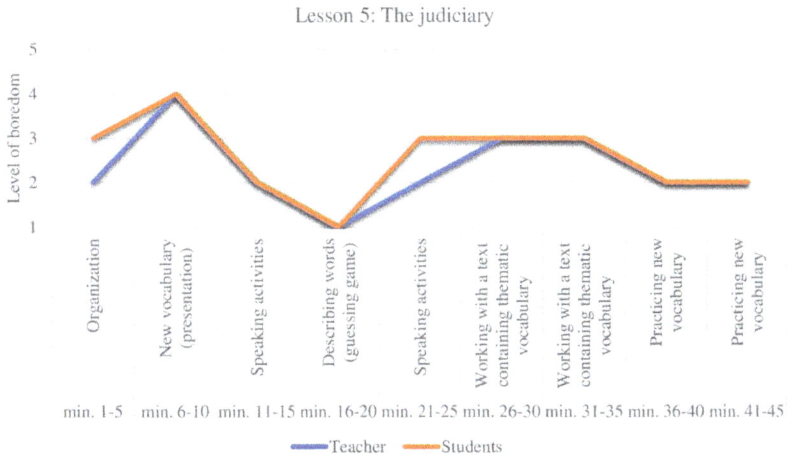

Figure 10 Teacher and student boredom during Lesson 5

of the teacher during presentation of new vocabulary related to the judiciary and reached its highest level (4 points, minutes 6–10). The feeling of boredom started to decrease during the subsequent speaking activity (2 points, minutes 11–15) and a language game (1 point, minutes 16–20) in which the students were requested to guess a set of words based on their descriptions in English. This was followed by a 3-point increase in the level of boredom observed by the teacher among the students and a 2-point rise in the teacher self-reported intensity of the negative emotion in question during a speaking activity in which the students discussed Aesop quotes (minutes 21–25). The experience of teacher boredom drew level with student boredom during an activity concerning a text containing vocabulary related to the lesson topic (minutes 26–35). The intensity of boredom dropped by one point at the start of a new vocabulary activity and remained at the same level until the end of the lesson (2 points, minutes 36–45). The highest levels of boredom during Lesson 5 were accounted for by the teacher in the following way: "I noticed the highest level of boredom when introducing new vocabulary. I think this is unfortunately inevitable. I know that it bores the students and this feeling also affects me".

As can be seen in Figure 11, the first half of Lesson 6 proved to be more boring both for the teacher and the students when compared with the second half (3 points in minutes 1–25 vs. 2 points in minutes 26–45). The analysis of the information concerning the content of Lesson 6 included in the lesson report revealed that the higher level of boredom was related to the implementation of rules for the formation and use of the passive voice presented by the teacher. Such a situation was also expressed by the teacher in her self-evaluation of the lesson in question. She commented: "A lot of new pieces of information made the students confused and bored. It's hard to say what to do to reduce the level of boredom in this situation. This also affected me when I saw my students being bored. Although the boredom level was moderate, it is also difficult to say what to do to reduce its level".

As far as Lesson 7 is concerned, the intensity of boredom reported by the teacher and her perception of this negative emotion among the students was low and the same in both cases (see Figure 12). The teacher and the students seemed to be somewhat bored (2 points) in the initial minutes of the lesson, somewhere towards the end of the first half of the lesson and at the end of it. These were situations related to organizational issues and the revision of the information concerning the passive voice (minutes 1–10), performing a text-related activities (minutes 16–25) and the conclusion of the lesson in which the teacher summarized the main points of the topic and set a homework assignment (minutes 41–45). The teacher commented: "The level of boredom was almost unnoticeable. The level of boredom motivated the students to work. Student involvement is also motivating for the teacher. The preparation of more difficult exercises significantly reduces the level of boredom as well as praising the students".

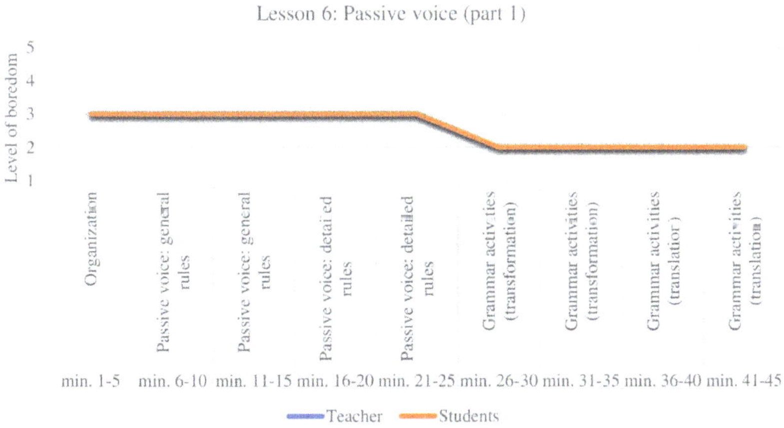

Figure 11 Teacher and student boredom during Lesson 6

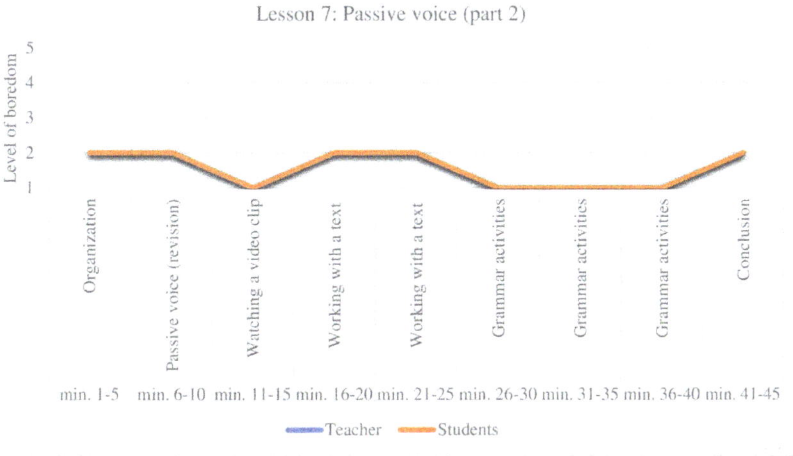

Figure 12 Teacher and student boredom during Lesson 7

Teacher 2

The mean levels of teacher and student boredom during each lesson as well as the participant's general self-reported clevels of the experience of boredom and her perception of this negative emotion experienced by the learners were, on the whole, low and comparable since they amounted to 1.51 and 1.64, respectively (see Figure 13 and Table 6). In addition, the highest and lowest overall levels of boredom were

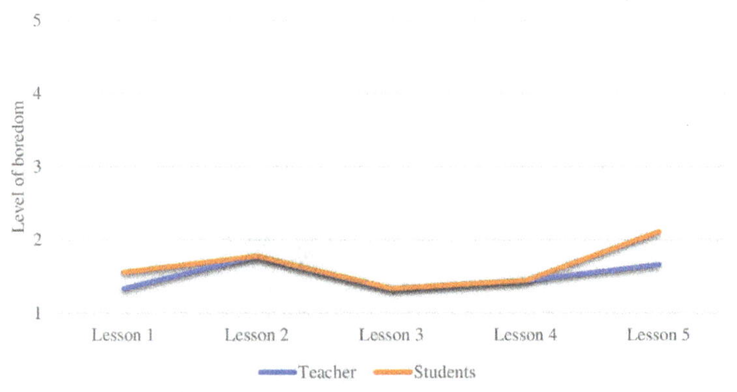

Figure 13 The experience of Teacher 2 boredom and her perception of boredom experienced by the students during English lessons

Table 6 Overall means (*M*) and standard deviation (*SD*) values for boredom experienced by Teacher 2 and her perception of boredom experienced by the students during English lessons

	Lesson 1	Lesson 2	Lesson 3	Lesson 4	Lesson 5	Overall
			M (*SD*)			
Teacher	1.33 (.50)	1.78 (.44)	1.33 (.50)	1.44 (.53)	1.67 (.50)	1.51 (.21)
Students	1.56 (.53)	1.78 (.44)	1.33 (.50)	1.44 (.53)	2.11 (.78)	1.64 (.31)

reported by the teacher in Lesson 2 (1.78) as well as Lesson 1 and Lesson 3 (each 1.33), respectively. When it comes to the highest and lowest levels of boredom perceived by the teacher among her learners, they occurred in Lesson 5 (2.11) and Lesson 3 (33), respectively.

As regards self-reported levels of boredom experienced by Teacher 2 and her perception of the negative emotion under study among her learners during Lesson 1, the analysis of the data showed that both the teacher and the students felt a bit bored (2 points) throughout the first 15 minutes of the lesson dedicated to organizational issues, a short warm-up discussion activity regarding posting a comment on a website as well as reading and translating an example of an online comment (see Figure 14). The next activity in which the students were asked to read a text and analyze its vocabulary and content as well as perform an activity summarizing main points regarding posting online comments (minutes 16–25) did not evoke any feelings of boredom among the participants. As can be seen in Figure 14, some changes, albeit on a very low level (i.e., 2 points, minutes 26–35), were only detected among the students during the last activity in which they further practiced writing online comments. The last five minutes of the lesson, devoted to a short conclusion, ended with no

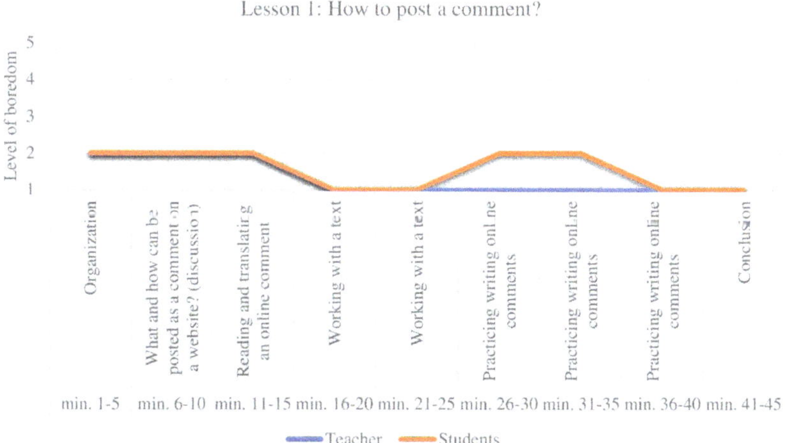

Figure 14 Teacher and student boredom during Lesson 1

feelings of the emotion under study on the part of the teacher as well as the students. The teacher commented: "The most boring part of the lesson was connected with reading, and the least boring one was linked with students' activities and/or their own experiences … I had to correct students' comments almost all the time. I also prepared a lot of activities which prevented the students and me from being bored".

When it comes to Lesson 2, the intensity of boredom reported by the teacher and her perception of this aversive emotion among her students was very low and the same in both cases (see Figure 15). The teacher and the students appeared to be slightly bored (2 points) in the first five minutes of the lesson, somewhere in the middle of its first half and from minute 26 until the end of the lesson. These were situations connected with organizational issues, getting information about Central Park from the coursebook (minutes 11–20), a couple of listening activities (minutes 26–40) and a conclusion in which the teacher went over the main points of the lesson and set a homework assignment (minutes 41–45). The slight experience of boredom observed in Lesson 2 was commented upon by the teacher in the following way: "Boredom was observed when the students listened to the text for the second time. Most students listened carefully to this text for the first time but they concentrated less on it when they were asked to listen to it again. The same can be said about myself".

Figure 16 shows that during Lesson 3 the experience of boredom went hand in hand, regardless of whether it was self-reported by the teacher or perceived among the learners. The figure also shows that the self-reported experience of teacher boredom and her perception of this negative emotion among her students, even though

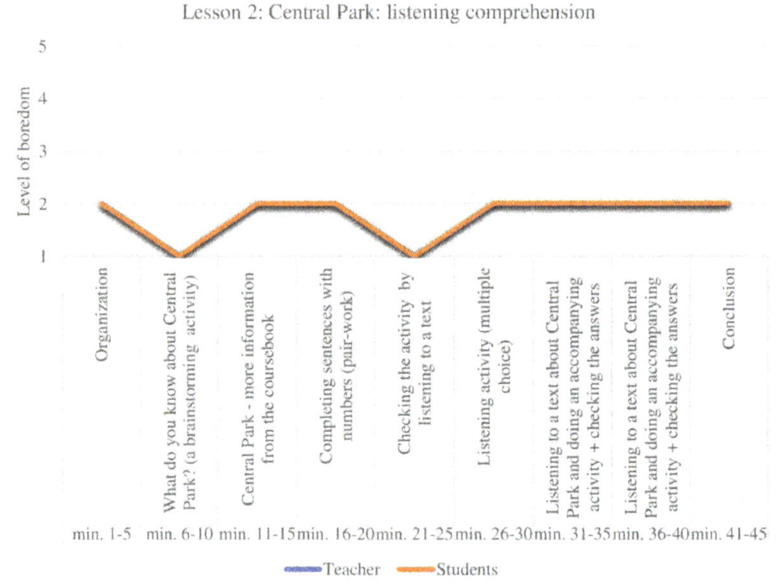

Figure 15 Teacher and student boredom during Lesson 2

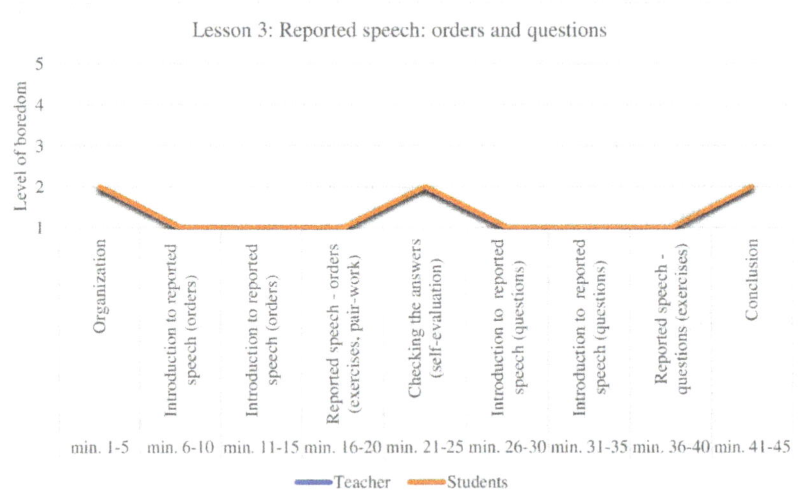

Figure 16 Teacher and student boredom during Lesson 3

on a very low level, was only present in the initial minutes of the lesson devoted to organizational issues (2 points, minutes 1–5), in the middle of the lesson (2 points, minutes 21–25), when answers to a previous exercise were checked by the teacher and the students were asked to self-evaluate, and at the end of the lesson when the teacher summarized the main points of it and set the homework assignment. The teacher remarked: "The students worked actively because the material was divided into parts and the way the issues related to the lesson topic explained by me made them listen carefully and with involvement. Joint work and the feeling that my students can understand a quite difficult lesson gave a sense of satisfaction. I had no time for boredom".

The intensity of boredom self-reported by the teacher and perceived by her among the students during Lesson 4 was similar to Lesson 3 (see Figure 17). Both the teacher and the students experienced a very low level of boredom at the beginning of the lesson which dealt with organizational issues (2 points, minutes 1–5), in the middle of it (2 points, minutes 21–25), when the teacher checked the answers to the activity the students were requested to perform in minutes 16–20 and then self-evaluate, and finally for the last 10 minutes of Lesson 4 (2 points, minutes 36–45) dedicated to checking the answers to the activity performed by the students before and their self-evaluation as well as conclusion. The lesson was commented upon by the teacher in the following way: "The students felt comfortable while working in pairs because they could help each other, jointly work out some things and finish an exercise together. I also was involved in the lesson all the time".

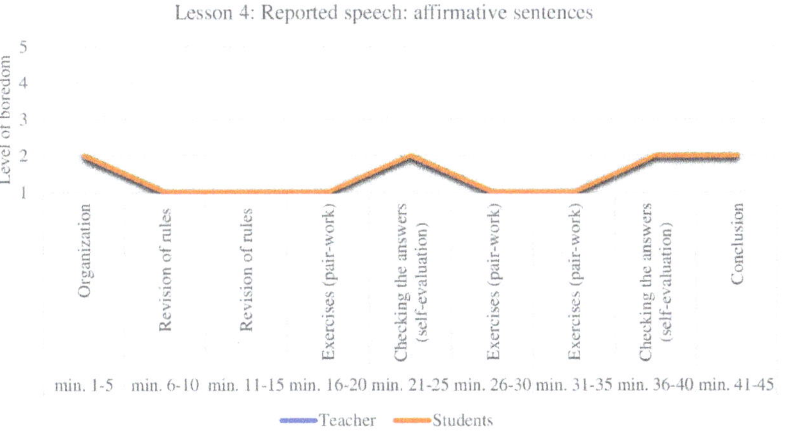

Figure 17 Teacher and student boredom during Lesson 4

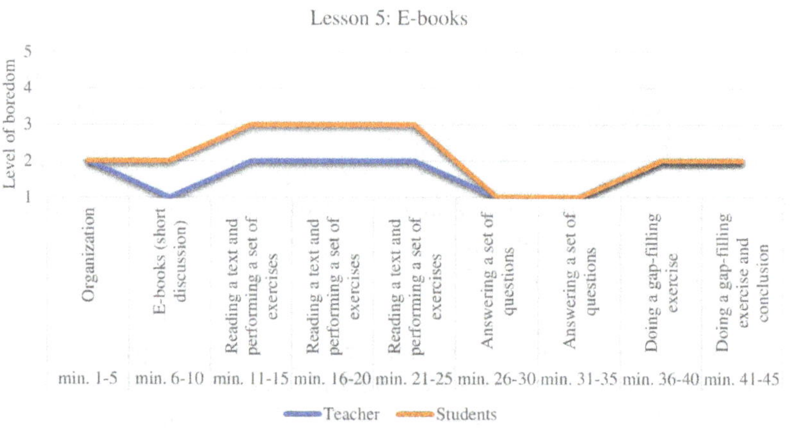

Figure 18 Teacher and student boredom during Lesson 5

As can be seen in Figure 18, except for the initial part of Lesson 5 in which both the teacher and the students seemed to experience comparable levels of boredom (2 points, minutes 1–5), the ongoing 20 minutes of the lesson in question turned out to be slightly more boring for the students than the teacher when compared with the second half (2 points in minutes 6–10 and 1 point in minutes 6–10 as well as 3 points in minutes 11–25 and 2 points in minutes 11–25 for the students and the teacher vs. 1 point in minutes 26–30 and 2 points in minutes 36–45 for both the students and the teacher). The analysis of the data related to the content of Lesson 5 contained in the lesson report showed that the higher levels of boredom observed by the teacher among her students concerned the discussion of e-books (minutes 6–10) and a part of the lesson when the students were requested to read a text and perform a set of accompanying activities (i.e., summarizing each part of the text with a couple of sentences, translating parts of the text and writing down new vocabulary) (minutes 11–25). The reading phase of the lesson was also a bit boring for the teacher. Some feelings of boredom were also generated at the end of the lesson dedicated to a gap-filling activity and conclusion. The teacher remarked: "Working with a text is usually tiring. I observed that better students were more active but weaker students seemed to be bored. I think the text was quite difficult and demanding for them. The feeling of boredom among the students had an influence on me too. However, I managed not to succumb to this feeling by trying to control the way students work".

> **Reflective Break**
> - When do you think your students (may) experience the most boredom during lessons? What causes it?
> - When (if ever) do you experience the most boredom during lessons? What causes this negative emotion?
> - Based on your own experience, do you find any results emerging from the two teachers' reports surprising? Why?

5.6 DISCUSSION

The study sought to provide answers to seven research questions (RQs) which by and large focused upon the experience of boredom in the eyes of L2 teachers and the ways in which this negative emotion can be combated, whether it is manifested by learners or teachers. The aim of the present section is to discuss these RQs and interpret the findings, whenever possible linking them to the existing empirical evidence. Reflective Breaks are added after the discussion of each RQ to encourage the readers to further reflect on the results of the study and to link them to their own experiences.

5.6.1 RQ1: What is the Participants' Overall Proneness to Boredom?

Quantitative analysis of the responses to the BPS (Farmer & Sundberg, 1986) demonstrated that the sample as a whole manifested low levels of boredom proneness ($M = 2.22$) and for as many as 76 teachers (71.70%) the average of responses to the items included in the scale amounted to 2.02. Such results as well as the *SD* value also indicate that there was little individual variation among the respondents in this respect. These findings are not easy to account for and interpret in view of the fact that just a handful of studies have investigated teacher boredom and, to the best knowledge of the present authors, this empirical investigation is the first to employ the BPS to determine L2 teachers' overall propensity to succumb to this aversive emotion. In fact, the only study that has targeted teachers' boredom in the L2 classroom, undertaken by Dumančić (2018), was qualitative in nature and it aimed to identify the causes and manifestations of this emotional state as well as the coping strategies employed to tackle it.

One possible explanation for the reported low tendency to experience boredom could be the characteristics of the sample investigated in this study. After all, the participants were on average in the mid-thirties (average age = 36.49), while teaching experience for the entire group oscillated around 12 years ($M = 12.43$). In could therefore be safely assumed that the pernicious effects of demotivation (e.g., Kim & Kim, 2022) as well as burnout (e.g., Sato, Fernández Castillo, & Oyanedel, 2022) were yet unlikely to be felt by the vast majority of the teachers, which could have lowered their overall propensity to feel bored. Even though the BPS is intended to tap into the tendency to experience this negative emotion in a wide variety of situations, the job of a teacher, particularly an L2 teacher, is highly distinctive in that it is likely to permeate various spheres of individuals' lives that extend far beyond the school setting as such (e.g., preparation for classes, looking for sources and materials, improving ones' own TL proficiency) (Borg, 2006; Johnson, 2015; MacIntyre et al., 2019; Mercer, 2020). In consequence, the score on the scale may be, at least to some extent, reflective of overall proneness to boredom with respect to different aspects of teaching, with the important caveat that a dedicated instrument would need to be developed to verify this assumption. It should also be noted that research in psychology has shown boredom proneness to be affected by some cognitive and affective factors, one of them being age (e.g., Isacescu, Struk, & Danckert, 2017; Vondanovich & Kass, 1990), although such empirical investigations have not really targeted teachers.

Reflective Break

- Do you consider yourself as a person with a high or low tendency to experience boredom? Please justify your opinion.
- Do you agree that in the case of L2 teachers there is a close relationship between their overall tendency to succumb to boredom and the extent to which they experience this negative emotion in their jobs? Why?

5.6.2 RQ2: What are the Causes and Manifestations of Boredom Experienced by L2 Learners in English Lessons in the Eyes of the Language Teachers and How Does This Negative Emotion Manifest Itself?

Thematic analysis of the responses to the open-ended-queries in the teacher questionnaire allowed identification of three major categories of issues underlying the causes of boredom manifested by L2 learners from the perspective of the participating teachers, that is, (1) *triggers of boredom*, (2) *indicators of boredom* and (3) *who/what is to blame*? With respect to the first category (1), which is by and large reflective of the overall causes of boredom, the main triggers of this negative emotion, ordered according to the frequency of mentions in the responses were as follows: *language skills and subsystems* (in particular reading, listening, writing and grammar), *the use of coursebooks* (predictable and uninteresting content), *fatigue* (issues related to weekly schedule), *overchallenge* (excessive amounts and difficulty of things to be covered in English lessons), *backlog* (gaps in TL knowledge resulting from instruction at earlier stages of education), *remote learning induced by the COVID-19 pandemic* (no face-to-face contact, scant opportunities for spontaneous interaction, technical problems), *disparity in the level of English proficiency* (mixed-level classes), *out-of-school learning* (the private tuition received), as well as *test preparation* (the focus on the final exams at the end of elementary or secondary school). In the view of the teachers, the main manifestations of boredom (2) were *the lack of engagement* (scant attention, involvement or readiness to contribute to classroom activities), *inappropriate or unrelated behavior* which took on a wide variety of forms (talking about irrelevant things with peers, playing with smartphones, daydreaming), as well as *body language* (yawning, bored facial expressions, etc.). Finally, when it comes to the culprits of the occurrence of boredom in L2 classes (3), the teachers *mainly blamed themselves* (uninteresting lessons, repetitive topics, tasks and activities, failure to pitch instruction at the right level, lack of preparation) and, to a much lesser extent, *their students* (no cooperation, lack of preparation for class, low level of TL proficiency, personality-related factors, fatigue) or *things beyond their control* (the need to follow the national curriculum and cover all required topics, grammar structures, vocabulary, etc.).

Many of the causes of boredom identified by the teachers fit in with most of the theoretical accounts of this negative emotion that were elaborated upon in Chapter 3, such as the under-stimulation model (Larson & Richards, 1991), the forced-effort model (Hill & Perkins, 1985), the attentional theory of boredom proneness (Eastwood et al., 2007), the emotion theory (Eastwood et al., 2007, 2012), the control-value theory of achievement emotions (Pekrun, 2006) or the menton theory of engagement and boredom (Davies & Fortney, 2012). This is because, for instance, the need to focus on tasks geared to the level of less proficient learners is bound to result in lack of arousal, involvement and stimulation, reliance on uninteresting and repetitive coursebook activities, which still requires considerable effort that learners may view as unwarranted, is likely to lead to subjective monotony and inattention, while limited opportunities for face-to-face interaction might lead to difficulties in self-regulating emotions. Overall, in line with the tenets of the control-value theory of achievement emotions (Pekrun, 2006), the teachers to a large extent viewed boredom as resulting from unpropitious control appraisals (e.g., learners' self-efficacy with respect to the tasks being performed) and value appraisals (e.g., learners' limited appreciation of controlled grammar practice). When we take a close look at the manifestations of boredom mentioned in the questionnaire responses, it would appear that it for the most part took the form of slightly unpleasant but relatively harmless calibrating boredom as well as much more unpleasant and detrimental reactant boredom. It could also be argued that the apparently quite innocuous signs such as yawning or facial expressions could be indicative of apathetic boredom, where a combination of low levels of well-being, satisfaction or any positive emotions might signal a more permanent, extremely pernicious approach to L2 learning (cf. Goetz et al., 2014). Finally, in terms of the boredom-coping strategies identified by Nett et al. (2010), the analysis suggests that, in the eyes of the teachers, most of the learners fell into the category of evaders or criticizers, with the crucial caveat that constructive efforts to combat boredom made by reappraisers may often be hidden from view and the nature of the question might have prevented the participants from even contemplating them.

The causes and manifestations of boredom identified in the present investigation mirror to a large extent those revealed in other studies on L2 boredom in traditional and online contexts. For example, excessive focus on certain TL skills and subsystems, in particular grammar, reading and listening, the use of overchallenging tasks, repetitive coursebook activities, remote instruction, fatigue or teachers' approach and instructional practices have been reported as sources of boredom by, among others, Derakhshan et al. (2021, 2022b), Kruk (2016), Kruk et al. (2022b), Kruk et al. (2021), Kruk and Zawodniak (2017, 2020), or Nakamura et al. (2021). More generally, the causes and manifestations of boredom uncovered in the present study by and large fit in with the two factors underlying this negative emotion that Pawlak et al. (2020b) reported for the Polish educational setting, that is, disengagement, monotony and repetitiveness as well as lack of satisfaction and challenge.

At the same time, the present findings also differ from previous empirical evidence in two ways. First, some of the causes of boredom reported in prior studies failed to be mentioned by the teachers or were just alluded to mainly in passing. For instance, the teachers placed relatively little emphasis on learner-related factors apart from TL proficiency and somewhat vaguely conceived personality, although some earlier studies have pointed to the potential impact of general boredom proneness, learning styles, negative attitudes or lack of creativity (e.g., Pawlak et al., 2020a, 2020b). Another example in this respect is that, in contrast to previous research (e.g., Derakhshan et al., 2022b; Li, 2021; Zawodniak et al., 2021), the analysis failed to identify unchallenging tasks or activities as a trigger of boredom. Second, the participating teachers highlighted the importance of boredom-inducing factors that have not come to the fore in previous empirical investigations. These included backlog or things that needed catching up on because they had failed to be grasped previously (e.g., in lower grades or at lower educational levels), private tutoring, preparation for examinations or the requirements of national curricula with respect to L2 education. A plausible explanation for at least some of these divergences is that, while the bulk of prior research has been conducted with university students, mainly English majors, the current study focused on L2 learning in different types of schools. It should come as no surprise, for example, that lack of challenge did not figure as a prominent cause of boredom in this context, given the fact that L2 learners represented in most cases lower levels of TL proficiency than university-level participants.

> **Reflective Break**
> - Which causes and manifestations of boredom mentioned by the teachers have you observed among your students? Can you think of any that were not revealed in the present study?

5.6.3 RQ3: What Efforts to Reduce Student Boredom do Language Teachers Undertake?

The participants identified five main strategies that they fell back upon to deal with the feeling of boredom that their students manifested. These included, in the order of frequency of references in the responses to the questionnaire items: (1) resorting to the *use of additional materials*, especially authentic ones afforded by computer-based technologies, (2) *diversification* with respect to the learning activities, instructional techniques or the modes of classroom organization (i.e., switching to pair work), (3) *changing the course of the class* through making an immediate interactive decision or envisaging a different course of action in the future, (4) *making the lesson more dynamic* (e.g., by means of quick activating exercises), (5) *using humor* (e.g., telling jokes) and (6) *other* strategies confined to individual teachers, such as making gestures, relying on the element of surprise, introducing interesting facts about the TL, improving the rapport with students, praising or rewarding.

Although these findings are not easy to interpret given the paucity of relevant studies, whether in the field of educational psychology or in the domain of L2 learning and teaching, an attempt can be made to evaluate them against the background of the potential solutions to boredom that were overviewed in Chapter 3 as well as the extremely scant empirical evidence included in Chapter 4. On the whole, it would seem that the respondents tended to opt for a *reactive* rather than *proactive* approach to dealing with this aversive emotion. This means that the participants for the most part prioritized concrete steps that could be taken to combat boredom once they became cognizant of its diverse manifestations rather than trying to prevent or at least minimize its occurrence in the first place. This is because the questionnaire responses did not yield any instances indicative of attempts to sensitize students to the experience of this negative phenomenon by, for example, encouraging conscious reflection in this respect, also in relation to other academic emotions (cf. Daschmann et al., 2011; Weinerman & Kenner, 2016; Westgate & Wilson, 2018). No evidence was also found for endeavoring to identify boredom-coping profiles in advance, such as those that were proposed by Nett et al. (2021), to create opportunities for L2 learners to take volitional control of the assigned tasks and activities by reconsidering their goals and values (Bartels et al., 2009; Pekrun et al., 2010), or for partly delegating responsibility for what happens during language lessons to the students (Goetz et al., 2014; Mennim, 2017), which would by and large be tantamount to developing learner autonomy (Little, 2022). Such a situation is unfortunate since, while finding effective ways of reducing the manifestations of boredom is clearly important, prevention is surely better than cure and might turn out to be more beneficial in the long run (cf. Daschmann et al., 2014).

These results can be related to the empirical investigation conducted by Pawlak et al. (2021), which, to the present authors' best knowledge, is the only other attempt to date to tap into the ways in which L2 teachers deal with the occurrence of boredom in their classroom. Although some of the strategies were akin to those identified in the current study (e.g., adjusting learning tasks, using humor, making classes interactive), others were more premeditated (i.e., proactive) and more reflective of longer-term commitment to combating boredom (e.g., introducing controversial topics, improving teaching style, helping students come up with individual study programs). Also in this case, however, such discrepancies can likely be attributed to the fact that Pawlak et al.'s (2021) empirical investigation involved university students who were simply more likely to articulate their needs which could later be accommodated to some extent as a way of reducing boredom.

> **Reflective Break**
> - Which of the strategies mentioned by the teachers in this study do you or would you use to deal with boredom in your own classroom?
> - What else do you or would you do to combat boredom among your students?
> - Do you agree with the conclusion that the reactive approach to dealing with boredom on its own may not be sufficient to address the problem? Why or why not?

5.6.4 RQ4: What are the Causes and Indicators of Boredom Experienced by L2 Teachers During English Lessons?

The analysis allowed identification of five major triggers of boredom that the teachers succumbed to during their classes. The most frequently mentioned and thus the most important in the eyes of the participants proved to be the *act of teaching* as such, which included four more specific causes, that is, *repetitiveness* (i.e., focusing on the same TL features or the same content in several lessons in a row), *teaching resources* (i.e., mostly reliance on run-of-the-mill, uninteresting coursebooks), *teaching specific elements of the TL* (i.e., in particular grammar structures because of exams) and *remote teaching* necessitated by the pandemic (i.e., presumably related to, as was the case with the students, the lack of opportunities for face-to-face interactions). The remaining causes of boredom included *language learners* who were uninterested, uninvolved, uncooperative or weak in terms of TL proficiency, *teacher passivity*, which inevitably came into play when learners were requested to work on their own (e.g., performing a writing task, working on an activity from the coursebook), *external factors*, which were somewhat idiosyncratic in nature and were related, for example, to the weather or personal circumstances, and, finally, *other considerations*, linked in particular to the functioning of the school on an institutional level (e.g., staff meetings, bureaucracy). In the opinion of the teachers, the boredom which afflicted them brought with it both physical and psychological consequences, such as fatigue, difficulty in concentrating, decrease in motivation, impatience or even a sense of failure, but, luckily, such manifestations were temporary rather than permanent in nature and typically disappeared once the triggers of this negative emotion were no longer present.

The findings provide a basis for several important observations. First, even though most of the theoretical accounts of boredom discussed in Chapter 2 and referred to earlier in the present chapter have been put forward to account for the occurrence of boredom among learners, including those studying additional languages, some of them can also be fallen back on to explain the causes of this negative emotion among L2 teachers. To give an example, it is warranted to assume that, in line with the tenets of the under-stimulation model (Larson & Richards, 1991) or the attentional theory of boredom proneness (Eastwood et al., 2007), just as is the case with learners, teachers may easily be affected by boredom when they perceive the classroom activities used (e.g., repetitive tasks included in the coursebook, mundane exercises focusing on a given grammar structure) as uninteresting or uninvolving. It could also be assumed that high levels of boredom prevailing in one part of a lesson as a result of the activities mentioned above may bring about efforts to change the situation by introducing a task that is likely to be more engaging for both learners and teachers themselves, a phenomenon that can be accounted for in terms of the dimensional model (Pekrun et al., 2010; cf. Bench & Lench, 2013). Second, it is surely noteworthy that, irrespective of a specific trigger of this negative emotion, the experience of boredom was for the most part transitory and thus likely to dissipate with the onset of a new activity or the next phase of the lesson. On the one hand, this once again highlights the relevance of the dimensional model but it also underscores the fact that, as has already been mentioned in relation to RQ1, the participants of the present study cannot be regarded as being on the whole demotivated or suffering from teacher burnout. On the other hand, such a situation might bode well for their ability to deal with boredom experienced by their students because, as postulated by the crossover theory (Hatfield et al., 1994), emotional contagion might reduce the likelihood of the occurrence of this aversive emotion somewhat irrespective of the specific steps that can be embarked upon to reduce it. Third, by and large, the causes and manifestations of L2 teacher boredom revealed in the present research project mirror those reported by Dumančić (2018) in the Croatian context, although the specific labels employed could have been different and the transient nature of this negative emotion might not have been emphasized. This could indicate that the root causes of boredom as well as the ways in which it influences classroom behaviors might be universal, at least in the case of elementary and secondary school teachers rather than university lecturers. Obviously, this assumption needs to be tested empirically in future investigations, all the more so because research into teacher boredom is in its nascent stages.

Reflective Break
- How do you relate to the causes and manifestations of teacher boredom that emerged from this study? Can you add others based on your own teaching experience?

5.6.5 RQ5: What do L2 Teachers do to Combat the Boredom They Experience During Their English Classes?

When it comes to dealing with the negative emotion of boredom that they experienced, the teachers reported a number of strategies that, based on the results of thematic analysis, were grouped into three main categories: *right here, right now solutions*, representing the most frequent reactions, by far, which can be seen as stop-gap measures intended to reduce boredom "on the spot" (e.g., changing the activities employed or joining learners in performing them), *predetermined solutions*, which were preemptive in nature and were broadly related to designing the English classes taught by, for example, being on the lookout for new ideas and materials, drawing upon technological advances or striving to introduce variety, and *engaging in activities that were not directly linked to the lesson*, such as filling out the register, drinking coffee, planning tasks and activities for the next class or sometimes even contemplating what to do later in the day.

The main point of reference when evaluating these findings is the study conducted by Dumančić (2018) in the Croatian context, which, to the best knowledge of the present authors, constitutes the only attempt thus far to look into the strategies that L2 teachers fall back upon to cope with their own boredom. On the whole, it immediately becomes clear that the repertoire of such strategies reported by the Polish teachers in this research project was much more limited and that the solutions they mentioned were much less specific. This is because the analysis failed to yield examples of suppression, cognitive change or absence of desire to self-regulate one's emotions as well as instances of resorting to such concrete actions as playing music or introducing physical activity. Two possible, even if contradictory, explanations of such differences immediately come to mind: (1) the Polish participants could have been somewhat less concerned about the disruptive effect of boredom on their classes, a situation that cannot be easily accounted for based on the collected data, and (2) they might have been less willing to recognize the detrimental contribution of this aversive emotion and in particular the fact that they may have chosen to ignore it, as reliance on suppression or avoidance could indicate. In addition, it would appear that, similarly to dealing with student boredom, the teachers tended to opt for a more reactive approach to their own experience of this negative emotion in L2 classes rather than embracing a more proactive state which could also possibly be more effective.

> **Reflective Break**
> - Do you use any of the strategies mentioned by the participants to cope with your own boredom during L2 lessons?
> - Would you rather suppress your feeling of boredom or try to actively combat it? Why?

5.6.6 RQ6: Is There a Relationship Between Boredom as Experienced by Students and Teachers?

The participants were far from unanimous in recognizing the link between boredom that afflicted their students and their own experience of this aversive emotion. In fact, only 49% of the teachers were of the opinion that such a link exists, which explains the paucity of the data, all the more so because the responses provided in support of the existence of this relationship were admittedly scarce. This said, thematic analysis of these responses indicated that teachers were more likely to succumb to boredom in situations when their learners were in general withdrawn, uninterested, uninvolved or unmotivated, all of which showed that learning English was far from being their top priority. In addition, they were also likely to experience boredom when learners manifested negative reactions to specific activities implemented in the course of a lesson, such as lack of cooperation, reluctance to get engaged in the task in hand or telltale physical symptoms such as yawning or checking the time. Some indirect evidence for the link between student and teacher boredom also derives from the responses to other queries included in the questionnaire and discussed earlier in this chapter in the sense that this negative emotion had similar causes. In particular, it is evident that, both in the case of learners and teachers, boredom was likely to be triggered by repetitive and uninteresting activities, excessive use of the coursebook, the need to practice certain TL skills and subsystems (e.g., grammar), but also to some extent the overall approach of the L2 teacher.

On the whole, the analysis did provide some support for the claims of the crossover theory and the related concept of emotional contagion (Barsade, 2002; Hatfield et al., 1994), although, in the view of the participants, this process was apparently unidirectional, with the boredom experienced and manifested by L2 learners bringing about a parallel emotional state in L2 teachers. It is warranted to assume, however, that the feeling of boredom is a double-edged sword and that L2 teachers are likely to bring about this aversive experience in their learners. Even though, perhaps owing to its design, the present study failed to provide ample support in this respect, this is surely an issue that should be specifically addressed by future research projects.

> **Reflective Break**
> - In your opinion, is there a relationship between student and teacher boredom in L2 classes?
> - If so, is it always the case that learners' boredom brings about teacher boredom or can this also work the other way around?

5.6.7 RQ7: How does Boredom Experienced by Teachers Change During a Language Lesson and from One Lesson to Another?

The answer to this research question was possible thanks to the data obtained from two sources: (1) one of the open-ended items in the questionnaire that was responded to by all the participants and (2) the lesson reports that were completed by two teachers in which they were requested to indicate the levels of boredom exhibited by themselves as well as their students at five-minute intervals, offer comments on the contents of a specific lesson (i.e., foci, activities, modes of work), and provide short boredom-related narratives on the basis of a set of prompts. The data coming from both of these sources provided evidence for the dynamicity of boredom in L2 lessons as well as offering insights into overall patterns of such changes and factors responsible for them.

On a more general level, the majority of the 106 participants responding to the open-ended query were of the opinion that the intensity of boredom manifested by learners was the highest towards the end of a class (42.45%), a situation that they attributed to fatigue, dropping motivation or anticipation of the break or the following class. About one third of the teachers (31.13%) viewed the mid part of the class to be the most boredom-inducing due to the repetitive nature of coursebook activities or the necessity of covering things exceeding their learners' current level of TL proficiency. Only a minority of the participants (8.49%) considered the beginning of a class to be the most boring for students because of the procedural issues that needed to be taken care of at this stage (e.g., taking attendance). Such findings are not surprising since they are largely consistent with the results of previous studies of boredom adopting both a macro-perspective, where general patterns were sought on the basis of data obtained from large numbers of participants, and a micro-perspective, where boredom was traced in a situated manner in regularly scheduled classes (e.g., Derakhshan et al., 2021; Kruk, 2016; see section 3 in Chapter 4, for the explanation of the two perspectives on research into L2 boredom). More importantly, however, crude as they might be, such data clearly suggest that, irrespective of learners' overall proneness to experience boredom (Farmer & Sundberg, 1986), this negative emotion is dynamic and state-like, tending to fluctuate in response to what transpires in a particular lesson.

Much more revealing insights concerning the dynamicity of boredom can be derived from the lesson reports completed by the two teachers who had volunteered to provide such information. Despite the fact that the data were collected in the course of 12 classes taught by both teachers and there was naturally some amount of variability, it is still possible to offer several observations and interpretations. First, the self-perceived indications of learner and teacher boredom on the 5-point scale revealed that this negative emotion was indeed in a state of flux, both from one lesson to the next and within the confines of the same class, with the important caveat that the amplitude of such changes was limited due to the low overall levels of boredom reported by the participants both for themselves and their learners (1.95 and 1.97, respectively in the case of Teacher 1, and 1.51 and 1.64, respectively in the case of Teacher 2). Second, the reasons for such fluctuations correspond for the most part to the causes of boredom highlighted in the responses of the 106 participants to the open-ended items in this study but also mirror to a considerable extent the results of previous empirical investigations, which, however, have only targeted L2 learners (e.g., Kruk, 2021a; Kruk & Zawodniak, 2020; Pawlak et al., 2020d). In particular, the levels of boredom were likely to be on the increase in lessons devoted to practicing TL subsystems, such as grammar or vocabulary, as well as those dedicated to the development of receptive skills (i.e., reading and listening) but also the skill of writing. What is interesting, similar conclusions can be reached about the classes that were investigated in the present research project. Third, the patterns of teacher and student boredom overlapped in most cases, which once again provides support for the crossover theory (cf. Hatfield et al., 1994). In cases where differences were detected in this respect, they were primarily related to *teacher passivity*, or situations in which the teacher did not exactly know what to do when the students (at least some of them) were involved in performing the assigned tasks and activities, a finding which, yet again, is in line with the outcomes reported above. Fourth, examining the values of standard deviation (.21–.55), it becomes clear that the two teachers were quite consistent in their perceptions of their students' boredom as well as their own over time. This said, it should be emphasized once again that the two teachers had self-selected to provide data about the experience of boredom during their classes, which indicates that they were highly dedicated and enthusiastic. This must have undoubtedly colored their perceptions of the feeling of boredom that they themselves believed they experienced or that was in their opinion manifested by their students.

> **Reflective Break**
> - In your opinion, which part of the L2 classes that you conduct is the most boredom-provoking for your students? Why do you think they are the most bored at this particular point in time?
> - When you look at your L2 classes from a wider perspective, which of them do you perceive as the most boring for your students? While answering this question, think about activity types, L2 material and topics your classes are usually devoted to.
> - How do you perceive your experience of boredom as compared to that of your students? Is it more or less intense than in the case of your students?
> - Do you think your own and/or your students' boredom is a contagious experience? Provide one or two examples in this respect.

5.7 LIMITATIONS OF THE STUDY

The present study is among the first to have addressed boredom both in L2 learning and teaching and therefore it should not be overly surprising that it suffers from a number of weaknesses that should be taken heed of in research projects with the same or similar focus undertaken in the future. First, even though the number of participants was respectable and it exceeded 100, which is definitely sufficient in a largely qualitative study, the teachers had decided to self-select in response to a call posted on Facebook, which in itself could have affected the results of the study. This problem is even more acute in the case of the two participants who consented to fill out reports concerning the classes that they taught as it could reasonably be assumed that they were much more dedicated and enthusiastic than most of their colleagues, which must have skewed the findings of this part of the study in some way. Second, the data obtained in this investigation could have been enriched by, for example, including interviews with some of the participants as they could have surely shed more light on the occurrence of boredom among learners and teachers and the strategies employed to mitigate this negative emotion. However, it was incredibly difficult to get Polish teachers of English to fill out the anonymous questionnaire, not to mention providing reports on the lessons they taught, with the effect that other ways of data collection were not really contemplated. Third, although this was not one of its aims, the study would have surely benefitted from an attempt to develop and validate a scale that would tap into the experience of boredom among L2 teachers, a task that future research should definitely try to accomplish. Fourth, due to the nature of this study, no attempt could be made to determine how the participating teachers' perceptions were mediated by their individual profiles (e.g., beliefs, strategies, personality, other emotions) that could be determined on the basis of research into IDs as such (cf. Dörnyei & Ryan, 2015). Fifth, there are teacher-related variables, such as well-being (Mercer, 2021), burnout or demotivation (Kim & Kim, 2022) that were not considered in this investigation but should be surely given attention in future research projects on L2 teacher boredom. For example, SLA researchers may look into the extent to which L2 teacher boredom is likely to contribute to the state of emotional exhaustion and personal inefficacy or they may investigate whether the options for enhancing L2 teacher well-being can become helpful in coping with the experience of boredom (cf. Greenier et al., 2021; Kostoulas & Lämmerer, 2020). Sixth, the study was undertaken in a very specific educational and national context, with the effect that its results may not be fully applicable to other settings.

Reflective Break
- Having read the report of the study (or at least its parts), what do you consider to be its greatest drawback?

5.8 WHAT DOES IT ALL MEAN?

Before we move on to the discussion of how teachers can engage with reflective practice with respect to L2 boredom in the next chapter of the book, it is useful to highlight some of the most crucial insights emanating from the research project as they will somewhat naturally provide points of departure for such reflection. These are as follows:

- the teachers manifested a low tendency to experience boredom in general, which can be related to their age (i.e., mid-thirties) and teaching experience (ca. 12 years);
- the causes and symptoms of learners' boredom from the perspective of the participating teachers could largely be explained in terms of theoretical accounts of this negative emotion (see Chapter 3) and to a large extent mirrored the findings of previous studies; the discrepancies that were revealed

stemmed in all likelihood from the fact that data were drawn from L2 teachers at different educational levels, not just universities;

- the teachers tended to adopt a reactive rather than proactive approach to combating the boredom experienced by their learners; in other words, they mostly focused on cure rather than prevention;
- the factors impacting teachers' boredom could also mostly be accounted for against the backdrop of theories developed in educational psychology (see Chapter 2) and they can be regarded as to a large extent universal; the experience of boredom as reported by the participants was for the most part transitory, which might indicate that they are better able to combat this negative emotion among their learners;
- the inventory of strategies used by the participating teachers to cope with their boredom was limited and such strategies were typically described in general terms; this might indicate that the teachers were not overly concerned with the detrimental effects of this emotion or that they were reluctant to admit that they experienced it in the first place and mostly chose to ignore it;
- although the responses were far from unanimous, there was some evidence for the link between L2 boredom manifested by learners and teachers; the teachers, however, saw this relationship as unidirectional, with learner boredom triggering their own boredom, while there are grounds to believe that the influence is reciprocal;
- L2 boredom was shown to fluctuate during the classes conducted by the two teachers as well as from one class to the next, with reasons for those fluctuations mirroring those identified in previous research; the intensity of this negative emotion was on the whole low for both students and teachers and its patterns were in most cases similar for both groups; such findings, however, could be the corollary of the fact that the two teachers who had volunteered to provide classroom data were highly dedicated and motivated.

Reflective Break
- Which of the takeaways from the study listed above do you see as the most surprising and why?

CONCLUSION

The present chapter has been devoted to the presentation and discussion of the findings of the study which sought to tap into boredom in L2 classes from the perspective of teachers. More specifically, this empirical investigation aimed to shed light on the causes and manifestations of this negative emotion experienced by learners and teachers as well as the strategies that can be drawn on in both cases to mitigate its occurrence. In addition, the research project intended to determine whether boredom was subject to change as a result of internal and external factors, both in the case of L2 teachers and their learners. On the whole, although this study is surely not free from limitations, it has undoubtedly provided invaluable insights into the ways in which boredom is perceived by L2 teachers and the ways of reducing it, even if those teachers were recruited from one educational context. In particular, it was revealed that the causes and manifestations of boredom as well as the ways of dealing with this aversive emotion mirror to a large extent those that were revealed in prior studies. Such findings provide a basis for concrete pedagogical proposals that will be outlined in the following chapter but also offer an impetus for future empirical investigations that will be tackled in the conclusion to this book.

Chapter 6

Integrating Theory and Practice: Reflective Practice with Respect to Boredom

INTRODUCTION

While the initial four chapters of the present book provided the necessary review of the literature concerning the role of positive and negative emotions, in particular boredom, in L2 pedagogy, the previous one was empirical in nature and reported the results of a study which looked at this aversive emotion from the standpoint of language teachers. The purpose of this final chapter is twofold. First, it relates the experience of boredom in language classrooms as well as ways of preventing and combating it that can provide a springboard for stimulating reflective practice in L2 education (Farrell, 2014b, 2018, 2019, 2022). Second, it brings together theoretical and empirical perspectives in order to provide specific guidelines on dealing with boredom experienced by L2 learners and teachers in the classroom in an attempt to offer a coherent model of pedagogical interventions in this respect. In effect, this chapter will be admittedly more practical in nature than the remainder of the volume. With all of this in mind, it will open with an attempt to briefly discuss issues in reflective practice and to illustrate how awareness of the different aspects of boredom can be tied to promoting reflection in L2 learning and teaching. This will be followed by a set of principles that can be embraced and concrete steps that can be taken in order to both prevent and diminish the experience of this negative emotion by learners and teachers.

6.1 ISSUES IN REFLECTIVE PRACTICE IN L2 TEACHING

Farrell (2007) defined reflective teaching in the following, very accessible way: "When teachers reflect on their teaching, generally they take the time to stop and think about what is happening in their practice to make sense of it so that they can learn from their professional experiences" (p. 2). Recently, he provided a more elaborate characterization of the construct, according to which reflective practice is "a cognitive process accompanied by a set of attitudes in which teachers systematically collect data about their practice, and, while engaging in dialogue with others, use the data to make informed decisions about their practice both inside and outside the classroom" (Farrell, 2014b, p. 123). Leaving the details aside, the two definitions clearly indicate that reflective practitioners are characterized by a mindset, ability, readiness and in some cases also the wherewithal that allow them to systematically engage in thinking about and discussing their instructional practices in the hope of improving on them and thus making the processes of L2 teaching and learning more effective.

Even though many teachers, including L2 teachers, might consider such reflection to be superfluous and in fact think that it only further adds to the multitude of tasks they need to complete on a daily basis (e.g., planning lessons, developing tests, grading papers, dealing with institutional mandates and filling out necessary documentation), adopting such a reflective approach has a number of evident benefits. In the first place, it helps avoid or at least minimize the danger of suffering from burnout as a result of following the same routines, based on the knowledge gained during teacher education programs, dominant traditions, externally imposed requirements or perhaps impulse-driven choices made over and over again. Equally importantly, engaging in reflective practice has the potential to enhance understanding of teaching practices, even when they are based on theoretically or empirically driven recommendations, to improve decision-making over different time scales (e.g., with respect to an entire course, a sequence of classes or an activity being performed in a particular lesson), to enhance self-confidence in relation to the choice of instructional options as well as other actions taken in the classroom and in many cases also to make a major contribution to professional growth (cf. Farrell, 2007, 2011, 2013, 2018, 2019). Finally, it could also be argued that, when reflective teaching translates into more enjoyable, more engaging, better organized and, above all, more effective instruction, this can enhance the teacher's well-being, or happiness about and satisfaction with this demanding job (cf. Mercer & Gregersen, 2020).

Over the years several theoretical accounts of teacher reflection have been proposed. For one thing, there is a consensus that three distinct levels of reflection can be distinguished even if different labels are employed to describe them (Farrell, 2007; Jay & Johnson, 2002; Larrivee, 2008). These levels include *descriptive reflection*, which is focused on a particular problem or situation, *conceptual* or *comparative reflection*, with an emphasis on the rationale for practice, which involves reexamination of belief systems, and *critical reflection*, in which case the broader context is also considered including all the players in the educational process (i.e., students, teachers, institution, parents, broader community, etc.). Specialists have also identified several approaches to reflection such as (1) *technical rationality*, where teachers' skills and actions are analyzed in relation to some theoretical or empirical basis, (2) *reflection-in-action*, where professional problems are handled on the spot as they occur in the classroom, (3) *reflection-on-action*, where teachers' behaviors or reactions are recollected and considered a posteriori after a given class has been taught, (4) *reflection-for-action*, in which case a more proactive approach is adopted and future courses of action are contemplated, often drawing on the results of other modes of reflection and (5) *action research*, where teachers engage in self-reflective inquiry into their instructional practices with the aim of improving on them (cf. Banegas & Consoli, 2020; Chien, 2013; Crookes, 2013; Farrell, 2013, 2014b; Hatton & Smith, 1995; Schön, 1983; Yang, 2009).

A number of models and frameworks of reflection have also been proposed. One of the most widely known is undoubtedly the model of reflective inquiry offered by Dewey (1933). According to this model, reflection is facilitated by adhering to the following five stages: (1) *suggestion*, where a situation is identified as problematic and initial thoughts concerning a possible solution are generated and entertained, (2) *intellectualization*, which involves refining the problem that has been encountered by posing questions pertaining to its source or nature, (3) *guiding idea*, where an initial hypothesis is formed, further evidence is collected and, if need be, perhaps also contrasted against the relevant literature, (4) *reasoning*, whereby different ideas are put together and a potential solution to the problem is generated even if it turns out not to be the optimal one, and (5) *hypothesis testing*, where the final, refined idea is conceived of and implemented, with its effect on the elimination of the problem being observed and thought about; if successful, it is retained and, if not, the cycle is set in motion yet again (cf. Farrell, 2014b).

While the contribution of the theoretical proposals and models outlined above can by no means be denied, the point of reference for further discussion will be the *framework for reflecting on practice* developed by Farrell (2014b), which is holistic in nature and, in the view of the present authors, is best suited to provide a point of departure for reflective practice with respect to the experience of boredom in teaching and learning an L2 as well as efforts aimed at avoiding or diminishing the negative effects of this aversive emotion. The model encompasses five different stages or levels of reflection, which are interconnected, affect each other and together constitute a comprehensive mechanism which in its entirety accounts for various aspects of reflection. What is particularly important, the model applies in equal measure to teachers at different stages of their careers who possess varying degrees of experience. The components of the framework are briefly characterized below (Farrell, 2014b):

1. *Philosophy*, which is related to influences that have contributed to the development of teachers as persons throughout the span of their lives, such as culture, religion, socioeconomic background, family, personal values but also perhaps, although this is not included in the original model, their personality; in order to understand their own philosophy and gain the necessary self-knowledge, teachers need to engage in self-reflection or contemplation which will increase the level of awareness of their decisions in the classroom and the sources of such decisions; such mindfulness can be stimulated by means of meditation techniques, reflective writing or teacher narratives, sometimes with a focus on critical incidents, persons or phases that may have impacted their careers.

2. *Principles*, which are reflective of the assumptions, beliefs and conceptions about L2 learning and teaching held by teachers, with all these three elements interacting to affect the actions, decisions as well as other instructional choices made in their classrooms; since, due to the numerous activities that teachers are expected to fulfill every day or their workload, they are unlikely to consciously and regularly reflect upon such issues, it is necessary to provide them with opportunities to do so; as Richards and Lockhart (1994) elucidate, this can be done by "posing questions about how and why things are the way they are, what value systems they represent, what alternatives might be available, and what the limitations are of doing things one way as opposed to another" (p. 6); such goals can be accomplished by, for example, encouraging teachers to talk about "role model teachers", to examine their maxims, or working principles, to articulate their beliefs, perhaps in response to inventories of such beliefs, or to explore their metaphors (e.g., the teacher as knowledge provider or artist).

3. *Theory*, which underlies the instructional options and resources that teachers fall back upon when it comes to introducing and practicing different TL skills or honing different language skills (e.g., grammar is best taught by following the presentation – practice – production sequence, or the PPP), planning language classes, deciding on forms of assessment, etc.; theories can derive from teacher education programs but they can also get formed based on experience; since, yet again, many teachers may not be fully cognizant of such theories or seldom have the time or opportunity to stop and contemplate them, specific steps need to be taken so that they can be articulated; for example, teachers can be asked to reflect on the entirety of lesson planning through *forward planning* (first content and then teaching methods), *central planning* (first teaching methods and then content) or *backward planning* (first outcomes and then activities to be included); they can also be requested to identify and examine critical incidents, understood as

unexpected and unplanned events during lessons that are vividly kept in memory; this can be done in collaboration with other teachers, by responding to questionnaires specifically designed for this purpose, collecting situations when lessons break down and can no longer proceed in an effective way, or reporting and analyzing specific cases (cf. Brookfield, 1995; Richards, 2013; Richards & Farrell, 2005).

4. *Practice*, which represents the aspects of teaching that are amenable to observation and inspection such as teachers' actions and behaviors in the classroom as well as learners' reactions to such instructional practices (e.g., their engagement, however it is conceptualized, or disengagement); obviously, actions and behaviors of this kind are closely related to and influenced by the less visible elements described above, that is, philosophy, principles and theory; when examining their observable instructional practices, teachers can engage in reflection-in-action or reflection-on-action, which can subsequently provide a basis for reflection-for-action (see above); reflection at this stage can be facilitated through observations that can be conducted by teachers themselves (self-observation), their peers (peer observation), which can involve team teaching, lesson study and peer coaching, or with the help of audio- or video-recording; another possibility is conducting action research projects that can in some cases involve collaboration among teachers (cf. Bailey, 2001; Johnson, 2009; Richards, 1990; Richards & Farrell, 2005; Richards & Lockhart, 1994).

5. *Beyond practice*, which is related to external influences on instructional practices; such influences can manifest themselves, for example, at the level of a particular school, local community or countrywide educational policy; they can reflect, among others, the interests of specific groups (e.g., teachers in an institution, principals or parents), ideological agendas (e.g., the promotion of a specific L2 at the expense of others) as well as economic and organizational issues (e.g., limited funding, time constraints, room availability); in this way, reflective practice is extended beyond individuals and involves critical dialog with others, which allows careful evaluation and reflection but also provides a crucial impulse for collaborative learning (Crow & Smith, 2005); such critical reflection can be fostered by formation of teacher reflection groups, which can be combined with journal writing and lesson observation.

There are two important points that need to be articulated about this framework but also about reflection more generally. First, reflective practice can be directed at the entirety of the teaching process but also at its very specific aspects (e.g., teaching grammar or vocabulary, assessment or emotions, in particular boredom which is the most relevant to this discussion). Second, the framework is predicated on the assumption that teachers vary in the extent to which they choose to engage in reflection, either because of contextual constraints or because of their psychological makeup or simply attitudes toward the need for reflective practice vis-à-vis the burdens placed on them in professional and personal lives.

Reflection break
- To what extent do you engage in reflection on your teaching practice at the five levels included in the model described in this section?
- In your opinion, what factors encourage and discourage such reflection?
- Which of the techniques for stimulating reflection mentioned in this section are you familiar with and try to use? Which of them do you view as easy or difficult to take advantage of in your professional context? Why?

6.2 EXPLORING LINKS BETWEEN REFLECTIVE PRACTICE AND L2 BOREDOM

A crucial question that needs to be addressed at this point is how dealing with boredom fits in with the framework outlined above or, rather, how this framework can be employed to stimulate reflection on how this negative emotion can be prevented or combated in the case of both learners and teachers. At the level of *philosophy*, there is an issue as to whether the value system that teachers cherish assumes that emotions, whether positive or negative, including boredom, should get in the way of everyday functioning, also with respect to L2 education. There is also the question concerning predispositions that can be viewed as more trait-like than state-like in nature, such as general boredom proneness (Farmer & Sundberg, 1986), as well as personality. It could reasonably be argued, for example, that teachers who are generally more likely to succumb to boredom are also more likely to experience this negative emotion in the classroom and also be less likely to react to it when they observe it among their students. However, this does not have to be the case if such teachers are characterized by what is referred to in the Big Five Model (McCrae & Costa, 2003) of personality as openness to experience since their curiosity, open-mindedness, awareness of their own feelings or need for change might to some extent counterbalance the overall tendency to feel bored. At the same time, these traits might also impact teachers' readiness to engage in reflection on boredom in the first place. For instance, those who are themselves less prone to boredom and more open to experience might be more likely to reflect on this negative emotion, its causes, manifestations and effects, with respect to both themselves and their learners.

Whatever the case might be, reliance on appropriate techniques, such as reflective writing, is likely to enhance teachers' self-knowledge in this respect.

Moving on to the level of *principles*, teachers might vary quite considerably in how they perceive the role of various emotions, including boredom, in the process of L2 learning and teaching. There are surely practitioners who, perhaps under the influence of their own experiences as L2 learners (Richards & Lockhart, 1994), are convinced of the contribution of affective factors and the need to effectively deal with them on a daily basis in the classroom, but many other teachers might view them as largely irrelevant for a variety of reasons. Some of them, for example, might believe that effective L2 learning is mainly the outcome of cognitive processes, factors affecting these processes (e.g., aptitude, learning styles, learning strategies) and the instructional techniques employed, while others might recognize the role of emotions at least to some extent but might consciously choose to ignore them, either because of lack of time or the conviction that it is not their job to tamper with learners' emotional sphere, often, yet again, as a reflection of their own individual profiles or perhaps previous learning experiences. Such assumptions, beliefs and conceptions in relation to L2 boredom can be brought to consciousness when teachers are given a chance to ruminate on how the principles they often implicitly subscribe to impact their take on this negative emotion and ways of responding to it by, for instance, pondering over their working principles, thinking about role models or coming up with metaphors concerning their jobs.

Reflection on L2 boredom is also relevant at the stage of *theory* because the instructional choices that teachers make in their classrooms are reflective to a greater or lesser extent of the theoretical positions that were conveyed to them in teacher educational programs, even if such theories or hypotheses may not have been fully understood or only some of their elements are in fact remembered, often quite vaguely. Obviously, instructional practices can also draw upon "unofficial" theories or "theories-in-use" (Argyris & Schön, 1974) which teachers may have formed on the basis of their experience, sometimes intuitively linking them with "official" theories referred to above. Therefore, the decision to contemplate the causes and manifestations of boredom or ways of combating this negative emotion can be grounded, for instance, in the affective filter hypothesis (Krashen, 1987), the broaden-and-build theory (Fredrickson, 1998) or the control-value theory of achievement emotions (Pekrun, 2006). Alternatively, it may derive from previous teaching situations in which, when more or less deliberately ignored, boredom spun out of control and became transformed from its indifferent, calibrating or searching variants to much more detrimental reactant or apathetic types (Goetz et al., 2014). In order to become aware of the link between the theories they adhere to and their approach to L2 boredom, teachers can be encouraged to reflect on lesson planning in an attempt to see whether their plans leave room for dealing with this negative phenomenon (but perhaps other emotions as well), to identify critical incidents in which boredom may have played a crucial role, or to discuss with other teachers cases when extremely acute teacher or student boredom may have caused language lessons to go off track.

When it comes to the stage of *practice*, it is here that reflection with respect to boredom, whether experienced by learners, teachers or both parties, has the potential to become the most immediate and also the most tangible. This is because observation of the instructional practices in which teachers themselves or their colleagues engage provides an invaluable opportunity to determine much more precisely the reasons why boredom should become a problem in the first place, pinpoint its symptoms and perhaps also observe whether the negative emotion can be nipped in the bud, ameliorated to some extent or eliminated with the help of some pedagogical interventions. For example, when a language lesson is actually in progress, teachers do not only have to speculate about the hypothetical influence of their philosophy, principles or theories on how they perceive boredom or what they choose to do about it, but they can in fact find out in real time which topics, activities and tasks or student groupings are more boredom-inducing than others and whether introducing some changes in this respect will be beneficial. Such reflection, whether in the form of reflection-in-action or reflection-on-action can be stimulated by self- and peer-observation, lesson study or team teaching as well as drawing on audio- and video-recordings of the classes being taught. Insights obtained from these reflective practices can then be used in the course as an impulse for reflection-for-practice, where, for instance, techniques for preventing or coping with boredom can be contemplated.

Reflective practice with respect to boredom can also be linked to external influences on instructional practices that are referred to in Farrell's (2014b) model as the *beyond practice* stage. While such influences are bound to be context-dependent, however broadly this context may be defined (e.g., on national level, in terms of a specific community or a particular school), they can also determine the extent to which positive and negative emotions, including boredom, can even be viewed as an issue that is worthy of serious consideration, let alone deserving of taking specific steps to be addressed in one way or another. For instance, school principals or parents might be of the opinion that teachers should basically confine themselves to practicing TL subsystems or skills rather than trying to interfere with learners' emotions, not least because they do not have the requisite qualifications to do so. Moreover, such sentiments may be shared by many students themselves, especially older ones, not to mention the fact that acute time constraints and examination requirements may effectively preclude giving attention to affective issues, with emotions such as boredom thus being ignored in the classroom. In order to fully understand the nature of such influences and potentially devise ways of circumventing them, collaboration between teachers can be encouraged in the form of teacher development groups (Farrell, 2018), accompanied by other reflection-prompting techniques, such as observation of lessons or journal writing.

As highlighted when describing the framework for reflective practice in the previous section, it can by no means be taken for granted that every teacher in every context will engage in reflection on L2 boredom and that this reflection will encompass all the five stages included in the model. This is because, for example, some teachers may simply be reluctant to reflect on their instructional practices in general and, even when they are convinced to do so, they might prefer to focus on issues related to the teaching of TL skills and subsystems as most relevant to students' success on final examinations. Engaging in reflective practice might also prove to be a daunting challenge for novice teachers who struggle to simply survive in the classroom in the first place and who are thus more likely to think about those aspects of everyday teaching that can ensure such survival, with boredom being a very unlikely candidate. Finally, boredom as well as other emotions are perhaps the most likely to be reflected upon with respect to everyday practice rather than the remaining stages of the model for the simple reason that this might hold the promise of effectively dealing with this negative emotion.

Reflective Break

- Do you ever reflect on boredom manifested by your students but also yourself in your teaching? What form does such reflection take?
- How realistic is it to reflect on learner and teacher boredom at the five stages described above? Please justify your opinion.

6.3 DEALING WITH BOREDOM IN L2 CLASSROOMS: THEORY, RESEARCH AND TEACHERS' VOICES

The aim of the present section is to provide a set of tentative guidelines that can be followed in order to prevent the occurrence of boredom in the L2 classroom or to reduce its negative effects once this distressing emotion begins to manifest itself, both in the case of learners and teachers. Those pedagogical recommendations are based on the theoretical accounts of boredom and the empirical evidence that have been overviewed in Chapters 2–4 of this book as well as the results of the study that was reported in Chapter 5. For the sake of clarity but also in recognition of the fact that the nature, manifestations and consequences of boredom experienced by L2 learners and teachers are at least in some cases distinct, these recommendations are presented separately for these two groups. This said, it should be borne in mind that, even though the participants of the investigation conducted for the purpose of this book were far from unanimous in their views on the connection between learner and teacher boredom, and they mostly viewed the influence as unidirectional (i.e., boredom experienced by learners bringing about this negative emotion in teachers), emotional contagion can work in both directions. Therefore, it appears reasonable that efforts to reduce boredom should be coordinated in the sense that they should be directed at this negative phenomenon both in the case of learners and teachers. It should also be stressed at this juncture that the extent to which the guidelines can be followed will depend both on their feasibility in a given instructional setting (e.g., the amount of time available, the need to focus on external requirements) and philosophy, principles, belief systems, as well as theories subscribed to by the teachers themselves, a constellation that can only be fully comprehended and perhaps changed to some extent through conscious reflection.

6.3.1 Dealing with Learner Boredom

When discussing ways of confronting the negative emotion of boredom afflicting learners in the L2 classroom, a vital distinction must be made between a *proactive* and *reactive* approach, a differentiation that was stressed when discussing the findings of the empirical investigation in Chapter 5. In accordance with the logical assumption that prevention is usually better than cure, teachers should first and foremost take steps to minimize the likelihood that high levels of learner boredom will occur in their lessons. One way to achieve this goal is to *sensitize students to the experience of boredom* in the L2 classroom, both more generally and with respect to specific tasks and activities. This could involve, for example, getting learners to discuss the positive and negative emotions that they experience in the process of learning an additional language in an institutional context but also outside the classroom with a specific focus on boredom and the way it interacts with other emotions. Brief discussions of this kind could also be retrospective in nature and take place periodically in relation to very specific instructional practices that have been employed in the classroom as well as homework assignments as this would allow students to focus more concretely on specific activities, topics, lesson foci or classroom organization modes. One could also envisage administering short surveys that could be used for this purpose, with the crucial caveat that this could be exceedingly time-consuming and could thus best be done only perhaps once in a semester. Another possibility is *to tap into the levels of boredom and its antecedents* by means of some of the tools that have been developed by researchers, such as the *Boredom Proneness Scale* (Farmer & Sundberg, 1986) or the *Boredom in Practical English Language Classes – Revised Questionnaire* (Pawlak et al., 2020) as this can help teachers assess the gravity of the problem and get at least an initial idea concerning the causes of this negative emotion. Once it has been established that boredom constitutes a major problem in a particular learner group, an attempt can be made to *identify the prevalent boredom-coping profiles* of the students falling back on the division into evaders, criticizers and reappraisers proposed by Nett et al. (2010) and described in detail in Chapter 3. Determining such profiles is important as it may help teachers decide on the most beneficial course of action with respect to the need for reliance on boredom-coping strategies and choosing those that might be the most beneficial in this context.

While many teachers might quite reasonably argue that the procedures described above are overly time-consuming and it is simply not practicable to implement them on a regular basis in the vast majority of L2 classrooms, efforts to prevent boredom from occurring do not have to be confined to a direct focus on this negative emotion or even other emotions as well. In fact, this goal can also be achieved somewhat "along the way" when planning and implementing classes, choosing specific instructional practices, assigning homework as well as raising L2 learners' awareness of such practices. Perhaps the most obvious solution would be to *introduce as much variety as possible* as this brings with it a number of benefits (e.g., catering for individual learner differences), one of which is that learners will not so easily succumb to boredom. In fact, even activities that have been shown to be very boredom-inducing in many studies, including the present investigation, such as practicing grammar structures or developing reading skills, do not have to generate excessive bored reactions if they are adeptly integrated into classes and interwoven with other tasks (e.g., exercises focusing on a grammar feature could be separated with speaking activities), but also if they are conducted in different ways (e.g., different types of reading or listening comprehension items are utilized). This applies in equal measure to homework assignments which, when repetitive, could become a major source of after-class boredom in L2 learning (cf. Pawlak et al., 2022a). Diversification of instructional practices can also involve *reliance on additional resources*. This could simply indicate going beyond the contents of the coursebook by introducing additional activities and materials, but, as the results of the study reported in the previous chapter have clearly demonstrated, in most cases, it is likely to entail the use of new technologies. Reliance on such technologies allows, among other things, greater access to authentic resources, often in audiovisual form, as well as the option for practicing TL skills and subsystems in more attractive and engaging ways with the help of various applications, Internet websites and devices that students simply cannot live without, in particular smartphones.

There are a number of other solutions that can be drawn upon to reduce boredom, many of which can be associated with what is commonly seen as more effective instruction or actions aimed at fostering learner autonomy. Although it is simply not possible to give justice to all such options here, some of them are surely worth highlighting. One of them is *attempting to match the level of difficulty of the tasks and activities implemented in the classroom to learners' TL proficiency* as much as possible. While this is by no means intended to suggest that students should not be challenged or that there is no need to periodically revise what they have already been taught, it is evident from theoretical accounts of boredom (e.g., Larson & Richards, 1991) as well as the existing empirical evidence (e.g., Pawlak et al., 2020) that both underchallenging and overchallenging tasks are among the main culprits of boredom. For example, teachers may fall back on compulsory + optional or open-ended strategies (Ur, 1996). In the former case, learners are given a task and are told that only one part of it has to be performed by all students, whereas the rest is done only by some (e.g., more proficient) learners. In the latter case, answers that students are expected to provide are not limited in number. Teachers can also try *to make classes more interactive* by, for example, including numerous discussion tasks, and *to strike a balance between teacher- and learner-centered lesson stages* as well as *between activities aimed at honing receptive and productive skills*. Another possibility is *raising learners' awareness of their goals* in learning a particular L2 and how specific tasks and activities used in the classroom can facilitate the attainment of these goals. Even though numerous techniques could be implemented with this purpose in mind, particularly useful appears to be *visualization*, which would not only be instrumental in stimulating a search for novelty and meaning but would also assist learners in creating more tangible ideal L2 selves (cf. Csizér, 2020; Dörnyei, 2009; Henry, 2020). Teachers can also *delegate responsibility* for some of the things that transpire in the classroom to their students, by, for example, asking them to look for materials related to a specific topic or engage in peer teaching. In this way teachers could also capitalize on the tuition that learners might have informally received in one way or another. A related idea is *introducing an element of choice* by occasionally allowing students to choose the focus of a given class or its part, but also by including once in a while a period of time when they can engage with things of their own choosing based on several alternatives proposed by the teacher (e.g., activities devoted to vocabulary or grammar, reading for pleasure, creative writing, a communicative task). Finally, worth mentioning is also *negotiating certain aspects of the course* with students (e.g., the degree of reliance on the coursebook, the choice of topics to be covered or the resources that can provide a springboard for discussing such topics) as well as *devising individual study plans* for some students, perhaps those that are far more advanced than the rest of the class or those that are most visibly lagging behind.

Obviously, no matter what teachers may strive to do to attempt to prevent boredom from occurring in their L2 classrooms, it is inevitable that some learners will succumb to this negative emotion in some situations, either because the focus of a lesson might be inherently boring (e.g., the need to concentrate on exam preparation or the practice of a specific TL feature) or because some of the topics and tasks will be viewed as inherently tedious by individual learners. There are several courses of action that can be taken in such situations, an important caveat being that they have to be adjusted to a specific learner group, a particular student, as well as the focus and nature of the class being taught. Perhaps the most obvious way of implementing such a reactive approach is *introducing change* when signs of boredom occur and appear to be affecting the majority of the students. Such change could be immediate, as is the case when the teacher chooses to abandon a current activity and switch to a different one, or delayed, in which case a decision is made to abandon, when possible, tasks that are visibly boredom-inducing in a subsequent class with a similar focus with another learner group or in lessons that are taught to the same group of learners in the future. Bringing about change is also closely related to another way of reducing boredom mentioned by the participants of the study reported in Chapter 5, namely, an attempt to *make language lessons more dynamic*. This could be done, for example, by *introducing activities that require learners to move around the room* (e.g., telling about an unforgettable day in their lives to as many peers as possible) or *opting for short tasks that could be completed in a few minutes* (e.g., a brief discussion on a controversial topic or a short communicative game) but which would help break the monotony and the inherently mundane character of things that may simply have to be covered in class (e.g., some points of grammar or specific writing genres). Teachers can also resort to a number of other techniques, such as *using humor* (e.g., telling jokes or funny stories) on condition that they make sure that what they find funny is likely to be funny for their students, *drawing on the element of surprise* (e.g., the text that students read or listen to might be chosen in such a way as to contradict their initial beliefs, predictions or expectations) and also perhaps *introducing short breaks* when students are becoming evidently inattentive or distracted. While this might be regarded as highly controversial, one could also envisage *deliberately extending an activity that is highly boredom-inducing* so that students become more eager to confront a new, different and perhaps more challenging task. For example, learners might be more eager to engage in a decision task performed in groups after having spent a considerable amount of time on an activity focusing on modal verbs. Finally, when thinking of ways of diminishing the likelihood of the occurrence of boredom outside the classroom, students could be provided with options that would make the process more engaging, such as the need to draw on Internet-based resources, as the case would be when performing various types of WebQuests (cf. Aydin, 2015).

Reflective Break
- Which of the guidelines suggested above do you find the most and the least realistic in your context? Why?

> • Which of the steps intended to reduce learner boredom do you use in your own teaching? Can you give a few examples?

6.3.2 Dealing with Teacher Boredom

Offering guidelines on combating L2 teacher boredom is a formidable challenge because the theories of boredom discussed in Chapter 3 have been primarily proposed to account for this negative emotion in the case of learners and there is a paucity of research, whether in the field of educational psychology or SLA, that would have focused on boredom among practitioners. This said, some recommendations can still be made at this juncture based on the results of the empirical investigation reported in Chapter 5, the scant empirical evidence that was overviewed in Chapter 4 as well as the solutions that have been suggested with respect to learner boredom. Also in this case, there are grounds to assume that stymying boredom from the get-go by reducing the likelihood of its occurrence is a much more effective option than trying to deal with it once its symptoms have started to manifest themselves. Many of the steps that can be taken to prevent this negative emotion mirror those that teachers could fall back on to avert it among their students, which is hardly surprising in view of the interdependency of emotions displayed by individuals. This could entail, for instance, *consciously reflecting on the role of emotions, in particular boredom*, in the process of L2 instruction, also with respect to which topics, tasks and activities could be the most likely to be tedious when used repetitively and with little reflection. Thus, teachers could try *to self-diagnose their general boredom proneness* or their propensity to succumb to this aversive emotion once a suitable scale has been developed for this purpose. Once it has been determined that their chances of getting bored are high, they can *establish their boredom-coping profiles*, which could be instrumental in effectively managing this negative emotion.

As is the case with learners, teacher boredom can be warded off by changing some of the practices directly associated with L2 instruction. For example, these could include:

- *varying the teaching routine, introducing additional, more interesting materials and resources* that go beyond the contents included in coursebooks, capitalizing on the virtually unlimited opportunities afforded by new technologies;
- *enhancing interaction in the classroom* with the help of different types of communication-based tasks or frequent reliance upon pair and group work;
- *providing copious opportunities for the use of the grammar and vocabulary taught in communication*;
- *involving learners in conducting lessons or their parts*, which could entail, for instance, asking students who are top of their class to introduce and explain

selected points of grammar or having volunteers design lessons around their hobbies;

- *negotiating with the students* the amount and nature of homework assignments, the topics to be covered in class or the objectives they would like to achieve within a certain timeframe (e.g., individual study plans).

All these steps are important in view of the fact that the participants of this study pointed to repetitiveness, overreliance on mundane resources and the need to introduce and practice specific elements of the TL as major causes of boredom. In a somewhat similar vein, since teacher passivity was listed as one of the triggers of this negative emotion, teachers would be well advised to *plan in advance what they intend to do when students are busy* working on a test, a writing assignment or a listening or reading activity.

As was the case with learners, since it is simply not possible to anticipate and minimize the negative consequences of boredom in advance in all instances, teachers also need to have at their disposal techniques that would enable them to combat this aversive emotion "on the spot". Perhaps the most obvious solution in this case, one that was frequently mentioned by the participants of this study, is *changing the way in which a particular class is being conducted*, which, quite unsurprisingly, mirrors the most common boredom-coping strategy used with learners. These changes could affect various aspects of a lesson and involve, for example, a switch to a different activity with a similar focus, introduction of a totally new task, perhaps one that would require spontaneous communication, a transition to a different mode of classroom organization (most likely from whole-class teaching to pair and group work), or implementation of activities involving movement or simply some form of physical exercise. Another possibility is *to get actively involved* in the tasks performed by learners whenever such an opportunity presents itself. This mostly applies to pair and group-work tasks based on different forms of discussion or decision-making to which teachers could make a contribution when circulating around the room as well as games in which they could join in as active participants. When the situation gets out of hand in the sense that learners start to act in a disruptive manner or completely switch off in response to boredom, *teachers might need to improvise*, which could involve using humor, telling jokes, introducing interesting tidbits about the country where the TL is spoken, initiating a short discussion on a highly controversial topic or, if everything else fails, changing the focus of the class completely by moving to a different unit in the coursebook. In view of the fact that some classes may be inherently boring for teachers who have to cover all the things comprised by the core curriculum or go over the same coursebook activities over and over again, it might be necessary sometimes *to consciously suppress the feeling of boredom* simply to prevent it from spreading among students. One thing that could help it is to put oneself in the shoes of learners in order to remind oneself of the challenges of the process of L2 learning and the need to put up with things that are inherently boring in order to ultimately succeed in this undertaking.

Reflective Break
- Which of the recommendations listed above do you find the most and the least realistic in your context? Why?
- Which of the techniques intended to reduce teacher boredom do you use? Please provide examples. Which of them would you be willing to employ? Why?

CONCLUSION

The present chapter has been primarily practical in nature and it has sought to attain two main goals, that is, to illustrate how reflection on L2 boredom can be related to the model of reflective practice proposed by Farrell (2014b) and to provide a set of principles and guidelines for preventing as well as coping with learner and teacher boredom. What needs to be stressed at this juncture is the fact that the extent to which L2 boredom can be reflected upon, prevented or combated in the classroom or outside is bound to hinge upon the philosophy, beliefs systems as well as official and unofficial theories adhered to by practitioners, and the circumstances in which they have to function on a daily basis in their professional contexts (e.g., the number of contact classes, curriculum-related demands, examination requirements, expectations of parents and educational authorities). The present authors are fully aware that, given more pressing priorities, such as the need to cover a number of TL features, develop different language skills and enhance communicative ability, let alone all the other challenges that the job of the teacher involves in any setting, it would be wishful thinking to assume that L2 boredom will become a very frequent object of reflective practices or pedagogical interventions emanating from such practices. This having been said, we are also convinced that L2 boredom can have such a detrimental effect on the quality of L2 learning inside and outside the classroom as well as the outcomes of this process that it surely deserves to be contemplated, hampered and combated in everyday teaching practice. It is our hope that the suggestions for reflection included in this chapter will help raise teachers' cognizance of this negative emotion and encourage at least some of them to try to ameliorate the problems that it inevitably brings with it.

Chapter 7

Awareness-raising Activities Stimulating Reflection on L2 Boredom

INTRODUCTION

While the guidelines for reducing learner and teacher boredom provided in Chapter 6 are undoubtedly valuable, it is also undeniable that they are extremely difficult to implement in everyday classroom practice. For one thing, teachers in most cases are obliged to adhere to an externally imposed curriculum which primarily focuses on the development of TL subsystems and skills in order to prepare students for different examinations, leaving little room and time for other issues. Even when such "additional issues" are to some extent taken into consideration, perhaps because they are included as educational goals in curricula, teachers are much more likely to zoom in on those that, in their view, have the potential to enhance the process of L2 teaching and learning as well as the outcomes of this process. As a result, while they might be ready to engage to some extent in, for example, instruction in selected learning or testing strategies, the promotion of learner autonomy, the implementation of information and computer technologies, the individualization of instructional practices or the development of intercultural competence, dealing with emotions, including boredom, is likely to take a back seat. In addition, teachers might feel unprepared to interfere with their learners' affect and therefore reluctant to do this, all the more so because not all students might be enthusiastic about such interventions. In view of all of these challenges, there are grounds to assume that the very first step in getting teachers to notice boredom for what it really is and to in fact attempt to combat it should involve encouraging them to engage in reflection on the causes and manifestations of this aversive emotion as well as the potential coping strategies, preferably at all the levels of the model proposed by Farrell (2018) described in Chapter 6. This goal can be attained to some degree with the assistance of the awareness-raising activities that are presented in this chapter.

Although a division is maintained between activities that can be used to encourage reflection on student and teacher boredom, given the link between the two, the former can also provide an important stimulus for the latter.

7.1 STIMULATING REFLECTION ON LEARNER BOREDOM

7.1.1 Identifying Causes and Symptoms of Boredom Among Learners Through Discussion

Teachers organize a short 15–20-minute discussion in three or four classes they teach with the purpose of determining the main causes of boredom among their students. The discussion can be preceded with a short 5-minute pair-work activity in which students would be invited to talk about the emotions that accompany them in the process of L2 learning with a specific focus on boredom. The discussion following this pair-work task should focus more squarely on the main triggers of this negative emotion and the ways in which it might manifest itself. The students might be presented with a list of sample questions which would function as prompts, such as, for example, "What emotions (e.g., enjoyment, boredom) do you usually experience during language lessons?", "What usually triggers the experience of emotions (e.g., curiosity, boredom)?", "How do such emotions (e.g., anxiety, boredom) reveal themselves?", "Do negative emotions (e.g., boredom) exceed positive ones (e.g., enjoyment)?". Either the TL taught or, when feasible, the students' mother tongue can be used for this purpose. The outcome should be a tentative list of causes and symptoms of boredom that the teacher could later reflect upon.

7.1.2 Identifying Causes and Symptoms of Boredom Among Learners Through Observation

Teachers observe 5–6 lessons they teach to different learner groups, concentrating on boredom that their learners experience. In particular, they try to capture the manifestations of boredom and to associate them with what transpires in class at a specific point in time (e.g., organization mode, topics discussed, TL subsystems and skills practiced, tasks and activities employed, stage of the lesson, etc.). The outcome could be a list of potential causes and symptoms of boredom matched to the aspects of L2 lessons that may be the most boredom-inducing. The list could then be possibly compared with a list drawn up by other teachers and lead to the development of a *checklist* of boredom-related symptoms together with their potential causes and aspects of instruction most likely responsible for the emergence of this negative emotion. The checklist could contain three columns as in the example below.

Symptoms of boredom	Potential causes	Related aspects of instruction
Disruptive behaviors	*Waning concentration*	*Long reading activity*
.....	.....	.....
.....	.....	.....

7.1.3 Checklist-Based Discussion

The present task constitutes a follow-up to the previous activity in section 1.2. Teachers try to find solutions to the identified causes and symptoms of learner boredom through mutual discussion. The checklist might be posted on a school website, included in a Facebook group or distributed through different applications (e.g., Twitter, WhatsApp). The identified solutions could also subsequently be posted or distributed by means of the same websites, platforms and apps.

7.1.4 Identifying Causes of and Reactions to Learner Boredom Through Critical Incidents

Either alone or together with colleagues teachers reflect on several lessons they have recently taught and try to think of situations in which learners' boredom necessitated a change in the way that a particular lesson was conducted, perhaps forcing them to deviate from the original plan or to react in an unprecedented way (e.g., transition to a different activity, change of grouping patterns or even total abandonment of the initial objectives). Once these critical episodes have been identified, teachers try to decide what made them realize that boredom was having a detrimental effect on the lesson and what may have triggered this negative emotion. They also recall their reactions to learners' bored behaviors, evaluate those reactions and reflect whether a better solution could have been applied in that specific situation. They also attempt to come up with tangible takeaways for the future.

7.1.5 Identifying Subtypes of Learner Boredom Through Reflective Journals and Discussion Groups

Teachers keep journals over the period spanning 2–4 weeks with the aim of stepping back into their recent teaching experience and descriptively classifying their students' bored behaviors into indifferent boredom, calibrating boredom, searching boredom, reactant boredom and apathetic boredom (see Chapter 2, section 2.2.). To be more precise, when making entries in their journals, they try to ascribe observed manifestations of boredom to particular subtypes of this negative emotion (e.g., acts of resistance or disruptive behavior – reactant boredom, off-task behaviors

– calibrating boredom). Having done this, they meet (either in person or online, or a combination of both settings) in groups of 3–4 teachers in order to jointly reflect on their observations and connect the identified subtypes of boredom to its sources, possibly those that were identified in Activities 1.1., 1.2 and 1.3. The activity designed in this way is expected to enhance teachers' understanding of the intricacies of learner boredom in terms of cause-and-effect relationships between its antecedents and types.

7.1.6 Measuring Student Boredom – Getting to Know Students' Inclinations

Teachers use different questionnaires which aim to tap into boredom and identify factors that are responsible for it and which have been employed by researchers (see Chapter 4). The use of such tools would help them gain insights into the general proclivity to experience boredom (e.g., *Boredom Proneness Scale*; Farmer & Sundberg, 1986), its occurrence in the L2 classroom (e.g., *Boredom in Practical English Classes – Revised*; Pawlak et al., 2020b) as well as when learners try to improve their TL skills on their own (e.g., *Boredom in Learning English Outside of School Questionnaire*; Pawlak et al., 2022a). Obviously, depending on the proficiency level of learners in a given group, such instruments might have to be translated into the students' mother tongue. Information obtained in this way could help teachers get to know their students' inclinations in relation to experiencing boredom and identify the most important triggers of this negative emotion. Such awareness could provide a basis for planning boredom-free lessons or at least such in which the danger of the occurrence of this negative emotion would be minimized.

7.1.7 Brainstorming Strategies for Coping with Boredom Among Learners in a Reflection Group

Teachers in the same schools or within a professional network create a development group in which they brainstorm and reflect on strategies that can be applied to deal with boredom among learners. Once a list of such boredom-coping strategies has been compiled, teachers discuss their effectiveness, share their experiences in using them and hold a discussion on the feasibility of implementing them in their own contexts, taking into account local realities. Since strategies for dealing with learner boredom may not be easy to talk about, not least because they are not likely to be teachers' top priority, a good point of departure for stimulating such discussion could be the guidelines for preventing and reducing boredom among learners that were presented in section 3.1. of Chapter 6. The outcome of the activity could be a tentative list of boredom-coping strategies ordered in accordance with their efficacy and feasibility. Such a list could subsequently be modified and updated over time based on teachers' experiences in implementing them.

7.1.8 Dealing with Boredom Among Learners with the Help of a Critical Friend

Two fellow teachers in the same school or professional network team up to evaluate the steps taken in order to combat boredom in their respective classrooms. Based on the outcomes of the preceding activities (Activities 1.1–1.4 above), they initially negotiate and agree on a plan of action intended to prevent bored behaviors and react to them once they have occurred. The plan is later implemented, to the extent to which it is feasible, in their respective classes, which they observe, evaluate and comment on. The discussion following such classes serves as a basis for the refinement of the preliminary course of action and devising a more comprehensive plan for combating learner boredom that can be consistently implemented in their future classes but also shared with other colleagues in the school or the network, often with the help of the Internet and social media

7.1.9 Preventing Boredom Among Learners – Making L2 Instruction More Interactive

Teachers, individually, with critical friends or in groups, go over a unit or two in the coursebook used with a given learner group as well as the curriculum on the basis of which the coursebook was written. Based on the descriptions of some of the studies discussed in Chapter 4, they make an effort to identify topics, tasks and activities that may turn out to be particularly conducive to bringing about bored behaviors in the classroom. Once these elements have been pinpointed, they try to make alterations by introducing a component that would make L2 instruction more interactive and allow relatively spontaneous communication. For example, teaching students how to write an argumentative essay could be interspersed with group-work tasks in which the pros and cons of different choices would be discussed or decisions would be made concerning some controversial issues. It is also possible to harness the potential of new technologies for this purpose (e.g., messengers or virtual worlds). For instance, instead of having students perform a mundane and repetitive communicative activity in pairs in the classroom (e.g., act out a role play), teachers could ask them to collaborate with L2 learners from a different school and set up an online connection via Skype or MS Teams. They could also invite their students to a specific location in a virtual world (e.g., Second Life, Active Worlds) to perform a given task in a simulating place (e.g., in a shop, at the cinema, in a park, in a famous museum). The lessons in which such modified tasks and activities are employed would later be observed with a focus on the occurrence of boredom and further changes would be made if necessary.

7.1.10 Preventing Boredom Among Learners – Negotiating with Students

Teachers make an effort to proactively combat boredom among their learners by occasionally negotiating with them the foci of regular classes as well as the nature and scope of homework assignments. With respect to lesson content, learners could be asked, for example, to add their own topics to be discussed in class, to find their own additional resources to complement the materials included in the coursebooks and additional materials or to identify areas of the TL that are in need of remedial teaching. In relation to homework, students could be requested to make suggestions concerning its focus, the deadlines or the ways it should be checked in the classroom. They can also be given a choice of several assignments with different foci and choose those that they view as the most interesting, engaging, relevant or simply useful. Several rounds of such negotiation could then be followed up on with a short discussion of their effects on students' boredom.

7.1.11 Preventing Boredom Among Learners by Attracting their Attention to this Negative Emotion

This is a three-stage activity that allows learners to better regulate their emotions in relation to boredom. The first stage consists of sensitizing students to the phenomenon of boredom together with its various causes and detrimental consequences. To this end, teachers encourage a whole-class discussion on boredom in L2 learning and at its starting point elicit from students possible definitions of this emotion. Then students are asked to provide examples of their own experiences of boredom and try to identify the triggers that led to them in a particular situation. In the second stage, students are divided into groups of 3 to 4 in which they come up with activities that in their opinion would keep them interested and engaged. In the third stage, members of each group present their ideas to other students in a whole-class session, they compare and evaluate their ideas and try to come up with reasons why specific activities are stimulating or, alternatively, still boring and how some of them could be enhanced even further to pique interest and engagement.

7.1.12 Combating Boredom in the Classroom – Analyzing Cases and Reflecting on/for Action

Teachers in the same school or professional network agree to observe or video-record several of their lessons and to identify situations in which student boredom might have had a negative impact on what transpired in the classroom or even led to the derailment of an entire class. Alternatively, teachers could provide written reports of such situations which they have recently experienced and share them in groups created through social media (e.g., Facebook, WhatsApp). Data of this kind would serve as stimuli for a discussion about the effectiveness of colleagues' reactions to the problem and the ways in which such reactions could have been improved upon. This would allow the development of guidelines for coping with boredom in the future which could later be updated if need be as a result of subsequent discussions.

7.1.13 Combating Boredom in the Classroom – Leading Learners up the Garden Path

This activity capitalizes on a way of teaching grammar, known as the *garden path technique* (Tomasello & Herron, 1989), in which learners are deliberately led to make an error in an effort to make the process of learning more memorable. For example, they could be given a list of regular verbs and asked to change them into the past tense, after which an irregular verb would be included which would likely generate an error. By the same token, teachers can occasionally choose activities that have to be completed in the classroom, even if they tend to be repetitive and tedious, such as different forms of grammar and vocabulary practice, and then deliberately prolong them to generate high levels of boredom. Such activities would then be followed by tasks that are important, challenging and perhaps also likely to induce boredom under normal circumstances but the element of novelty could cancel out this deleterious effect and enhance students' engagement in the new challenges. Obviously, it is up to teachers to decide on suitable tasks and activities to be used for this purpose since what is tedious and challenging could be defined very differently in different learner groups. Even though such practices can be viewed as controversial, it should be recalled that they are in line with the tenets of the multidimensional model (Pekrun et al., 2010).

7.2 STIMULATING REFLECTION ON TEACHER BOREDOM

7.2.1 Measuring Teacher Boredom – Getting to Know Teachers' Inclinations

In order to get attuned to contemplating their boredom in the L2 classroom, teachers could make use of different tools which would allow them to better understand their general boredom proneness (e.g., *Boredom Proneness Scale*; Farmer & Sundberg, 1986). Such information would contribute to raising awareness of their own propensity to succumb to this negative emotion and sensitize them to its different causes. This would be the first necessary step to considering boredom in connection to instructional activities implemented as part of L2 instruction.

7.2.2 Thinking About Boredom in one's own L2 Learning – A Retrospective Perspective

Teachers reflect on the feeling of boredom from a retrospective perspective by contemplating the experience of this negative emotion in their own L2 learning. This could take the form of writing narratives in which they would think back to and reflect on instances of feeling bored at each educational level (e.g., elementary school, secondary school, university). More specifically, they would be invited to describe in what way and why they experienced boredom but also what they did, if anything, to overcome it. In order to aid their reflection, they may consider a set of questions, such as, for example, "Who caused boredom?", "What caused boredom?", or "In what situations did you experience the most boredom?". The information obtained in this way may then be used to compare the identified causes and manifestations of boredom with those reported by their students (see subsections 1.1., 1.2. above) in order to better understand this negative emotion and try to develop ways to combat it.

7.2.3 Identifying Causes of and Solutions to Teacher Boredom – Reflective Journals

Teachers keep journals over the period of 2–4 weeks with the purpose of identifying situations in the classroom in which they experience boredom as well as the steps they take to tackle this negative emotion. Entries in such journals could be made with various frequency and be related to a particular lesson or a sequence of lessons. They could be made more specific by means of prompts such as: "In what situations did I feel bored when teaching today?", "What triggered this negative situation?"

or "How did I react?". The responses then serve as a springboard for reflection on whether more effective solutions can be found and whether the boredom-inducing situation could have been tackled differently, perhaps more effectively. Subsequently, such insights can be compared with those of other teachers, which can pave the way for developing more effective guidelines for successfully preventing and coping with boredom in a wider range of contexts.

7.2.4 Identifying Causes of and Solutions to Teacher Boredom Through Peer Observation

Teachers cooperate with critical friends, that is, other teachers in their schools or within professional networks. They take turns observing several (3–4) classes focusing on situations in which their colleagues manifest symptoms of boredom, the ways they try to overcome this negative emotion and the potential effects of such instances on the students. They take notes in the process to which they add their own comments and evaluations. The teachers subsequently meet (in person or online), exchange their notes, comments, observations and evaluations, discuss the effectiveness of their strategies and try to brainstorm the ways in which the occurrence of boredom could have been prevented in the first place as well as other, possibly more efficacious courses of action could have been embarked on to cope with this negative emotion.

7.2.5 Identifying Causes of and Solutions to Teacher Boredom Through Reflection on Specific Cases

Teachers write up one or two short classroom-based scenarios, such that are based on their own experiences or simply contrived, in which they themselves or their colleagues have succumbed to boredom, the actions that were taken in order to handle these situations and the lessons that have been drawn to prevent the detrimental effects of this negative emotion in the future. They swap these scenarios with a critical friend, their colleagues in the same school or other teachers within a professional network, and together attempt to speculate on the reasons for the occurrence of boredom, evaluate the boredom-coping strategies employed and discuss the ways in which the likelihood that such situations will be repeated in future lessons can be minimized. The main focus is on how instructional practices as well as the roles they perform with respect to those practices can be amended in order to decrease teacher boredom or perhaps even eliminate it altogether in some cases.

7.2.6 Preventing Teacher Boredom Through Collaborative Search for Solutions to Problematic Situations

This is a three-stage pair-work activity that begins with teachers writing a description of two situations in which they found themselves the most bored in the lessons they taught. In the second stage, they swap the descriptions with fellow teachers in their schools or within professional networks who approach and interpret them from a different angle, adding their own comments and suggestions meant to indicate what they would do to minimize the experience of boredom if they were in their colleagues' shoes. Finally, the third stage consists of studying each other's comments and suggestions, and argumentatively discussing these in relation to one's own expectations, self-perceived teaching achievements and/or plans for self-development as L2 teachers. Looking at their own boredom through the prism of their colleagues' lived experiences may not only help teachers cope with this negative emotion more effectively but also broaden their perspective on the challenges and pitfalls of the L2 teaching profession.

7.2.7 Preventing Teacher Boredom Through Reflecting on Positive and Negative Emotions in the L2 Classroom

A group of teachers in the same schools or within a professional network determine what emotions they most commonly display during the lessons they teach and try to provide reasons for this state of affairs. Then they prepare, negotiate and exemplify a list of things which could contribute to the manifestation of such emotions, either related to a given class being taught or the broader context. In case the teachers come to the conclusion that their negative emotions, including boredom, constituted a reflection of their students' emotions, they discuss whether they should try to interfere with (i.e., direct, enhance, suppress, etc.) emotions experienced by their learners and in what situations this should happen. In particular, they could focus on how more positive emotions could be enhanced both among students and themselves.

7.2.8 Preventing Boredom Through Reflecting on and Reacting to Learners' Coping Profiles

This activity is based on the assumption that L2 learners' reactions to boredom might impact the way in which teachers experience and react to this negative emotion. Teachers work in small groups of 3 to 4 with the aim of identifying their students' boredom-coping profiles and deciding on how this knowledge can be used to prevent or minimize this negative emotion in the learning process. They describe the most typical bored behaviors displayed by their students and collaborate to categorize them into *evaders*, *criticizers* and/or *reappraisers* (see section 2.2. in Chapter 3). If need be, they might introduce an entirely new category and perhaps even come up with a completely new way of grouping their learners in accordance with how they approach and respond to L2 boredom. Subsequently, the teachers share comments on how they usually react to their students' manifestations of boredom categorized in these ways and whether there may be a link between these manifestations and their own boredom. Finally, they brainstorm ways in which different boredom-coping profiles can be handled more effectively than may have been the case before. In consequence, adequate reactions to bored students' behaviors may lead to a decrease in teacher boredom.

7.2.9 Combating Teacher Boredom – Reflecting on the Reciprocal Nature of Teacher and Student Emotions

Working in small groups of 3 to 4, teachers reflect on and discuss situations in which their students' bored behaviors impacted their own experience of boredom, thus contributing to the phenomenon of emotional contagion (the carryover of positive and negative emotions between people). They try to compare their respective observations and brainstorm options for reducing those of student behaviors that are likely to increase teacher boredom. A tangible outcome of this activity is a checklist including student behaviors leading to teacher boredom, reasons for these behaviors as well as proposed solutions (see the example below). Optionally, to enhance teachers' understanding of the reciprocal effect between their own emotions and those manifested by their students, teachers could be asked to reflect on, discuss and exemplify the relationship between the former's and the latter's enjoyment and/ or anxiety.

Student-oriented sources of teacher boredom	Related aspects of instruction	Remedial actions
Passivity	Too many closed activities	Introducing challenge and novelty
Coming unprepared to class	Uninteresting and/ or repetitive homework assignments	Inquiring students about their homework-related expectations/adding variety to homework assignments
.....	.....	.....

7.2.10 Preventing Boredom Among Teachers Through Reflection on Control-Value Appraisals of Their Own Work

In this activity, which draws upon the assumptions of the control-value theory of achievement emotions (Pekrun, 2006, see Chapter 3, section 1.5.), teachers prepare written narratives dedicated to two distinct L2 teaching episodes. One of them refers to a situation which they found to be manageable and controllable, and which, at the same time, was important and meaningful for them. By contrast, in the second episode, they are requested to specify a situation when they had the impression that what was going on in the classroom was out of their control and did not appeal to them as a valuable experience. Then teachers meet in groups of 3 to 4 and comparatively discuss the episodes, trying to figure out whether a sense of little control and value may have led to the negative emotion of boredom. Finally, they collectively reflect on the danger of teacher boredom caused by students' control-value appraisals of L2 activities, and discuss ways of positively addressing these appraisals, having in mind students' needs, expectations, strengths as well as weaknesses.

7.2.11 Shifting Focus Through a Small Lens – Self-Reported Experience of Boredom in a Lesson

Teachers self-observe a sequence of lessons they conduct, make notes and list issues which trigger the feeling of boredom in connection with specific activities, procedures, etc. Then they are asked to indicate when the aversive emotion of boredom is the most likely to occur during a lesson (e.g., in its initial or final stages). In addition, they try to indicate the intensity of this emotion on a scale ranging from 0 (no boredom) to 10 (maximum boredom). The grid below may be beneficial in recording the observations. After conducting the classes, teachers try to carefully analyze the data and think about what changes should be undertaken to alleviate (the intensity of) the feeling of boredom during particular procedures and phases of a lesson.

Procedures, activities, …	Time + boredom intensity (0 – no boredom, 10 = maximum boredom)
	Beginning
	Middle
	End

7.2.12 Painting a Picture of a (Not) Bored Teacher

Teachers make a list of individual teacher characteristics which can contribute to the experience of boredom in the L2 classroom. They are invited to compare their lists with those compiled by their colleagues (in teacher groups, either face-to-face or online) and to decide which of these characteristics may be related to themselves, the teachers they know or teacher(s) who taught them in the past. They also consider ways of overcoming those "bored" traits.

CONCLUSION

The present chapter has provided examples of hands-on tasks and activities that can be used to stimulate teachers' reflection on L2 boredom, as experienced by their learners and themselves. In our view, these activities have the potential not only to help practitioners better understand the causes and symptoms of boredom and to make them cognizant of how its occurrence can be dependent on the overall emotional climate in the L2 classroom, but also to encourage them to come up with effective pedagogical interventions and coping strategies that can be employed to alleviate this negative emotion. We would like to emphasize that although the activities are sometimes linked to each other, most of them constitute stand-alone tasks that can be employed in different ways depending on specific needs. Many of them will prove useful for individual readers interested in determining how L2 boredom affects L2 learning and teaching and what they can do to cope with it. Some of the tasks can also be included in teacher training courses or workshops specifically addressing the role of emotions in the L2 classroom. There is also a (still remote) possibility that at some point workshops will be organized for pre- and in-service teachers with a direct focus on boredom, in which case the activities could provide much of the content covered in such a course.

Chapter 8
Conclusion

The main aim of the present book has been to examine teachers' perspectives on boredom in the L2 classroom and to highlight the need for reflective practice with respect to this negative emotion, thus filling an evident gap in existing empirical evidence. Specifically, our intention was to shed light on the ways in which L2 teachers at different educational levels view the causes and symptoms of boredom afflicting their learners as well as themselves, the link between this emotion experienced by the two groups, and strategies that can be employed to prevent and combat this negative phenomenon in both cases. The overview of the literature in the theoretical part of the volume (Chapters 1–4) demonstrated several important issues: (1) both positive and negative emotions shape the process of L2 learning in the classroom and outside and neither should therefore be neglected, (2) there are many intersections between boredom experienced in general education and in L2 learning and teaching, (3) despite such intersections, L2 boredom represents a distinctive and highly complex construct that remains to be conceptualized with respect to other ID factors that have been investigated in SLA (e.g., engagement, motivation, willingness to communicate, grit etc.), (4) it is not immediately clear how this negative emotion should most beneficially be addressed irrespective of the context in which it manifests itself and (5) despite constantly increasing empirical evidence, research into L2 boredom is still in its infancy, particularly with respect to teachers' perspectives on learners' experience of this aversive emotion and their own boredom as such as well as effective strategies that can be employed to deal with this negative emotion in both cases.

The research project reported in Chapter 5 produced a wealth of empirical evidence which also provides a basis for several important observations: (1) the extent to which teachers succumb to boredom in the L2 classroom is related to their general boredom proneness, which might be trait-like in character but is also reflective of age and teaching experience, (2) even though some of the triggers and symptoms of learner and teacher boredom are distinct, many of them tend to overlap, (3) in a similar vein, learner boredom and teacher boredom tend to fluctuate in single classes and sequences of successive classes, with the patterns being strikingly similar, (4) while many teachers recognize the link between their own boredom and that displayed by learners, they mostly see this impact as unidirectional, rarely contemplating the eventuality that their own bored behaviors can affect their learners and thus the quality of L2 instruction and (5) the boredom-coping strategies used by practitioners tend to be reactive rather than proactive in nature.

While both the theoretical and empirical parts of the book offered a basis for concrete recommendations for preventing and coping with both learner and teacher boredom as well as guidelines for reflective practice in this regard, it must be emphasized that the extent to which such pedagogical interventions or reflective practices can be drawn upon is bound to differ as a function of the instructional setting as well as the importance that practitioners attach to the affective dimension of L2 learning. In fact, it could easily be argued that L2 teachers have to deal with more pressing issues than boredom, which is not to say that researchers should give up on highlighting the ways in which this negative emotion can be successfully tackled. This said, teacher reflection is crucial in this respect, a point that this book has attempted to highlight on many occasions. We are confident that the concrete guidelines offered in Chapter 6 and the awareness-raising activities included in Chapter 7 will provide a so-much-needed impulse for reflective teaching practice with respect to L2 boredom.

Obviously, the study reported in this book admittedly constitutes only one modest step on the way to extending our understanding of teachers' perceptions of boredom in L2 learning and teaching as well as the ways that this negative emotion can most effectively be ameliorated in the language classroom but also outside educational settings. When we consider the limitations of the research project that were outlined in Chapter 5, it becomes quite clear that there is an urgent need for more studies that would seek to attempt to address this thorny issue. As regards the foci of such empirical investigations, one of the most pressing challenges involves the development of a scale that could be used to tap into the intensity of teacher boredom but to also identify the factor structure of this negative emotion in this case, building on similar efforts in the case of learner boredom (Pawlak et al., 2020b, 2022a). It would also be insightful to relate the extent to which teachers experience boredom to other facets of their individual learner profiles, such as the wide range of ID factors that have been explored in SLA studies (e.g., beliefs, learning styles, personality, motivation, grit; cf. Dörnyei & Ryan 2015; Griffiths & Soruç, 2020), but also variables that have been investigated specifically in relation to teachers, such as burnout, demotivation or well-being. In addition, there is a need to examine the efficacy of the employment of boredom-coping strategies and techniques for encouraging teacher reflection on reducing the negative effects of L2 boredom. Equally important is extending the investigation of teachers' perceptions of boredom to other national and educational contexts.

Moving on to methodological issues, future studies in this area should involve more participants selected in more representative and reliable ways than just posting an invitation on the Facebook page of one of the researchers. In particular, it would make sense to obtain more data on how L2 boredom fluctuates over time, taking into account longer time spans and different learner groups. Moreover, there is a need to rely on more varied data collection instruments such as interviews, stimulated recalls or lesson observations. All of this is of crucial importance because teachers might be more convinced to reflect on L2 boredom and actually take steps to cope with this negative emotion if they are presented with concrete empirical evidence that pedagogical interventions in this respect can benefit both them and their learners. While it is obvious that the experience of boredom cannot be totally eliminated from L2 classrooms, not least because teachers might have other, much more urgent priorities, there are certainly ways of reducing its detrimental effects or perhaps even capitalizing on it to enhance L2 instruction. This belief was the main impetus for us to embark on writing this book and we are hopeful that it will encourage teachers in different settings to accord L2 boredom the importance that it surely deserves.

Appendix 1

TEACHER BOREDOM QUESTIONNAIRE (TBQ)

Part One

1. Female/Male
2. Age:
3. Type of school you work in (e.g., elementary, secondary)
4. Degree: bachelor/MA/PhD/other:
5. Work experience (*How long have you been teaching English?*):
6. Your career level: internship teacher/contract teacher/nominated teacher/ diploma teacher.
7. Do you develop professionally? If yes, what do you do?

Part Two

1. It is easy for me to concentrate on my activities.
2. Frequently when I am working, I find myself worrying about other things.
3. Time always seems to be passing slowly.
4. I often find myself at "loose ends", not knowing what to do.
5. I am often trapped in situations where I have to do meaningless things.
6. Having to look at someone's home movies or travel slides bores me tremendously.
7. I have projects in mind all the time, things to do.
8. I find it easy to entertain myself.
9. Many things I have to do are repetitive and monotonous.
10. It takes more stimulation to get me going than most people.
11. I get a kick out of most things I do.
12. I am seldom excited about my work.

13. In any situation I can usually find something to do or see to keep me interested.
14. Much of the time I just sit around doing nothing.
15. I am good at waiting patiently.
16. I often find myself with nothing to do, time on my hands.
17. In situations where I have to wait, such as a line, I get very restless.
18. I often wake up with a new idea.
19. It would be very hard for me to find a job that is exciting enough.
20. I would like more challenging things to do in life.
21. I feel that I am working below my abilities most of the time.
22. Many people would say that I am a creative or imaginative person.
23. I have so many interests, I do not have time to do everything.
24. Among my friends, I am the one who keeps doing something the longest.
25. Unless I am doing something exciting, even dangerous, I feel half-dead and dull.
26. It takes a lot of change and variety to keep me really happy.
27. It seems that the same things are on television or the movies all the time; it is getting old.
28. When I was young, I was often in monotonous and tiresome situations.

Part Three

1. Have you observed any feelings of boredom in learning English during English lessons among your students? How were such feelings manifested? What could have caused them? Please provide examples and explain them.
2. Are your students bored the most at the beginning, middle or end of a lesson? Why is this the case?
3. During what types of activities (e.g., practicing specific language skills, language subsystems, tasks, forms of work) are your students the most likely to get bored? Why is this the case?
4. What is your reaction when you see students who are bored with English lessons?
5. How do you try to reduce the experience of boredom among students during English lessons? Please provide examples and explain.
6. If your students are bored during English lessons, do you feel responsible for it? Why or why not?
7. Do you feel bored while conducting English lessons? If so, what are the symptoms and causes of this negative experience? In what situations does it occur most often? Please provide examples and explain.

8. In your opinion, what factors are responsible for making you feel bored while conducting English lessons? Why?
9. If you experience feelings of boredom while conducting English lessons, how do you try to deal with this aversive emotion?
10. Over the years of your work as an English teacher, have you been experiencing more or less boredom? What have you been doing to reduce the intensity of boredom?
11. Do you see a relationship between your feeling bored while conducting English lessons and your students' boredom? How is it manifested? Provide examples.

Appendix 2

A LESSON REPORT

Part One

Teacher's name	Grade	Date	Number of students	Lesson's topic

Part Two

Minutes	Perceived levels of student boredom	Levels of teacher boredom	Modes of classroom organization, activities, etc.
1–5			
6–10			
11–15			
16–20			

21–25

26–30

31–35

36–40

41–45

Part Three

Please write a short narrative about the manifestations of observed boredom among the students as well as your feelings of boredom experienced while conducting a given lesson. Please respond to the following prompts: *What were the causes of boredom among your students?, What were you going to do to prevent the feeling of boredom from occurring among your students during the next lesson?, What caused the feeling of boredom you experienced when conducting the lesson?, What did you intend to do to prevent the feeling of boredom from accompanying you during the next lesson?*

References

Acee, T. W., Kim, H., Kim, H. J., Kim, J., Chu, H. R., Kim, M., … Riekenberg, J. J. (2010). Academic boredom in under- and over-challenging situations. *Contemporary Educational Psychology, 35*(1), 17–27.

Addison, R., & Brundrett, M. (2008). Motivation and demotivation of teachers in primary schools: The challenge of change. *Education, 36*(1), 79⬚94.

Ahmed, S. (2010). *The promise of happiness*. Durham, NC: Duke University Press.

Ainley, M. (2010). Interest in the dynamics of task behavior: Processes that link person and task in effective learning. In T. Urdan & S. A. Karabenick (Eds.), *Advances in motivation and achievement: The next decade of research in motivation and achievement* (Vol. 16A, pp. 235–264). Bingley, England: Emerald Group.

Alahmadi, S., Buttrick, N. R., Gilbert, D. T., Hardin, A. M., Westgate, E. C., & Wilson, T. D. (2017). You can do it if you really try: The effects of motivation on thinking for pleasure. *Motivation and Emotion, 41*, 545–561.

Ally, M. (2008). What is wrong with current theorizations of "boredom"? *Acta Academica, 40*(3), 35–66.

Andersen, P. A. (1999). *Non-verbal communication: Forms and functions.* Mountain View, CA: Mayfield.

Anderson, C., Keltner, D., & John, O. P., (2003). Emotional convergence between people over time. *Journal of Personality and Social Psychology, 84*(5), 1054–68. https://doi.org/10.1037/0022-3514.84.5.1054

Andrade, J. (2010). What does doodling do? *Applied Cognitive Psychology, 24*, 100–106.

Appleton, J. J., Christenson, S. L., & Furlong, M. J. (2008). Student engagement with school: Critical conceptual and methodological issues of the construct. *Psychology in the School, 45*, 369–386.

Argyris, C., & Schön, D. (1974). *Theory in practice: Increasing professional effectiveness.* Washington, DC: Jossey-Bass.

Aspinwall, L. G. (2001). Dealing with adversity: Self-regulation, coping, adaptation, and health. In A. Tesser & N. Schwarz (Eds.), *The Blackwell handbook of social psychology: Vol 1. Intrapersonal processes* (pp. 159–614). Maiden, MA: Blackwell.

Aubusson, P. (2008). *Teacher learning and development.* New York: Springer.

Aydin, S. (2012). Factors causing demotivation in EFL teaching process: A case study. *The Qualitative Report, 17*(101), 1–13.

Aydin, S. (2015). WebQuests as language-learning tools. *Computer Assisted Language Learning, 29,* 765–778. https://doi.org/10.1080/09588221.2015.1061019

Azad, S.B., & Ketabi, S. (2013). A comparative study of Iranian and Japanese English teachers' demotivation factors. *Pan-Pacific Association Applied Linguistics, 17*(1), 39–55.

Bailey, K. M. (2001). Action research, teacher research, and classroom research in language teaching. In M. Celce-Murcia (Ed.), *Teaching English as a second or foreign language* (3rd ed, pp. 489–498). Boston, MA: Heinle and Heinle.

Bakker, A. B. (2005). Flow among music teachers and their students: The crossover of peak experiences. *Journal of Vocational Behavior, 66*(1), 26–44. https://doi.org/10.1016/j.jvb.2003.11.001

Bakker, A. B., Westman, M., & Van Emmerik, Ij. H. (2009). Advancements in crossover theory. *Journal of Managerial Psychology, 24*(3), 206–219. https://doi.org/10.1108/02683940910939304

Banegas, D. L., & Consoli, S. (2020). Action research in language education. In J. McKinley & H. Rose (Eds.), *The Routledge handbook of research methods in applied linguistics* (pp. 176–187). London: Routledge.

Barbalet, J. M. (1999). Boredom and social meaning. *British Journal of Sociology, 50,* 631–646.

Barcelos, A. (2021). Revolutionary love and peace in the construction of an English teacher's professional identity. In R. Oxford, M. Olivero, & M. Harrison (Eds.), *Peacebuilding in language education* (pp. 96–109). Bristol: Multilingual Matters.

Barcelos, A. M. F., & Coelho, H. S. H. (2016). Language learning and teaching: What's love got to do with it? In P. D. MacIntyre, T. Gregersen, & S. Mercer (Eds.), *Positive psychology in SLA* (pp. 130–144). Bristol: Multilingual Matters.

Barnett, L. A., & Klitzing, S. W. (2006). Boredom in free time: Relationships with personality, affect, and motivation for different gender, racial, and ethnic student groups. *Leisure Science, 28,* 223–244.

Barsade, S. G. (2002). The ripple effect: Emotional contagion and its influence on group behavior. *Administrative Science Quarterly, 47*(4), 644–675. https://doi.org/10.2307/3094912

Bartels, J. M., Magun-Jackson, S., & Kemp, A. D. (2009). Volitional regulation and self-regulated learning: An examination of individual differences in approach-avoidance achievement motivation. *Electronic Journal of Research in Educational Psychology, 7*(18), 605–626.

Becker, E., Goetz, T., Morger, V., & Ranellucci, J. (2014). The importance of teachers' emotions and instructional behavior for their students' emotions: An experience sampling analysis. *Teaching and Teacher Education, 43,* 15–26. https://doi.org/10.1016/j.tate.2014.05.002

Bench, S. W., & Lench, H. C. (2013). On the function of boredom. *Behavioral Science, 3*(3), 459–472.

Berlyne, D. E. (1960). *Conflict, arousal, and curiosity.* New York: McGraw-Hill.

Berryhill, J., Linney, J. A., & Fromewick, J. (2009). The effects of education accountability on teachers: Are policies too-stress provoking for their own good? *International Journal of Education Policy and Leadership, 4*(5), 1–14.

Bielak J., & Mystkowska-Wiertelak, A. (2020). Investigating language learners' emotion-regulation strategies with the help of the vignette methodology. *System, 90,* 102208.

Borg, S. (2006). The distinctive characteristics of foreign language teachers. *Language Teaching Research, 10*(1), 3–31. https://doi.org/10.1191/1362168806lr182oa

Botes, E., Dewaele, J.-M., & Greiff, S. (2021). The development and validation of the short form of the foreign language enjoyment scale. *The Modern Language Journal, 105*(4). https://doi.org/10.1111/modl.12741

Boudreau, C., P. D. MacIntyre, & Dewaele, J.-M. (2018). Enjoyment and anxiety in second language communication: An idiodynamic approach. *Studies in Second Language Learning and Teaching 8*(1), 149–170.

Brans, K., Koval, P., Verduyn, P., Lim, Y. L., & Kuppens, P. (2013). The regulation of negative and positive affect in daily life. *Emotion, 13*(5), 926–939. https://doi.org/10.1037/a0032400

Bridgeland, J., Bruce, M., & Hariharan, A. (2013). *The missing piece: A national teacher survey on how social and emotional learning can empower children and transform schools.* Chicago, IL: Civic Enterprises, with Peter D. Hart Research Associates, for the Collaborative for Academic, Social, and Emotional Learning (CASEL).

Brodsky, J. (1995). *On grief and reason: Essays.* New York: Farrar, Straus and Giroux.

Brookfield, S. (1995). *Becoming a critically reflective teacher.* San Francisco: Jossey-Bass.

Brown, H. D., & Heekyeong, L. (2015). *Teaching by principles: An interactive approach to language pedagogy.* Pearson.

Brown, K. W., & Ryan, R. M. (2003). The benefits of being present: Mindfulness and its role in psychological well-being. *Journal of Personality and Social Psychology, 84,* 822–848.

Caldwell, L. L., Darling, N., Payne, L. L., & Dowdy, B. (1999). "Why are you bored?": An examination of psychological and social control causes of boredom among adolescents. *Journal of Leisure Research, 31,* 103–121.

Chabot, S. (2008). Love and revolution. *Critical Sociology, 34*(6), 803–828.

Chahkandi, F., Rasekh, A. E., &Tavakoli, M. (2016). Efficacious EFL teachers' goals and strategies for emotion management: The role of culture in focus. *Iranian Journal of Applied Linguistics (IJAL), 19*(1), 35–72.

Chambers, G. (1993). Taking the "de" out of demotivation. *Language Learning Journal, 7,* 13–16.

Chamot, A. U., & Harris, V. (Eds.). (2019). *Learning strategy instruction in the language classroom: issues and implementation.* Bristol: Multilingual Matters.

Chapman, K. E. (2013). *Boredom in the German foreign language classroom* (Unpublished doctoral dissertation). Madison, WI: University of Wisconsin-Madison.

Cheyne, J. A., Carriere, J. S., & Smilek, D. (2006). Absent-mindedness: Lapses of conscious awareness and everyday cognitive failures. *Consciousness and Cognition, 15*(3), 578–592.

Chien, C. (2013). Analysis of a language teacher's journal of classroom practice as reflective practice. *Reflective Practice, 14*(1), 131–143.

Ching, C. L., & Chan, V. L. (2020). Positive emotions, positive feelings and health: A life philosophy. *Linguistics and Culture Review*, *4*(1), 1–14. https://doi.org/10.37028/ling-cure.v4n1.16

Christenson, S. L., Reschly, A. L., & Wylie, C. (2012). Preface. In S. L. Christenson, A. L. Reschly, & C. Wylie (Eds.), *Handbook of research on students engagement* (pp. v-ix). New York, NY: Springer.

Cohen, A. D., Oxford, R. L., & Chi, J. C. (2002). Learning style survey. Retrieved from https://carla.umn.edu/maxsa/documents/LearningStyleSurvey_MAXSA.pdf

Cook, T. (2006). *An investigation of shame and anxiety in learning English as a second language* (Unpublished doctoral dissertation). University of Southern California, Los Angeles, CA.

Coşkun, A., & Yüksel, Y. (2021). Examining English as a foreign language students' boredom in terms of different variables. *Acuity: Journal of English Language Pedagogy, Literature and Culture*, *7*(1), 19–36. https://doi.org/10.35974/acuity.v7i2.2539

Crookes, G. (2013). *Critical ELT in action: Foundations, promises, praxis.* New York: Routledge.

Crow, J., & Smith, L. (2005). Co-teaching in higher education: Reflective conversations on shared experience as continued professional development for lecturers and health and social care students. *Reflective Practice*, *6*(4), 491–506.

Csikszentmihalyi, M. (1990). Flow: The psychology of optimal experience. HarperPerennial; New York.

Csizér, K. (2020). The L2 motivational self system. In M. Lamb, K. Csizér, A. Henry, & S. Ryan (Eds.). (2020). *The Palgrave handbook of motivation for language learning* (pp. 71–93). Palgrave Macmillan.

Cummins, R. (2010). Subjective wellbeing, homeostatically protected mood and depression: A synthesis. *Journal of Happiness Studies*, *11*, 1–17. https://doi.org/10.1007/s10902-009-9167-0

Dahlen, E. R., Martin, R. C., Ragan, K., & Kuhlman,. M. (2004). Boredom proneness in anger and aggression: Effects of impulsiveness and sensation seeking. *Personality and Individual Differences*, *37*(8), 1615–1627.

Damrad-Frye, R., & Laird, J. D. (1989). The experience of boredom: The role of the self-perception of attention. *Journal of Personality & Social Psychology*, *57*(2), 315–320.

Daniels, L. M., Tze, M. C., & Goetz, T. (2015). Examining boredom: Different causes for different coping profiles. *Learning and Individual Differences*, *37*, 255–261.

Daschmann, E. C., Goetz, T., & Stupnisky, R. H. (2011). Testing the predictors of boredom at school: Development and validation of the precursors to boredom scales. *British Journal of Educational Psychology*, *81*, 421–440.

Daschmann, E. C., Goetz, T., & Stupnisky, R. H. (2014). Exploring the antecedents of boredom: Do teachers know why students are bored? *Teaching and Teacher Education*, *39*, 22–30. http://dx.doi.org/10.1016/j.tate.2013.11.009

Davies, J., & Fortney, M. (2012). *The Menton theory of engagement and boredom* (pp. 131–143). Poster presented at the First Annual Conference on Advances in Cognitive Systems, Palo Alto, CA.

Dettmers, S., Trautwein, U., Lüdtke, O., Goetz, T., Frenzel, A. C., & Pekrun, R. (2011). Students' emotions during homework in mathematics: Testing a theoretical model of antecedents and achievement outcomes. *Contemporary Educational Psychology*, *36*(1), 25–35.

Derakhshan, A., Kruk, M., Mehdizadeh, M., & Pawlak, M. (2021). Boredom in online classes in the Iranian EFL context: Sources and solutions. *System*, *101*. 102556 https://doi.org/10.1016/j.system.2021.102556

Derakhshan, A., Eslami, Z. R., Curle, S., & Zhaleh, K. (2022a). Exploring the predictive role of teacher immediacy and stroke behaviors in English as a foreign language university students' academic burnout. *Studies in Second Language Learning and Teaching*, *12*(1), 87–115.

Derakhshan, A., Kruk, M., Mehdizadeh, M., & Pawlak, M. (2022b). Activity-induced boredom in online EFL classes. *ELT Journal*, *76*(1), 58–68. https://doi.org/10.1093/elt/ccab072

Dewaele, J.-M. (2002). Psychological and sociodemographic correlates of communicative anxiety in L2 and L3 production. *International Journal of Bilingualism*, *6*(1), 23–38.

Dewaele, J.-M., Botes, E., & Greiff, S. (2022). Sources and effects of foreign language enjoyment, anxiety and boredom: A structural equation modelling approach. *Studies in Second Language Acquisition*. https://doi.org/10.1017/S0272263122000328

Dewaele, J. M., Chen, X., Padilla, A. M., & Lake, J. (2019). The flowering of positive psychology in foreign language teaching and acquisition research. *Frontiers in Psychology*, *10*(212). https://doi.org/10.3389/fpsyg.2019.02128

Dewaele J. M., & Dewaele L. (2017). The dynamic interactions in foreign language classroom anxiety and foreign language enjoyment of pupils aged 12 to 18: A pseudo-longitudinal investigation. *Journal of EuroSLA*, *1*, 11–22.

Dewaele, J.-M., Franco Magdalena, A., & Saito, K. (2019). The effect of perception of Teacher characteristics on Spanish EFL Learners' Anxiety and Enjoyment. *Modern Language Journal*, *103*, 412–427.

Dewaele, J.-M., & Li, C. (2021). Teacher enthusiasm and students' social-behavioral learning engagement: The mediating role of student enjoyment and boredom in Chinese EFL classes. *Language Teaching Research*, *25*(6), 922–945. https://doi.org/10.1177/13621688211014538

Dewaele, J.-M., & MacIntyre, P. D. (2014). The two faces of Janus? Anxiety and enjoyment in the foreign language classroom. *Studies in Second Language Learning and Teaching*, *4*, 237–274.

Dewaele, J. M., & MacIntyre, P. D. (2016). Foreign language enjoyment and anxiety: The right and left feet of the language learner. In T. Gregersen, P. D. MacIntyre, & S. Mercer (Eds.), *Positive Psychology in SLA* (pp. 215–236). Multilingual Matters.

Dewaele, J.-M., & MacIntyre, P.D. (2019). The predictive power of multicultural personality traits, learner and teacher variables on foreign language enjoyment and anxiety. In M. Sato & S. Loewen (Ed.), *Evidence-based second language pedagogy: A collection of instructed second language acquisition studies* (pp. 263–286). London: Routledge.

Dewaele, J.-M., & Pavelescu, L. M. (2019). The relationship between incommensurable emotions and willingness to communicate in English as a foreign language: A multiple case study. *Innovation in Language Learning and Teaching, 15*(1). https://doi.org/10.1080/17501229.2019.1675667

Dewey, J. (1933) *How we think: A restatement of the relation of reflective thinking to the educative process.* Boston: Houghton Mifflin.

Dodge, R., Daly, A., Huyton, J., & Sanders, L. (2012). The challenge of defining wellbeing. *International Journal of Wellbeing, 2*(3), 222–235. https://doi.org/10.5502/ijw.v2i3.4

Dörnyei, Z. (1998). *Demotivation in second and foreign language learning.* Paper presented at the TESOL '98 Conference, Seattle, WA.

Dörnyei, Z. (2005). *The psychology of the language learner: Individual differences in second language acquisition.* Mahwah, NJ: Lawrence Erlbaum Associates.

Dörnyei, Z. (2007). *Research methods in applied linguistics.* Oxford: Oxford University Press.

Dörnyei, Z. (2009). The L2 motivational self system. In Z. Dörnyei & E. Ushioda (Eds.), *Motivation, language identity and the L2 self* (pp. 9–42). Clevedon: Multilingual Matters.

Dörnyei, Z. (2019). Towards a better understanding of the L2 Learning Experience, the Cinderella of the L2 motivational self system. *Studies in Second Language Learning and Teaching, 9*(1), 19–30.

Dörnyei, Z., & Ryan, S. (2015). *The psychology of the language learner revisited.* Routledge.

Dörnyei, Z., & Ushioda, E. (2011). *Teaching and researching motivation* (2nd ed.). Oxon, UK: Routledge.

Dumančić, D. (2018). Investigating boredom among EFL teachers. ExELL (Explorations in English Language and Linguistics), *6*, 57–80. https://doi.org/10.2478/exell-2019-0006

Eastwood, J. D., Cavaliere, C., Fahlman, S. A., & Eastwood, A. E. (2007). A desire for desires: Boredom and its relation to alexithymia. *Personality and Individual Differences, 42*(6), 1035–1045.

Eastwood, J. D., Frischen, A., Fenske, M. J., & Smilek, D. (2012). The unengaged mind: Defining boredom in terms of attention. *Perspectives on Psychological Science, 7*(5), 482–495.

Ekman, P. (2003). *Emotions revealed.* New York: Holt.

Elahi Shirvan, M., Yazdanmehr, E., Taherian, T., Kruk, M., & Pawlak, M. (2021). Boredom in practical English language classes: A longitudinal confirmatory factor analysis-curve of factors model. *Applied Linguistics Review.* https://doi.org/10.1515/applirev-2021-0073

Ellis, T. (1997). *SLA research and language teaching.* Oxford: Oxford University Press.

Ellis, R. (2008). *The study of second language acquisition.* Oxford: Oxford University Press.

Ellis, R. (2010). A framework for investigating oral and written corrective feedback. *Studies in Second Language Acquisition, 32*, 335–349.

Eren, A., & Coskun, H. (2016). Students' level of boredom, boredom coping strategies, epistemic curiosity, and graded performance. *The Journal of Educational Research, 109*, 574–588.

Erlam, R. (2008). What do you researchers know about language teaching? Bridging the gap between SLA research and language pedagogy. *Innovation in Language Learning and Teaching, 2*, 253–267.

Estrada, C. A. Isen, A. M., & Young, M. J. (1997). Positive affect facilitates integration of information and decreases anchoring in reasoning among physicians. *Organizational Behavior and Human Decision Processes, 72,* 117–135.

Exeter, D. J., Ameratunga, S., Ratima, M., Morton, S., Dickson, M., Hsu, D., & Jackson, R. (2010). Student engagement in very large classes: The teachers' perspective. *Studies in Higher Education, 35*(7), 761–775.

Flook, L., Goldberg, S. B., Pinger, L., Bonus, K., & Davidson, R. J. (2013). Mindfulness for teachers: A pilot study to assess effects on stress, burnout, and teaching efficacy. *Mind, Brain and Education, 7*(3), 182–195.

Fahlman, S. A. (2009). *Development and validation of the Multidimensional State Boredom Scale* (Unpublished doctoral dissertation). Ottawa: York University.

Farmer, R. F., & Sundberg, N. D. (1986). Boredom proneness: The development and correlates of a new scale. *Journal of Personality Assessment, 50*(1), 4–17.

Farrell, T. S. C. (2007). *Reflective language teaching: From research to practice.* London: Continuum.

Farrell, T. S. C. (2011). Exploring the professional role identities of experienced ESL teachers through reflective practice. *System, 66,* 1–9.

Farrell, T. S. C. (2013). *Reflective writing for language teachers.* London: Equinox.

Farrell, T. S. C. (2014a). *Reflective practice in ESL teacher development groups: From practices to principles.* Basingstoke: Palgrave Macmillan.

Farrell, T. S. C. (2014b). *Promoting teacher reflection in second language education: A framework for TESOL professionals.* New York: Routledge.

Farrell, T. S. C. (2018). Reflective practice for language teachers. In John I. Liontas (Ed.), *The TESOL encyclopedia of English language teaching.* New York: Wiley. https://doi.org/10.1002/9781118784235.eelt0873

Farrell, T. S. C. (2019). *Reflective practice in ELT.* London: Equinox.

Farrell, T. S. C. (2022). *Reflective practice in language teaching.* Cambridge: Cambridge University Press.

Farrell, E., Peguero, G., Lindsey, R., & White, R. (1988). Giving voice to high school students: "Pressure and boredom, Ye know what I'm sayin?" *American Research Journal, 4,* 489–502.

Feldman Barrett, L. (2017). *How emotions are made: The secret life of the brain.* New York: Houghton Mifflin Harcourt.

Finn, J. D., & Zimmer, K. S. (2012). Student engagement: What is it? Why does it matter? In

S. L. Christenson, A. L. Reschly, & C. Wylie (Eds.), *Handbook of research on student engagement* (pp. 97–131). Springer Science + Business Media.

Fisher, C. D. (1993). Boredom at work: A neglected concept. *Human Relations, 46*(3), 395–417.

Fredrickson, B. L. (1998). What good are positive emotions? *Review of General Psychology, 2,* 300–319.

Fredrickson, B. (2001). The role of positive emotions in positive psychology: The broaden-and-build theory of positive emotions. American Psychologist, 56, 218–226. https://doi.org/10.1037//0003-066X.56.3.218

Fredrickson, B. L. (2003). The value of positive emotions: The emerging science of positive psychology looks into why it's good to feel good. *American Scientist, 91*, 330–335.

Fredrickson, B. L. (2004). The broaden-and-build theory of positive emotions. *Philosophical Transactions of the Royal Society of London Series B: Biological Sciences, 359*, 1367–1377.

Fredrickson, B. L., & Branigan, C. (2001). Positive emotions. In T. J. Mayne & G. A. Bonnano (Eds.), *Emotion: Current issues and future directions* (pp. 123–151). New York: Guilford Press.

Fredrickson, B. L., & Branigan, C. (2005). Positive emotions broaden the scope of attention and thought-action repertoires. *Cognition and Emotion, 19*(3), 313–332.

Fredrickson, B. L., & Joiner, T. (2002). Positive emotions trigger upward spirals toward emotional well-being. *Psychological Science, 13*, 172–175.

Fredrickson, B. L., Mancuso, R. A., Branigan, C., & Tugade, M. M. (2000). The undoing effect of positive emotions. *Motivation and Emotion, 24*(4), 237–258.

Frenzel, A. C., Goetz, T., Stephens, E. J., & Jacob, B. (2009). Antecedents and effects of teachers' emotional experiences: An integrative perspective and empirical test. In P. A. Schutz & M. Zembylas (Eds.), *Advances in teacher emotions research: The impact on teachers' lives* (pp. 129–148). New York: Springer.

Frenzel, A. C., Pekrun, R., & Goetz, T. (2007). Girls and mathematics: A "hopeless" issue? A control-value approach to gender differences in emotions towards mathematics. *European Journal of Psychology of Education, 22*, 497–514.

Frenzel, A. C., Pekrun, R., Goetz, T., Daniels, L. M., Durksen, T. L., Becker-Kurz, B., & Klassen, R. M. (2016). Measuring teachers' enjoyment, anger, and anxiety: The Teacher Emotions Scales (TES). *Contemporary Educational Psychology, 46*, 148–163. https://doi.org/10.1016/j.cedpsych.2016.05.003

Galmiche, D. (2017). Shame and SLA. *Apples – Journal of Applied Language Studies, 11*, 25–53.

Gana, K., Deletang, B., & Metais, L. (2000). Is boredom proneness associated with introspectiveness? *Social Behavior and Personality: An International Journal, 28*, 499–504.

Gao, X. A. (2010*). Strategic language learning: The roles of agency and context*. Multilingual Matters.

Gao, L. X., & Zhang, L. J. (2020). Teacher learning in difficult times: Examining foreign language teachers' cognitions about online teaching to tide over COVID-19. *Frontiers in Psychology, 11*, 2396. https://doi.org/10.3389/fpsyg.2020.549653

Gardner, H. (2004). *Changing minds: The art and science of changing our own and other people's minds*. Brighton, MA: Harvard Business School Press.

Gearing, N. (2019). Korean language learning demotivation among EFL instructors in South Korea. *Studies in Second Language Learning and Teaching, 9*(1), 199–223.

Georgoulas-Sherry, V., & Kelly, D. R. (2019). Resilience, grit, and hardiness: Determining The relationships amongst these constructs through structural equation modeling techniques. *Journal of Positive Psychology & Wellbeing, 3*(2), 165–178.

Gkonou, C., Dewaele, J.-M., & King, J. (Eds.). (2020). *The emotional rollercoaster of language teaching*. Bristol: Multilingual Matters.

Gkonou, C., & Miller, E.R. (2017). Caring and emotional labor: Language teachers' engagement with anxious learners in private language school classrooms. *Language Teaching Research*, *23*, 372–387.

Gkonou, C., & Miller, E.R. (2021). An exploration of language teacher reflection, emotion labor, and emotional capital. *TESOL Quarterly*, *55*, 134–155.

Goetz, T., & Frenzel, A. C. (2006). Phänomenologie schulischer Langeweile. *Zeitschrift fur Entwicklungspsychologie und Pädagogisch Psychologie*, 38, 149–153.

Goetz, T., Frenzel, A. C., Hall, N. C., Nett, U. E., Pekrun, R., & Lipnevich, A. A. (2014). Types of boredom: An experience sampling approach. *Motivation and Emotion*, *38*(3), 401–419.

Goetz, T., Frenzel, A. C., Pekrun, R., Hall, N. C., & Lüdtke, O. (2007). Between- and within- domain relations of students' academic emotions. *Journal of Educational Psychology*, *99*(4), 715–733.

Goetz, T., Nett, U. E., Martiny, S. E., Hall, N. C., Pekrun, R., Dettmers, S., & Trautwein, U. (2012). Students' emotions during homework: Structures, self-concept antecedents, and achievement outcomes. *Learning and Individual Differences*, *22*(2), 225–234.

Goldberg, Y. K., Eastwood, J. D., LaGuardia, J., & Danckert, J. (2011). Boredom: An emotional experience distinct from apathy, anhedonia, or depression. *Journal of Social and Clinical Psychology*, *30*(6), 647–666.

Goleman, D. (2006). *Emotional intelligence*. New York: Bantam Books.

Gordon, A., Wilkinson, R., McGown, A., & Jovanoska, S. (1997). The psychometric properties of the boredom proneness scale: An examination of its validity. *Psychological Studies*, *42*, 85–97.

Greenier, V., Derakhshan, A., & Fathi, J. (2021). Emotion regulation and psychological wellbeing in teacher work engagement: A case of British and Iranian English language teachers. *System*, *97*, 102446. https://doi.org/10.1016/j.system.2020.102446

Gregersen, T., & Macintyre, P. (2014). *Capitalizing on language learners' individuality: From premise to practice*. Bristol: Multilingual Matters.

Gregersen, T., MacIntyre, P. D., & Meza, M. D. (2014). The motion of emotion: Idiodynamic case studies of learners' foreign language anxiety. *Modern Language Journal*, *98*(2), 574–588.

Gregersen, T., Mercer, S., MacIntyre, P., Talbot, K., & Banga, C. A. (2020). Understanding language teacher wellbeing: An ESM study of daily stressors and uplifts. *Language Teaching Research*. https://doi.org/10.1177/1362168820965897

Gregory, A., Allen, J. P., Mikami, A. Y., Hafen, C. A., & Pianta, R. C. (2014). Effects of a professional development program on behavioral engagement of students in middle and high school. *Psychology in the Schools*, *51*(2), 143–163.

Griffiths, C., & Soruç, A. (2020). *Individual differences in language learning: A complex systems theory perspective*. London: Palgrave Macmillan.

Gruber, J., Mauss, I. B., & Tamir, M. (2011). A dark side of happiness? How, when, and why happiness is not always good. *Perspectives on Psychological Science, 6*, 222–233. https://doi.org/10.1177/1745691611406927

Hatton, N., & Smith, D. (1995). Reflection in teacher education: Towards definition and implementation. *Teaching and Teacher Education, 11*(1), 33–49.

Harper, S., & Quay, S. (2009). Beyond sameness, with engagement and outcomes for all: An introduction. In S. R. Harper & S. J. Quaye (Eds.), *Student engagement in higher education: Theoretical perspectives and practical approaches for diverse populations* (pp. 1–15). New York, NY: Routledge.

Harris, M. B. (2000). Correlates and characteristics of boredom proneness and boredom. *Journal of Applied Social Psychology, 30*, 576–598.

Hatfield, E., Cacioppo, J., & Rapson, R. (1994). *Emotional contagion.* New York: Cambridge University Press.

Heiss, C., Ziegler, M., Engbert, K., Gropel, P., & Brand, R. (2010). Self-leadership and volition: Distinct and potentially supplemental constructs. *Psychological Reports, 107*(2), 447–462. https://doi.org/10.2466/01.03.07.14

Hennig-Thurau, T., Groth, M., Paul, M., & Gremler, D. D. (2006). Are all smiles created equal? How emotional contagion and emotional labor affect service relationships. *Journal of Marketing, 70*(3), 58–73. https://doi.org/10.1509/jmkg.70.3.58

Henry, A. (2020). Directed motivational currents: Extending the theory of L2 vision. In M. Lamb, K. Csizér, A. Henry, & S. Ryan (Eds.). (2020). *The Palgrave handbook of motivation for language learning* (pp. 139–161). Palgrave Macmillan.

Henry, A., & Thorsen, C. (2018). Disaffection and agentic engagement: "Redesigning" activities to enable authentic self-expression. *Language Teaching Research.* http://doi.org/10.1177/1362168818795976

Hill, A. B., & Perkins, R. E. (1985). Towards a model of boredom. *British Journal of Psychology, 76*(2), 235–240. https://doi.org/10.1111/j.2044-8295.1985.tb01947.x

Hiver, P. (2016). The triumph over experience: Hope and hardiness in novice teachers. In P. D. MacIntyre, T. Gregersen, & S. Mercer (Eds.), *Positive psychology in SLA* (pp. 168–192). Bristol: Multilingual Matters.

Horwitz, E. K., Horwitz, M., & Cope, J. (1986). Foreign language classroom anxiety. *Modern Language Journal, 70*(1), 125–132.

Hunter, A., & Eastwood, J. D. (2016). Does state boredom cause failures of attention? Examining the relations between trait boredom, state boredom, and sustained attention. *Experimental Brain Research, 236*(9), 2483–2492. https://doi.org/10.1007/s00221-016-4749-7.

Isacescu, J., Struk, A. A., & Danckert, J. (2017). Cognitive and affective predictors of boredom proneness, *Cognition and Emotion, 31*(8), 1741–1748. https://doi.org/10.1080/02699931.2016.1259995

Järvelä, S., Järvenoja, H., Malmberg, J., & Hadwin, A. F. (2013). Exploring socially shared regulation in the context of collaboration. *Journal of Cognitive Education and Psychology, 12*(3), 67–286. https://doi.org/10.1891/1945-8959.12.3.267

Jang, H., Reeve, J., & Deci, E. L. (2010). Engaging students in learning activities: It is not autonomy support or structure but autonomy support and structure. *Journal of Educational Psychology, 92*(3), 588–600.

Jay, J. K., & Johnson, K. L. (2002). Capturing complexity: A typology of reflective practice for teacher education. *Teaching and Teacher Education, 18,* 73–85.

Jiang, Y. (2020). An investigation of the effect of teacher on Chinese university students' foreign language enjoyment. *Foreign Language World, 196,* 60–68.

Jiang, Y., & Dewaele, J.-M. (2019). How unique is the foreign language classroom enjoyment and anxiety of Chinese EFL learners? *System, 82,* 13–25.

Johnson, K. E. (2009). *Second language teacher education: A sociocultural perspective.* New York: Routledge.

Johnson, K. E. (2015). Reclaiming the relevance of L2 teacher education. *Modern Language Journal, 99*(3), 515–528

Kam, C. C-S., & Bond, M. H. (2008). Role of emotions and behavioral responses in mediating the impact of face loss on relationship deterioration: Are Chinese more face-sensitive than Americans? *Asian Journal of Social Psychology, 11,* 175–184.

Kane, M. J., & McVay, J. C. (2012). What mind wandering reveals about executive-control abilities and failures. *Current Directions in Psychological Science, 21,* 348–354. https://doi.org/10.1177/0963721412454875

Kanske, P., & Kotz, S. A. (2011). Conflict processing is modulated by positive emotion: ERP data from a flanker task. *Behavioral Brain Research, 219*(2), 382–6.

Kass, S. J., Wallace, J. C., & Vodanovich, S. J. (2003). Boredom proneness and sleep disorders as predictors of adult attention deficit scores. *Journal of Attention Disorders, 7,* 83–91.

Khajavy, G. H., MacIntyre, P. D., & Barabadi, E. (2018). Role of the emotions and classroom environment in willingness to communicate: Applying doubly latent multilevel analysis in second language acquisition research. *Studies in Second Language Acquisition 40*(3), 605–624.

Khajavy, G. H., MacIntyre, P. M., & Hariri, J. (2020). A closer look at grit and language mindset as predictors of foreign language achievement. *Studies in Second Language Acquisition, 43*(2), 379–402. https://doi.org/10.1017/S0272263120000480

Kim, S. H. (2013). The representations of boredom in T. S. Eliot's "The waste land". *Journal of T. S. Eliot Society of Korea, 23*(1), 175–195.

Kim, T.-Y., & Kim, Y. (2022). Dynamics of South Korean EFL teachers' initial career motives and demotivation. In Y. Kimura, Y. Young, T.-Y. Kim, & Y. Nakata (Eds.), *Language teacher motivation, autonomy and development in East Asia* (pp. 95–110). Cham: Springer.

Kostoulas, A., & Lämmerer, A. (2020). Resilience in language teaching: Adaptive and maladaptive outcomes in pre-service teachers. In C. Gkonou, J.-M. Dewaele, & J. King (Eds.), *The emotional rollercoaster of language teaching* (pp. 89–110). Bristol: Multilingual Matters.

Krashen, S. D. (1987). *Principles and practice in second language acquisition.* Oxford: Pergamon Press.

Kruk, M. (2016). Investigating the changing nature of boredom in the English language classroom: Results of a study. In A. Dłutek & D. Pietrzak (Eds.), *Nowy wymiar filologii* (Vol. 1, pp. 252–263). Płock: Wydawnictwo Naukowe Państwowej Wyższej Szkoły Zawodowej w Płocku.

Kruk, M. (2022). Dynamicity of perceived willingness to communicate, motivation, anxiety in Second Life: The case of two advanced learners of English. *Computer Assisted Language Learning. 35*(1–2), 190–216. https://doi.org/10.1080/09588221.2019.1677722

Kruk, M. (2021a). *Investigating dynamic relationships among individual difference variables in learning English as a foreign language in a virtual world.* Cham, Switzerland: Springer. https://doi.org/10.1007/978-3-030-65269-2

Kruk, M. (2021b). Variation in experiencing boredom during self-directed learning in a virtual world: The case of one English major. *Australian Review of Applied Linguistics. 44*(3), 289–308. https://doi.org/10.1075/aral.19050.kru

Kruk, M., & Pawlak, M. (2022). *Understanding emotions in English language learning in virtual worlds.* London: Routledge.

Kruk, M., Pawlak, M., Elahi Shirvan, M., Taherian, T., & Yazdanmehr, E. (2022a). Potential sources of foreign language learning boredom: A Q methodology study. *Studies in Second Language Learning and Teaching, 12*(1), 37–58. https://doi.org/10.14746/ssllt.2022.12.1.3

Kruk, M., Pawlak, M., Elahi Shirvan, M., Taherian, T., & Yazdanmehr, E. (2022b). A longitudinal study of foreign language enjoyment and boredom: A latent growth curve modeling. *Language Teaching Research.* https://doi.org/10.1177%2F13621688221082303

Kruk, M., Pawlak, M., & Zawodniak, J. (2021). Another look at boredom in the language instruction: The role of the predictable and the unexpected. *Studies in Second Language Learning and Teaching, 11*(1), 15–40. http://dx.doi.org/10.14746/ssllt.2021.11.1.2

Kruk, M., & Zawodniak, J. (2017). Nuda a praktyczna nauka języka angielskiego. *Neofilolog,49*(1), 115–131.

Kruk, M., & Zawodniak, J. (2018). Boredom in practical English language classes: Insights From interview data. In L. Szymański, J. Zawodniak, A. Łobodziec, & M. Smoluk (Eds.), *Interdisciplinary views on the English language, literature and culture* (pp. 177–191). Zielona Góra: Wydział Humanistyczny Uniwersytetu Zielonogórskiego.

Kruk, M., & Zawodniak, J. (2020). A comparative study of the experience of boredom in the L2 and L3 classroom. *English Teaching & Learning, 44*(4), 417–437. https://doi.org/10.1007/s42321-020-00056-0

Kuh, G. (2009). What student affairs professionals need to know about student engagement. *Journal of College Student Development, 50*(6), 683–706.

Lam, S. F., Wong, B. P. H., Yang, H., & Liu, Y. (2012). Understanding student engagement with a contextual model. In S. L. Christenson, A. L. Reschly & C. Wylie (Eds.), *Handbook of research on student engagement* (pp. 403–420). Boston, MA: Springer US.

Lamb, M. (2019). Motivational teaching strategies. In M. Lamb, K. Csizér, A. Henry, & S. Ryan (Eds.). *The Palgrave handbook of motivation for language learning* (pp. 287–305). Cham: Palgrave Macmillan.

Larrivee, B. (2008) Development of a tool to assess teachers' level of reflective practice. *Reflective Practice, 9*(3), 341–360.

Larsen-Freeman, D. (2000). *Techniques and principles in language teaching.* Oxford: Oxford University Press.

Larsen-Freeman, D. (2016). Classroom-oriented research from a complex systems perspective. *Studies in Second Language Learning and Teaching, 6,* 377–393.

Larsen-Freeman, D. (2019). On language learner agency: A complex dynamic systems theory perspective. *Modern Language Journal, 103*(S1), 61–79. https://doi. org/10.1111/modl.12536

Larson, R. W., & Richards, M. H. (1991). Boredom in the middle school years: Blaming schools versus blaming students. *American Journal of Education, 99*(4), 418–433.

Lazarus, R. S. (1991). *Emotion and adaptation.* Oxford: Oxford University Press.

Leary, M. R., Rogers, P. A., Canfield, R. W., & Coe, C. (1986). Boredom in interpersonal encounters: Antecedents and social implications. *Journal of Personality and Social* Psychology, *51,* 968–975.

LePera, N. (2011). Relationships between boredom proneness, mindfulness, anxiety, depression and substance use. *The New Psychology Bulletin, 8*(2), 15–25.

Lewis, M., Haviland-Jones, M., & Feldman Barrett, L. (Eds.). (2008). *Handbook of emotions* (3rd ed.). New York: Guilford Press.

Li, C. (2021). A control-value theory approach to boredom in English class among university students in China. *Modern Language Journal, 105,* 317–334. https://doi. org/10.1111/modl.12693

Li, C., Dewaele, J.-M., & Hu, Y. (2023). Foreign language learning boredom: Conceptualization and measurement. *Applied Linguistics Review, 14*(2), 223–249. https://doi. org/10.1515/applirev-2020-0124

Li, C., Huang, J., & Li, B. (2021). The predictive effects of classroom environment and trait emotional intelligence on foreign language enjoyment and anxiety. *System, 96,* 102393.

Li, C., Jiang, G., & Dewaele, J.-M. (2018). Understanding Chinese high school students' foreign language enjoyment: Validation of the Chinese version of the foreign enjoyment scale. *System, 76,* 183–196.

Li, C., & Wei, L. (2022). Anxiety, enjoyment, and boredom in language learning amongst junior secondary students in rural China: How do they contribute to L2 achievement? *Studies in Second Language Acquisition.* https://doi.org/10.1017/S0272263122000031

Litman, J. A. (2005). Curiosity and the pleasures of learning: Wanting and liking new information. *Cognition and Emotion, 19*(6), 793–814. https://doi.org/10.1080/02699930541000101

Litman, J. A., & Jimerson, T. L. (2004). The measurement of curiosity as a feeling of deprivation. *Journal of Personality Assessment, 82*(2), 147–157. https://doi.org/10.1207/s15327752jpa8202_3

Litman, J. A., Robinson, O. C., & Demetre, J. D. (2017). Intrapersonal curiosity: Inquisitiveness about the inner self. *Self and Identity, 16*(2), 231–250. https://doi.org/10.108 0/15298868.2016.1255250

Little, D. (2022). Language learner autonomy: Rethinking language teaching. *Language Teaching, 55*(1), 64–73. https://doi.org/10.1017/S0261444820000488

Loewenstein, G. (1994). The psychology of curiosity: A review and reinterpretation. *Psychological Bulletin, 116*(1), 75–98. https://doi.org/10.1037//0033-2909.116.1.75

Lopez, S., Snyder, C.R., Magyar-Moe, J., Edwards, L., Pedrotti, J., Janowski, K., Turner, J., & Pressgrove, C. (2004). Strategies for accentuating hope. In P. Linley & S. Joseph (Eds.), *Positive Psychology in practice* (pp. 388–404). Hoboken, NJ: Wiley.

Lyster, R., Saito, K., & Sato, M. (2013). Oral corrective feedback in second language classrooms. *Language Teaching, 46*(1), 1–40. https://doi.org/10.1017/S0261444812000365

MacIntyre, P. D. (2017). An overview of language anxiety research and trends in its development. In C. Gkonou, M. Daubney, & J.-M. Dewaele (Eds.), *New insights into language anxiety: Theory, research and educational implications* (pp. 11–30). Bristol: Multilingual Matters.

MacIntyre, P. D., & Gardner, R. C. (1991). Methods and results in the study of anxiety and language learning: A review of the literature. *Language Learning, 41*(1), 85–117.

MacIntyre, P. D., & Gregersen, T. (2012). Emotions that facilitate language learning: The positive-broadening power of the imagination. *Studies in Second Language Learning and Teaching, 2*(2), 193–213.

MacIntyre, P. D., Gregersen, T., & Mercer, S. (2019). Setting an agenda for positive psychology in SLA: theory, practice, and research. *Modern Language Journal, 103*, 262–274.

MacIntyre, P. D., Gregersen, T., & Mercer, S. (2020). Language teachers' coping strategies during the Covid-19 conversion to online teaching: Correlations with stress, wellbeing and negative emotions. *System, 94*, 102352. https://doi.org/10.1016/j.system.2020.102352

MacIntyre, P. D., & Mercer, S. (2014). Introducing positive psychology to SLA. *Studies in Second Language Learning and Teaching, 4*(2), 153–172.

MacIntyre, P. D., Noels, K. A., & Clément, R. (1997). Biases in self-ratings of second language proficiency: The role of language anxiety. *Language Learning, 47*(2), 265–287.

MacIntyre, P.D., Ross, J., Talbot, K., Mercer, S., Gregersen, T., & Banga, C. A. (2019). Stressors, personality and wellbeing among language teachers. *System, 82*, 26–38. https://doi.org/10.1016/j.system.2019.02.013

Macklem, G. L. (2015). *Boredom in the classroom: Addressing student motivation, self-regulation, and engagement in learning.* New York: Springer.

Mann, S., & Robinson, A. (2009). Boredom in the lecture theatre: An investigation into the contributors, moderators and outcomes of boredom amongst university students. *British Educational Research Journal, 35*(2), 243–258.

McNamara, O., Murray, J., & Jones, M. (Eds.) (2014). *Workplace learning in teacher education: International practice and policy.* New York: Springer Nature.

Maddi, S. R. (1970). The search for meaning. In W. J. Arnold & M. M. Page (Eds.), *The Nebraska Symposium on Motivation* (pp. 134–183). Lincoln, NE: University of Nebraska Press.

Mahatmya, D., Lohman, B. J., Matjasko, J. L., & Farb, A. F. (2012). Engagement across developmental periods. In S. L. Christenson, A. L. Reschly, & C. Wylie (Eds.), *Handbook of research on student engagement* (pp. 45–63). New York, NY: Springer.

Mahmoodzadeh, M., & Khajavy, G.H. (2019). Towards conceptualizing language learning curiosity in SLA: An empirical study. *Journal of Psycholinguistic Research*, *48*, 333–351.

Malkovsky, E., Merrifield, C., Goldberg, Y., & Danckert, J. (2012). Exploring the relationship between boredom and sustained attention. *Experimental Brain Research*, *221*(1), 59–67.

Martin, A. J. (2012). Part II commentary: Motivation and engagement: Conceptual, operational, and empirical clarity. In S. L. Christenson, A. L. Reschly, & C. Wylie (Eds.), *Handbook of research on student engagement* (pp. 303–311). New York, NY: Springer.

Martin, A. J., Anderson, J., Bobis, J., Way, J., & Vellar, R. (2012). Switching on and switching off in mathematics: An ecological study of future intent and disengagement among middle school students. *Journal of Educational Psychology*, *104*(1), 1–18.

Martin, M, Sadlo, G., & Stew, G. (2006). The phenomenon of boredom. *Qualitative Research in Psychology*, *3*, 193–211.

Maslach, C. (2015). Psychology of burnout. *International Encyclopedia of the Social and Behavioral Sciences*, *2*, 929–932.

Maslach, C., & Leiter, M. P. (2016). Burnout. In G. Fink (Ed.), *Stress: Concepts, cognition, emotion, and behavior* (pp. 351–357). San Diego: Academic Press.

McCrae, R. R., & Costa, P. T. Jr. (2003). *Personality in adulthood: A five-factor theory perspective* (2nd ed.). Guilford Press.

McCann, E. J., & Turner, J. E. (2004). Increasing student learning through volitional control. *Teachers College Record*, *106*(9), 1695–1714. https://doi.org/10.1111/j.1467-9620.2004.00401.x

Medgyes, P. (2017). The (ir)relevance of academic research for the language teacher. *ELT Journal*, *71*, 491–498. https://doi.org/10.1093/elt/ccx034

Mennim, P. (2017). Discourse-based evaluation of a classroom peer teaching project. *ELT Journal*, *71*, 37–49.

Mercer, S. (2020). The wellbeing of language teachers in the private sector: An ecological perspective. *Language Teaching Research*, 1–24. https://doi.org/10.1177/1362168820973510

Mercer, S. (2021). An agenda for well-being in ELT: An ecological perspective. *ELT Journal*, *75*(1), 14–21. https://doi.org/10.1093/elt/ccaa062

Mercer, S., & Gregersen, T. (2020). *Teacher wellbeing.* Oxford: Oxford University Press.

Mercer-Lynn, K. B., Hunter, J. A., & Eastwood, J. D. (2013). Is trait boredom redundant? *Journal of Social and Clinical Psychology*, *32*, 897–916.

Mercer, S., & Dörnyei, Z. (2020). *Engaging students in contemporary classrooms.* Cambridge: Cambridge University Press.

Merriam-Webster (2015). *Definition of shame.* https://www.merriam-webster.com/dictionary/shame

Muñoz-Basols, J. (2005). Learning through humor: Using humorous resources in the teaching of Foreign Languages. *The A.T.I.S. Bulletin*, 42–46.

Muris, P., & Meesters, C. (2014). Small or big in the eyes of the other: On the developmental psychopathology of self-conscious emotions as shame, guilt and pride. *Clinical Child and Family Psychology Review, 17*, 19–40. https://doi.org/10.1007/s10567-013-0137-z

Nakamura, S., Darasawang, P., & Reinders, H. (2021). The antecedents of boredom in L2 classroom learning. *System, 98*, 102469. https://doi.org/10.1016/j.system.2021.102469

Nassaji, H. (2012). The relationship between SLA research and language pedagogy: Teachers' perspectives. *Language Teaching Research, 16*. 337–365. https://doi.org/10.1177/1362168812436

Nett, U. E., Goetz, T., & Daniels, L. M. (2010). What to do when feeling bored? Students' strategies for coping with boredom. *Learning & Individual Differences, 20*(6), 626–638.

Nett, U. E., Goetz, T., & Hall, N. C. (2011). Coping with boredom in school: An experience sampling perspective. *Contemporary Educational Psychology, 36*, 49–59.

Neu, J. (1998). Boring from within: Endogenous versus reactive boredom. In W. F. Flack & J. D. Laird (Eds.), *Emotions in psychopathology: Theory and research* (pp. 158–170). London: Oxford University Press.

Newton, J. (2011). Maslow's hierarchy of basic needs. *The Neurotypical Site.* www.theneurotypical.com./maslows_basic_needs.html

O'Connor, D. (1967). The phenomena of boredom. *Journal of Existentialism, 7*, 381–399.

Oga-Baldwin, W. L. Q. (2019). Acting, thinking, feeling, making, collaborating: The engagement process in foreign language learning. *System, 89*, 102128. https://doi.org/10.1016/j.system.2019.102128

Oudeyer, P. Y., Gottlieb, J., & Lopes, M. (2016). Intrinsic motivation, curiosity, and learning: Theory and applications in educational technologies. *Progress in Brain Research, 229*, 257–284. https://doi.org/10. 1016/bs.pbr.2016.05.005

Oxford, R. L. (2014). What we can learn about strategies, language learning, and life from two extreme cases: The role of well-being theory. *Studies in Second Language Learning and Teaching, 4*(4), 593–615.

Oxford, R. L. (2015). Emotion as the amplifier and the primary motive: Some theories of emotion with relevance to language learning. *Studies in Second Language Learning and Teaching, 5*(3), 371–393.

Oxford R. L. (2016a). Powerfully positive: Searching for a model of language learner well-being. In D. Gabryś-Barker & D., Gałajda (Eds.), *Positive psychology perspectives on foreign language learning and teaching* (pp. 21–37). New York, NY: Springer.

Oxford R. L. (2016b). Toward a psychology of well-being for language learners: The "EMPHATICS" vision. In P. D. MacIntyre, T. Gregersen, & S. Mercer (Eds.), *Positive psychology in SLA* (pp. 10–87). Bristol: Multilingual Matters.

Oxford, R. L. (2021). Emotions. In T. Gregersen & S. Mercer (Eds.), *The Routledge handbook of the psychology of language learning and teaching* (pp. 176–188). New York: Routledge.

Papi, M. (2010). The L2 motivational self system, L2 anxiety, and motivated behavior: A Structural equation modeling approach. *System, 38*, 467–479.

Parker, P. D., Prkachin, K. M., & Prkachin, G. C. (2005). Processing of facial expressions of negative emotion in alexithymia: The influence of temporal constraint. *Journal of Personality, 73*(4), 1087–1107. https://doi.org/10.1111/j.1467-6494.2005.00339.

Patrick, H., Kaplan, A., & Ryan, A.-M. (2011). Positive classroom motivational environments: Convergence between mastery goal structure and classroom social climate. *Journal of Educational Psychology, 103*(2), 367–382.

Pavelescu, L. M., & Petrić, B. (2018). Love and enjoyment in context: Four case studies of adolescent EFL learners. *Studies in Second Language Learning and Teaching, Teaching, 8*(1), 73–101

Pawlak, M. (2009). Grammar learning strategies and language attainment: Seeking a relationship. *Research in Language, 7*, 43–60.

Pawlak, M. (2018). Grammar Learning Strategy Inventory *(GLSI):* Another look. *Studies in Second Language Learning and Teaching, 8*(2), 351–379

Pawlak, M. (2019). Investigating language learning strategies: Prospects, pitfalls and challenges. *Language Teaching Research.* https://doi.org/10.1177/1362168819876156

Pawlak, M. (2020a). Individual differences and good language teachers. In C. Griffiths & Z. Tajeddin (Eds.), *Lessons from good language teachers* (pp. 121–132). Cambridge: Cambridge University Press.

Pawlak, M. (2020b). Grammar and good language teachers. In C. Griffiths & Z. Tajeddin (Eds.), *Lessons from good language* teachers (pp. 219–231). Cambridge: Cambridge University Press.

Pawlak, M., & Biedroń, A. (2021). Verbal working memory as a predictor of explicit and implicit knowledge of English passive voice. In R. M. DeKeyser (Ed.), *Aptitude-treatment interaction in second language learning* (pp. 93–115). John Benjamins.

Pawlak, M., Derakhshan, A., Mehdizadeh, M., & Kruk, M. (2021). Boredom in online English language classes: Mediating variables and coping strategies. *Language Teaching Research.* https://doi.org/10.1177%2F13621688211064944

Pawlak, M., & Kruk, M. (2022). *Individual differences in computer assisted language learning research.* London: Routledge.

Pawlak, M., Kruk, M., Csizér, K., & Zawodniak, J. (2023). Investigating in-class and after-class boredom among advanced learners of English: intensity, interrelationships and learner profiles. *Applied Linguistics Review.* https://doi.org/10.1515/applirev-2022-0150

Pawlak, M., Kruk, M., & Zawodniak, J. (2020a). Individual trajectories of boredom in learning English as a foreign language at the university level: Insights from three students' self-reported experience. *Innovation in Language Learning and Teaching, 15*(3), 263–278. https://doi.org/10.1080/17501229.2020.1767108

Pawlak, M., Kruk, M., Zawodniak, J., & Pasikowski, S. (2020b). Investigating factors responsible for boredom in English classes: The case of advanced learners. *System, 97*, 102259. https://doi.org/10.1016/j.system.2020.102259

Pawlak, M., Kruk, M., Zawodniak, J., & Pasikowski, S. (2022a). Examining the underlying Structure of after-class boredom experienced by English majors. *System, 106*, 102769. https://doi.org/10.1016/j.system.2022.102769

Pawlak, M., Zarrinabadi, N., & Kruk, M. (2022b). Positive and negative emotions, L2 grit and perceived competence as predictors of L2 motivated behaviour. *Journal of Multilingual and Multicultural Development*, 1–17. https://doi.org/10.1080/01434632.2022.2091579

Pawlak, M., Zawodniak, J., & Kruk, M. (2020c). The neglected emotion of boredom in teaching English to advanced learners. *International Journal of Applied Linguistics, 30*(3), 497–509. https://doi.org/10.1111/ijal.12302

Pawlak, M., Zawodniak, J., & Kruk, M. (2020d). *Boredom in the foreign language classroom: A micro-perspective*. Springer.

Pawlak, M., Kruk, M., Csizér, K., & Zawodniak, J. (2023). Investigating in-class and after-class boredom among advanced learners of English: intensity, interrelationships and learner profiles. *Applied Linguistics Review*. https://doi.org/10.1515/applirev-2022-0150

Peixoto, F., Mata, L., Monteiro, V., Sanches, C., & Pekrun, R. (2015). The Achievement Emotions Questionnaire: Validation for pre-adolescent students. *European Journal of Developmental Psychology, 12*(4), 472–481. https://doi.org/10.1080/17405629.2015.1040757

Pekrun, R. (2006). The control-value theory of achievement emotions: Assumptions, corollaries, and implications for educational research and practice. *Educational Psychology Review, 18*(4), 315–341.

Pekrun, R., Frenzel, A. C., Perry, R. P., & Goetz, T. (2007). The control-value theory of achievement emotions: An integrative approach to emotions in education. In A. P. Schutz & R. Pekrun (Eds.), *Emotion in education* (pp. 13–36). Amsterdam: Academic Press.

Pekrun, R., Goetz, T., Daniels, L. M., Stupnisky, R. H, & Perry, R. P. (2010). Boredom in achievement settings: Exploring control-value antecedents and performance outcomes of a neglected emotion. *Journal of Educational Psychology, 102*(3), 531–549.

Pekrun, R., Goetz, T., Frenzel, A. C., Barchfeld, P., & Perry, R. P. (2011). Measuring emotions in students' learning and performance: The Achievement Emotions Questionnaire (AEQ). *Contemporary Educational Psychology, 36*(1), 36–48.

Pekrun, R., & Linnenbrink-Garcia, L. (2012). Academic emotions and student engagement. In S. L. Christenson, A. L. Reschly, & C. Wylie (Eds.), *Handbook of research on student engagement* (pp. 259–282). New York, NY: Springer.

Pekrun, R., & Stephens, E. J. (2009). Goals, emotions, and emotion regulation: Perspectives of the control-value theory. *Human Development, 52*, 357–365. https://doi.org/10.1159/000242349

Perkins, R. E., & Hill, A. B. (1985). Cognitive and affective aspects of boredom. *British Journal of Psychology, 76*(2), 221–234. https://doi.org/10.1111/j.2044-8295.1985.tb01946.x

Peterson, C., & Park, N. (2009). Classifying and measuring strengths of character. In S. J. Lopez & C. R. Snyder (Eds.), *Oxford library of psychology: Oxford handbook of positive psychology* (pp. 25–33). New York, NY: Oxford University Press.

Peterson, C., Maier, S. F., & Seligman, M. E. P. (1993). *Learned helplessness: A theory for the age of personal control*. New York: Oxford University Press.

Peterson, C., & Seligman, M. (2004). *Character strengths and virtues: A handbook and classification*. Oxford: Oxford University Press.

Piechurska-Kuciel, E. (2011). The relationship between language anxiety and the development of the speaking skill: Results of a longitudinal study. In M. Pawlak, E. Waniek-Klimczak, & J. Majer (Eds.), *Speaking and instructed foreign language Acquisition* (pp. 200–214). Bristol: Multilingual Matters.

Plutchik, R. (1980). *Emotion: A Psychoevolutionary synthesis.* New York, NY: Harper and Row.

Preckel, F., Götz, T., & Frenzel, A. (2010). Ability grouping of gifted students: Effect on academic self-concept and boredom. *British Journal of Educational Psychology, 80*(3), 451–472.

Putwain, D. W., Pekrun, R., Nicholson, L. J., Symes, W., Becker, S., & Marsh, H. W. (2018). Control-value appraisals, enjoyment, and boredom in mathematics: A longitudinal latent interaction analysis. *American Educational Research Journal, 55*, 1339–1368.

Richards, J. (1990). Beyond training: approaches to teacher education in language teaching. *Language Teacher, 14*, 3–8.

Richards, J. C. (2013). Curriculum approaches in language teaching: forward, central, and backward design. *RELC Journal 44*(1), 5–33.

Richards, J. C., & Farrell, T. S. C. (2005). *Professional development for language teachers: Strategies for teacher learning.* New York: Cambridge University Press.

Richards, J. C., & Lockhart, C. (1994). *Reflective teaching.* New York: Cambridge University Press.

Richards, J. C., & Lockhart, C. (1996). *Reflective teaching in the second language classroom.* Cambridge University Press.

Rieffe, C., & De Rooij, M. (2012). The longitudinal relationship between emotion awareness and internalising symptoms during late childhood. *European Child & Adolescent Psychiatry, 21*(6), 349–356. https://doi.org/10.1007/s00787-012-0267-8

Ross, A. S., & Rivers, D. J. (2018). Emotional experiences beyond the classroom: Interactions with the social world. *Studies in Second Language Learning and Teaching, 8*(1), 103–126.

Ross, A. S., & Stracke, E. (2016). Learner perceptions and experiences of pride in second language education. *Australian Review of Applied Linguistics 39*(3), 272–291. https://doi.org/10.1075/aral.39.3.04ros

Ryan, R. M., & Deci, E. L. (2000). Self-determination theory and the facilitation of intrinsic motivation, social development, and well-being. *American Psychologist, 55*(1), 68–78.

Sakai, H., & Kikuchi, K. (2009). An analysis of demotivators in the EFL classroom. *System, 37*, 57–69.

Sato, M., Fernández Castillo, F., & Oyanedel, J. C. (2022) Teacher motivation and burnout of English-as-a-foreign-language teachers: Do demotivators really demotivate them? *Frontiers in Psychology, 13*, 891452. https://doi.org/10.3389/fpsyg.2022.891452

Sato, M., & Loewen, S. (2022). The research-practice dialogue in second language learning and teaching: Past, present, and future. *Modern Language Journal, 106*, 509–527. https://doi.org/10.1111/modl.12791

Schopenhauer, A. (2008). *The world as will and representation* (vol. 1). (R. E., Aquila in collaboration with D. Carus, Trans.). New York: Longman. (Original work published 1819).

Schön, D. A. (1983). *The reflective practitioner: How professionals think in action.* New York: Basic Books.

Schreck, M. K. (2011). *You've got to reach them to teach them: Hard facts about the soft skills of student engagement.* Bloomington, IN: Solution Tree Press.

Scovel, T. (1991). The effect of affect on foreign language learning: A Review of the anxiety research. In E. K. Horwitz & D. J. Young (Eds.), *Language anxiety: From theory and research to classroom implications* (pp. 15–24). Englewood Cliffs, NJ: Prentice Hall.

Seli, P., Cheyne, J. A., Xu, M., Purdon, C., & Smilek, D. (2015). Motivation, intentionality, and mind wandering: Implications for assessments of task-unrelated thought. *Journal of Experimental Psychology: Learning, Memory, and Cognition, 41*, 1417–1425. http://dx.doi.org/10.1037/xlm0000116

Seligman, M. E. P. (2002). *Authentic happiness: Using the new positive psychology to realize your potential for lasting fulfillment.* New York: Free Press.

Seligman M. E. P. (2011). *Flourish: A visionary new understanding of happiness and well-being.* New York, NY: Atria/Simon & Schuster.

Seligman, M. E. P., & Csikszentmihalyi, M. (2000). Positive psychology: An introduction. *American Psychologist, 55*(1), 5–14.

Sharp, J. G., Hemmings, B., Kay, R., Murphy, B., & Elliott, S. (2017). Academic boredom among students in higher education: A mixed-methods exploration of characteristics, contributors and consequences. *Journal of Further and Higher Education, 41*(5), 657–677.

Shernoff, D. J. (2013). *Optimal learning environments to promote student engagement.* New York: Springer.

Shorey, H. S., Snyder, C. R., Rand, K. L., Hockemeyer, J. R., & Feldman, D. B. (2002). Somewhere over the rainbow: Hope theory weathers its first decade. *Psychological Inquiry. 13*(4), 322–331.

Simonton, K. L., & Garn, C. G. (2020). Control-value theory of achievement emotions: A closer look at student value appraisals and enjoyment. *Learning and Individual Differences, 81*, 315–341. https://doi.org/10.1007/s10648-006-9029-9

Sinatra, G. M., Heddy, B. C., & Lombardi, D. (2015). The challenges of defining and measuring student engagement in science. *Educational Psychologist, 50*(1), 1–13.

Skaalvik, E. M., & Skaalvik, S. (2011). Teacher job satisfaction and motivation to leave the teaching profession: Relations with school context, feeling of belonging, and emotional exhaustion. *Teaching and Teacher Education, 27*(6), 1029–1038.

Skinner, E. (2016). Engagement and disaffection as central to processes of motivational resilience and development. In K. R Wentzel & D. B. Miele (Eds.), *Handbook of motivation at school* (pp. 145–168). New York: Routledge.

Skinner, E. A., Kindermann, T. A., Connell, J. P., & Wellborn, J. G. (2009). Engagement and disaffection as organizational constructs in the dynamics of motivational development. In K. R. Wenzel & A. Wigfield (Eds.), *Handbook of motivation at school* (pp. 223–245). New York: Routledge.

Skinner, E. A., Kindermann, T. A., & Furrer, C. J. (2009). A motivational perspective on engagement and disaffection: Conceptualization and assessment of children's behavioral and emotional participation in academic activities in the classroom. *Educational and Psychological Measurement, 69*, 493–525.

Snyder, C.R. (2002). Hope theory: Rainbows in the mind. *Psychological Inquiry*, *13*(4), 249–275.

Spacks, P. M. (1995). *Boredom: The literary history of a state of mind.* Chicago, IL: The University of Chicago Press.

Spielberger, C. D., & Reheiser, E. C., (2009). Assessment of emotions: Anxiety, anger, depression, and curiosity. *Applied Psychology: Health and Well-being*, *1*(3), 271–302.

Sternberg, R. J., & Sternberg, K. (2012). *Cognitive psychology.* Belmont, CA: Wadsworth Cengage Learning.

Sugino, T. (2010). Teacher demotivational factors in the Japanese language teaching context. *Procedia Social and Behavioral Sciences*, *3*, 216–226.

Sulis, Mercer, S., Mairitsch, A., Babic, S., & Shin, S. (2021). Pre-service language teacher wellbeing as a complex dynamic system. *System*, *103*. 102642 https://doi.org/10.1016/j.system.2021.102642

Svalberg, A. M.-L. (2009). Engagement with language: Interrogating a construct. *Language Awareness*, *18*, 242–258.

Taguchi, T., Magid, M., & Papi, M. (2009). The L2 motivational self system among Japanese, Chinese and Iranian learners of English: A comparative study. In Z. Dörnyei & E. Ushioda (Eds.), *Motivation, language identity and the L2 self* (pp. 66–97). Bristol: Multilingual Matters.

Takkac Tulgar, A. (2018). The effects of curiosity on second language learning in terms of linguistic, social-cultural and pragmatic development. *Adnan Menderes Universitesi Eğitim Fakultesi Eğitim Bilimleri Dergisi*, *9*(2), 59–72.

Tamir, M., & Bigman, Y. (2014). Why might people want to feel bad? Motives in contra-hedonic emotion regulation. In W. G. Parrott (Ed.), *The positive side of negative emotions* (pp. 201–223). New York, NY: Guilford Press.

Tangney, J. P., & Dearing, R. L. (2003). *Shame and guilt.* New York: Guilford Press.

Taxer, J. L., & Frenzel, A. C. (2015). Facets of teachers' emotional lives: A quantitative investigation of teachers' genuine, faked, and hidden emotions. *Teaching and Teacher Education 49*, 78–88. http://dx.doi.org/10.1016/j.tate.2015.03.003

Teimouri, Y. (2018). Differential roles of shame and guilt in L2 learning. *Modern Language Journal*, *102*(4), 632–652.

Teimouri, Y., Plonsky, L., & Tabandeh, F. (2020). L2 Grit: Passion and perseverance for second-language learning. *Language Teaching Research.* https://doi.org/10.1177/1362168820921895

Todman, M. (2003). Boredom and psychotic disorders: Cognitive and motivational issues. *Psychiatry: Interpersonal and Biological Processes*, *66*(2), 146–167.

Tomasello, M., & Herron, C. (1989). Feedback for language transfer errors: The garden path technique. *Studies in Second Language Acquisition*, *11*, 385–395.

Toohey, P. (2011). *Boredom: A lively history.* New Haven, CT: Yale University Press.

Tracy, J. L., & Robins, R. W. (2004). Putting the self into self-conscious emotions: A Theoretical model. *Psychological Inquiry*, *15*(2), 103–125. https://doi.org/10.1207/s15327965pli1502_01

Trautwein, U., Lüdtke, O., Kastens, C., & Köller, O. (2006). Effort on homework in grades 5–9: Development, motivational antecedents, and the association with effort on classwork. *Child Development, 77*(4), 1094–1111.

Tugade, M. M., & Fredrickson, B. L. (2004). Resilient individuals use positive emotions to bounce back from negative emotional experiences. *Journal of Personality and Social Psychology, 86,* 320–333.

Tugade, M. M., & Fredrickson, B. L. (2007). Regulation of positive emotions: Emotion regulation strategies that promote resilience. *Journal of Happiness Studies: An Interdisciplinary Forum on Subjective Well-Being, 8*(3), 311–333. https://doi.org/10.1007/s10902-006-9015-4

Tulis, M., & Fulmer, S. M. (2013). Students' motivational and emotional experiences and their relationship to persistence during academic challenge in mathematics and reading. *Learning and Individual Differences, 27,* 35–46.

Ur, P. (1996). *A course in language teaching.* Cambridge University Press.

Van Ha, X., Murray, J. C., & Mehdi Riazi, A. (2021). High school EFL students' beliefs about oral corrective feedback: The role of gender, motivation and extraversion. *Studies in Second Language Learning and Teaching, 11*(2), 235–264. http://dx.doi.org/10.14746/ssllt.2021.11.2.4

van Tilburg, W. A. P., & Igou, E. R. (2011). On boredom and social identity. *Personality and Social Psychology Bulletin, 37*(12), 1679–1691.

van Tilburg, W. A., Igou, E. R., & Sedikides, C. (2013). In search of meaningfulness: Nostalgia as an antidote to boredom. *Emotion, 13,* 450–461. http://dx.doi.org/10.1037/a0030442

Veiga F. H., Reeve J., Wentzel K., Robu V. (2014). Assessing students' engagement: A review of instruments with psychometric qualities. In F. H. Veiga (Ed.), *First International conference of student engagement at school: Perspectives from psychology and education* (pp. 38–57). Lisbon, Portugal: Instituto do Educaçaoda Universidade de Lisboa.

Vodanovich, S. J. (2003). Psychometric measures of boredom: A review of the literature. *The Journal of Psychology, 137,* 569–601.

Vondanovich, S. J., & Kass, J. (1990). Age and gender differences in boredom proneness. *Journal of Social Behavior and Personality, 5,* 297–307.

Vodanovich, S. J., & Rupp, D. E. (1999). Are procrastinators prone to boredom? *Social Behavior and Personality, 27,* 11–16.

Vogel-Walcutt, J., Fiorella, L., Carper, T., & Schatz, S. (2012). The definition, assessment, and mitigation of state boredom within educational settings: A comprehensive review. *Educational Psychology Review, 24*(1), 89–111.

Wattana, S. (2013). *Talking while playing: The effects of computer games on interaction and willingness to communicate in English* (Doctoral dissertation, University of Canterbury). Retrieved from UC Research Repository. http://dx.doi.org/10.26021/9498

Watts, S., & Stenner, P. (2003). Q methodology, quantum theory and psychology. *Operant Subjectivity, 26*(1), 155–173.

Wegner, L. (2011). Through the lens of a peer: Understanding leisure boredom and risk behavior in adolescence. *South African Journal of Occupational Therapy, 41*(1), 18–24.

Wei, H., Gao, K., & Wang, W. (2019). Understanding the relationship between grit and foreign language performance among middle school students: The roles of foreign language enjoyment and classroom environment. *Frontiers in Psychology, 10.* https://doi.org/10.3389/fpsyg.2019.01508

Weinerman, J., & Kenner, C. (2016). Boredom: That which shall not be named. *Journal of Developmental Education, 40*(1), 18–23.

Weir, K. (2013, July/August). Never a dull moment: Things get interesting when psychologists take a closer look at boredom. *Monitor on Psychology, 44*(7), 54.

Westgate, E. C., & Wilson, T. D. (2018). Boring thoughts and bored minds: The MAC model of boredom and cognitive engagement. *Psychological Review, 125*(5), 689–713. https://doi.org/10.1037/rev0000097

Westgate, E. C., Wilson, T. D., & Gilbert, D. T. (2017). With a little help for our thoughts: Making it easier to think for pleasure. *Emotion, 17*, 828–839. http://dx.doi.org/10.1037/emo0000278

Westman, M. (2001). Stress and strain crossover. *Human Relations, 54*(6), 717–751.

Wettstein A., Kühne F., Tschacher W., & La Marca R. (2020). Ambulatory assessment of psychological and physiological stress on workdays and free days among teachers. A Preliminary Study. *Frontiers in Neuroscience, 14*, 112.

Wilson, P. A. (2016). Shame and collaborative learning in second language classes. *Konin Language Studies, 4*(3), 235–252.

Wilson, T. D., Reinhard, D. A., Westgate, E, Gilbert, D. T., Ellerbeck, N., Hahn, C., Brown, C. L., & Shaked, A. (2014). Just think: The challenges of the disengaged mind. *Science, 345*(6192), 75–77.

Woodrow, L. (2006). Anxiety and speaking English as a second language. *RELC Journal, 37*(3), 308–328.

Yang, S. (2009). Using blogs to enhance critical reflection and community of practice. *Educational Technology & Society, 12*(2), 11–21.

Yazdanmehr, E., Elahi Shirvan, M., & Saghafi, K. (2021). A process tracing study of the dynamic patterns of boredom in an online L3 course of German during COVID-19 pandemic. *Foreign Language Annals. 54*(3), 714–739. https://doi.org/10.1111/flan.12548

Yeager, J. M., Fisher, S., & Shearon, D. N. (2011). SMART strengths: *Building character, resilience and relationships in youth.* New York: Cogent Publishing.

Young, D. J. (1991). Creating a low-anxiety classroom environment: What does language anxiety research suggest? *Modern Language Journal, 75*(4), 426–437.

Zawodniak, J., Kruk, M., & Pawlak, M. (2021). Boredom as an aversive emotion experienced by English majors. *RELC Journal.* https://doi.org/10.1177/0033688220973732

Zinchenko, A., Obermeier, C., Kanske, P., Schröger, & Kotz, S. A. (2017). Positive emotion impedes emotional but not cognitive conflict processing. *Cognitive, Affective, & Behavioral Cognitive, Affective, & Behavioral Neuroscience, 17*, 665–677.

Index